Observer's Guides

ASTROPHOTOGRAPHY
An Introduction

H. J. P. ARNOLD

Series Editor Leif J. Robinson

Other *Sky & Telescope* Observer's Guides

Meteors, by Neil Bone
City Astronomy, by Robin Scagell

Published in the United States by Sky Publishing Corp.,
49 Bay State Rd., Cambridge, MA 02138

First published in Great Britain in 1995
by George Philip Limited,
an imprint of Reed Consumer Books Limited,
Michelin House, 81 Fulham Rd., London SW3 6RB
and Auckland, Melbourne, Singapore, and Toronto

ISBN 0-933346-73-5

Library of Congress Cataloging-in-Publication Data

Arnold, H. J. P. (Harry John Philip), 1932–
    Astrophotography : an introduction / H. J. P. Arnold.
        p.   cm. — (Sky & telescope observer's guides)
    Includes bibliographical references and index.
    ISBN 0-933346-73-5   (pbk : alk. paper)
    1. Astronomical photography. I. Title. II. Series.
QB121.A75   1995
  522'.63—dc20   94–42325

Edited by John Woodruff
Produced by Mandarin Offset
Printed in Hong Kong

Contents

Foreword

Astrophotography is simple, just a step beyond using an ordinary camera for everyday snapshots. The challenge is to record faithfully scenes that are illuminated by light that is often thousands of times dimmer than daylight.

Capturing the Sun, Moon, planets, and stars on film *has* to be easy: during my three decades at *Sky & Telescope* I've seen perhaps a hundred thousand photographs taken by men and women, young and old, veteran and novice. Not everyone can have worked hard taking those pictures. Most of the images were very ordinary and were never printed in the magazine. But that's not the point. Rather, those who submitted the photographs thought they were special enough to share with someone, just as you share your baby's picture with whomever will look at it.

I never became a serious astrophotographer simply because I saw daily the best that amateurs and professionals had to offer. That's not to say that I've never taken portraits of the night sky. My circumpolar star trails are probably as good as yours will be – which is another way of saying you can't miss!

Yet I envy the likes of William Sterne Jr, who always frames sequence shots of eclipses with elegant and dramatic foregrounds. And Akira Fujii, who for decades has produced the finest in sky portraiture and often tosses off genius concepts, like delineating the Earth's shadow during a total lunar eclipse through a multiple-exposure sequence. And Dennis di Cicco, who conceived of a year-long exposure which revealed the figure-of-eight analemma in the sky – the north–south peregrination of the Sun as twisted by the ellipticity of the Earth's orbit. All these superb expressions of astrophotography were done with simple, everyday equipment guided by great imagination and exquisite planning.

Astrophotography has never been easier. Cameras have more features than ever before, there is greater variety among lenses, films have unprecedented speed and sharpness. Simple camera platforms track the stars as they glide across the sky, and you can build one in an evening. Truly, at the beginner level, it's a point-and-shoot astronomical world, just as it is in everyday life.

"The reports of my death are greatly exaggerated," cracked Mark Twain. So is the rumour that astrophotography is becoming obsolete, being supplanted by solid-state electronic detectors. Sure, these devices are revolutionizing astro-imaging, for they allow unparalleled deep probings into the far reaches of the Universe and the capturing of the tiniest details on planets. Did you pick up on the missing qualifier there? I didn't say "by professionals" – nowadays amateurs can play in those ultimate waters too. But that's another story.

Yet very ordinary astrophotographers can reap the benefits of digital technology by taking pictures the old-fashioned way, on film, and then importing them into a computer where they can be toyed with at leisure. Enhance colour: right! Add contrast: right! Combine images: right! Digital processing can breathe new life into old images.

I see a happy future for astrophotography. Doug Arnold's book is just the ticket for me and thousands of others who want to stick a toe in the water but not take a plunge.

Leif J. Robinson
Editor, *Sky & Telescope* magazine

Preface

The pages of astronomy magazines contain beautiful and awe-inspiring pictures, many of which are the work not of professional astronomers but of amateurs. With rare exceptions, those who took the pictures owe nothing to luck and everything to application and hard work. But they all had to start somewhere, and this book is intended to help the newcomer to astrophotography along the first part of the road that may lead to publication in the astronomy magazines. Even if it does not, there is still the enormous satisfaction and enjoyment to be derived from one of the most fascinating hobbies.

Telescopes do not figure prominently in this book. Although they are the astronomer's chief tool, they require knowledge and skill to operate competently. I believe there is a valuable apprenticeship to be served by the budding astrophotographer using basic photographic equipment before attempting to use the telescope. The apprenticeship will not be dull, for many astronomical objects can be captured with just the photographic essentials – a fixed camera and interchangeable lenses – without recourse to any astronomical equipment. However, binoculars are a valuable accessory: not only do they enhance our eyesight, and have a wide field of view, but they can be also be used for other, non-astronomical purposes.

For this book there are two potential readerships. The first are amateur astronomers, or those who at least know something about astronomy already, who are contemplating a move into astrophotography. The second are amateur photographers who possibly know little or nothing about astronomy, but who have admired astronomical images and are wondering what is involved. Writing for two readerships inevitably means that for one or the other a few parts of the book will contain little that is new. For example, Chapter 1 ("The sky above") can be skipped by the astronomers, while the photographers may wish to pass over Chapter 13 ("Processing"). Even for the photographers, though, Chapter 2 ("Another world") is a reminder that in some ways astrophotography is very different from everyday photography.

This book is an expanded version of the text first published in 1988 as *Night Sky Photography*. Chapters 13, 14, and 15 are totally new, while Chapter 10 is almost completely new, and Chapters 12 and 16 have much new material. Other chapters have been modified and updated.

I expressed my thanks to those who contributed so helpfully during the preparation of *Night Sky Photography* in that volume, but I need to add more names here. R.J. Livesey (Director of the British Astronomical Association's Aurora Section), Lou Marsh (of the BAA's Lunar Section), and Paul Doherty helped with data and discussion, while in the US Dennis di Cicco (of *Sky & Telescope*) and Keith A. Boas (Senior Editor of Publications at Eastman Kodak) were also helpful. On purely photographic matters I received sound guidance from Geoffrey Crawley (Technical Manager, *British Journal of Photography*) and Peter Sutherst (formerly head of Technical Services in Kodak Limited's Professional Sales group). Both Geoffrey and Peter, together with Paul Doherty, were kind enough to review the entire text, and all made valuable suggestions for improvements.

H.J.P. Arnold

CHAPTER 1

The sky above

This chapter is intended to outline some of the salient features of the night sky and of the celestial objects in it that can be recorded on film. It is aimed principally at those with more photographic than astronomical knowledge, and the emphasis is on practical rather than theoretical considerations. By the chapter's end, I hope that the newcomer to astronomy will have a basic understanding of what is happening in the sky; books recommended in the Bibliography provide a more comprehensive treatment.

How big and how bright?

If a coin is held just in front of one of our eyes, it appears very large and blanks out a large area of the field of view. If the same coin is held at arm's length it appears much smaller, and if it is placed 100 metres (330 feet) away it might just be seen by those with excellent vision. However, the size of the coin has not altered in any way. We face this problem in describing the size of celestial objects. Some are very close in astronomical terms – a few hundred thousand kilometres. Others are so distant that special units of measurement, such as the *light year* (9.46 million million km/5.88 million million miles) and the *parsec* (30.9 million million km/19.2 million million miles), have been introduced for ease of reference. As luck would have it, there is an excellent example of the effect of distance in the Solar System. As seen from the Earth, the Sun and the Moon are about the same size, but the Moon's diameter is a mere 3476 km (2160 miles) compared with the Sun's almost 1.4 million km (865,000 miles).

It is obvious, therefore, that in describing the size of objects in the sky, and in relating their positions one to another, linear measurements cannot be used. We turn for help to the concept of the *celestial sphere*, shown in Figure 1.1. From ancient times it was imagined that the stars, grouped into constellations, and the planets were set in a sphere with the Earth at the centre. This is not true, of course, but the celestial sphere does present a method of sizing any object as seen from the Earth. As Figure 1.1 shows, we can imagine a circle with the same radius as the sphere running around its equator for 360°, and another passing through the celestial pole and through the point directly overhead, the *zenith*. The angle from horizon to horizon passing through the zenith is 180°, and from the horizon to the zenith, 90°. This provides an angular system of measurement in which the apparent size of a celestial object is given in terms of its angular extent on the

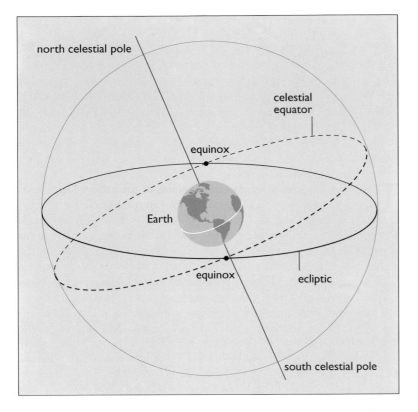

Figure 1.1 *The celestial sphere. When we look up at the night sky, it seems as if we are on the inside of a huge sphere that carries the stars and planets with it as it turns, once every 24 hours. The Earth's axis extended meets the sphere at the north and south celestial poles, and the plane of the Earth's equator similarly extended marks the celestial equator. The ecliptic (see page 11), the path followed by the Sun and the planets, is angled to the celestial equator, and the two points where these two circles cross are the equinoxes. The celestial sphere makes it possible to consider the sizes of celestial objects and the distances between them as angles.*

celestial sphere. The vertex of the measured angle is located at the observer's eye ("vertex" being a geometrical term for the point at which lines meet to make an angle.)

There are some helpful, rough-and-ready methods of estimating angular sizes that the newcomer can adopt. When the arm is fully extended, a clenched fist covers an area of sky about 10° across (nine fists to zenith!), and the little finger about 1° across. Since the angular diameter of the full Moon is around ½°, it is easily established that the lunar disk is hidden (or "occulted") by the little finger positioned at arm's length. Of course, the system is capable of much more accuracy than this. One degree is composed of 60 minutes (usually referred to as *arc minutes* to distinguish them from units of time), for which the symbol is ', and each minute is composed of 60 *arc seconds*, for which the symbol is ". Thus the angular size of both the Sun and the Moon is slightly more than 30 arc minutes. The planets are small enough as seen from the Earth to be measured in arc seconds; the stars are so distant that effectively they are points of light with no discernible size.

In discussing the size of objects above, the term *magnitude* was avoided quite deliberately because, rather perversely, astronomers use it to describe the brightness of celestial objects. The scale used is still basically that devised by the Greek astronomer and mathematician Hipparchus in the second century BC. He described the brightest stars that could be seen with the naked eye (Hipparchus lived almost two millennia before the invention of the telescope) as being of the first magnitude, and the faintest as of the sixth magnitude. The magnitude scale is now on a more precise footing, each successive magnitude change corresponding to a brightness difference of just over 2.5 times. A first-magnitude star is thus 100 times (i.e. 2.5 to the power 5) brighter than a sixth-magnitude star. Hence, the brighter the star, the lower the magnitude.

Not surprisingly, the system has been considerably refined since the time of Hipparchus. Magnitudes have been measured to decimal values (using instruments called photometers). The four brightest stars are accorded negative values: Sirius, the brightest star in the sky; Canopus, in the southern constellation Carina; Alpha Centauri, in another southern constellation, Centaurus; and Arcturus, in the northern constellation Boötes. Sirius is surpassed by Jupiter and Mars some of the time, depending on the planets' positions relative to the Sun and Earth, and by Venus, the full Moon, and the Sun all of the time. Sirius has a magnitude of -1.5, Venus at its brightest -4.7, the full Moon -12.7, and the Sun -26.7.

As with size, a note of caution has to be sounded on the matter of brightness. Stars differ enormously in luminosity and distance from Earth, so the magnitudes indicated above are what are referred to as *apparent* or *visual magnitudes*. Values have also been calculated for the magnitudes that stars would possess if they were viewed from a standard distance of 10 parsecs, and these are known as *absolute magnitudes*. The calculation for Sirius and Polaris is enlightening. To our eyes Polaris is a very ordinary star with an apparent magnitude of $+2.0$, compared with the -1.5 of Sirius. However, the absolute magnitude of Sirius is only $+1.4$, whereas that of Polaris is -4.6, which is almost as bright as the maximum apparent magnitude of Venus. Hence Polaris is in fact far more luminous than Sirius, but its far greater distance from Earth makes it appear much dimmer. More chastening still is the calculation for our star, the Sun. Viewed from 10 parsecs it would be magnitude $+4.8$: a dim, albeit naked-eye object.

Nonetheless, it is apparent magnitudes that are of the greatest concern to the budding astrophotographer. Cameras and films enable us to record stars far dimmer than those discernible to the human eye. Since our Galaxy is estimated to contain about 100,000 million stars it is extremely interesting to look at some of the numbers. There are 22 stars of first magnitude and brighter, 68 of second magnitude, 197 of third magnitude, 599 of fourth magnitude, 1976 of fifth magnitude, and 5830 of sixth magnitude – a total of 8692 stars which are, in theory, visible to the naked eye under ideal conditions. Now, we can see only about half of the celestial sphere at any particular time, and it is only near the zenith that the faintest of the sixth-magnitude stars will be visible. Away from the zenith, stars have to be viewed through more of the Earth's atmosphere, and a few degrees above the horizon only first-magnitude stars can be seen. The net result is that, from the UK or US, even under ideal conditions, no more than about 2600 stars are visible to us without the aid of binoculars or a telescope. From magnitude 6, the numbers grow rapidly: 16,000 seventh magnitude, 51,000 eighth magnitude, and over 160,000 ninth magnitude. It has been calculated that there are possibly 5 million stars of twelfth magnitude. Although we cannot see these faint stars individually with the naked eye, in total they contribute to the general luminosity of the night sky. This is nowhere more so than in the Milky Way, a band in the sky created by a line-of-sight effect as we look inwards towards the centre of the Galaxy from our position near the edge of one of the spiral arms.

The way we see

Before setting out to study the movement (real or apparent) of the stars and planets, and the part that the Earth itself plays, it will be helpful to describe briefly for the newcomer an important attribute of the human eye. The retina is the light-sensitive membrane at the back of the eye which receives the image formed by the lens. This quality is conferred by millions of sensitive elements of two different types – rods and cones, named after their characteristic shapes. The cones distinguish colour and operate best in bright light conditions. The rods cannot discriminate colour, and are most sensitive in low light conditions. Time is needed for the rods to accommodate to dark conditions, and this is referred to as *dark adaptation*.

The cones are concentrated in the central area of the retina and are the only elements in the fovea, a small area of the retina where the eye possesses its highest resolving power. Away from the fovea the rods rapidly begin to predominate. This explains one of the most important facts about looking at the night sky, and in particular searching for dim objects. If the observer looks directly at the area of interest, the object may not be resolved because of the cones' poor performance in low light conditions. However, if the eye is directed slightly to one side of the object's suspected position, the superior low light performance of the rods around the fovea is far more likely to result in the object being discriminated. This observing technique is known as *averted vision*, and is one of the most valuable techniques we can learn as we set out on our journey around the skies.

The map of the sky

Imagine that we are on a planet just like Earth, but that there is no Sun, so the planet's rotation brings no interruption of the permanent night. Just like Earth, this planet rotates from west to east (anticlockwise as seen from a vantage point over the north pole, clockwise from over the south pole). As the hours pass, a panorama of stars travels across the sky from east to west, until the time comes for the pattern to start being repeated. Relative to each other as seen from the Earth, the positions of the stars change very little over the centuries. It is not too difficult to project the positions of the stars on the imaginary celestial sphere onto flat, two-dimensional maps, as we do with maps of the Earth's surface.

The Earth's equator projected onto the celestial sphere forms the *celestial equator,* and the geographical poles projected form the *celestial poles* (see Figure 1.1). A coordinate system like latitude and longitude is needed. On star maps latitude becomes *declination,* abbreviated as dec, which is expressed in degrees, arc minutes, and arc seconds, prefixed by + or − to indicate position north or south of the celestial equator, up to a maximum of 90° at the celestial poles. The east-west equivalent of longitude is *right ascension,* abbreviated as RA, and is expressed in hours, minutes, and seconds, with a maximum of 24 hours, corresponding to the Earth's rotation period. Since one complete revolution equals 360°, 1 hour of right ascension represents 360°/24 = 15°. As with the Greenwich meridian marking the zero line in the longitude system on Earth, in mapping the stars the point or line selected for the commencement of the 24-hour clock is arbitrary. The choice actually has to do with the Sun, but since, for the moment, we are not permitting the Sun to exist, the explanation will follow later.

Over the course of a full rotation of our dayless planet, an observer at the north (or south) pole will see the pole star at the zenith, and the celestial equator will be on the horizon. The same half of the sky will always be visible (either the northern or the southern hemisphere only), and all the stars will revolve around the celestial pole with none rising or setting – that is, they will all be *circumpolar*. At the equator, an observer will see the entire celestial sphere over the course of the 24 hours in which the planet rotates. Every star will rise and set, and each will do so at a right angle to the eastern or western horizon. In between these two extreme locations, some stars will be circumpolar, like, for example, the stars of Ursa Major as seen from the UK, while others will rise and set at a slant angle to the horizon of 90° less the latitude. For example, at 40°N the slant angle will be 50° towards the south. (The slant angle for stars rising and setting as seen from the southern hemisphere is to the north.)

For a northern-hemisphere observer at 51°N, any star with a declination of +51° will be directly overhead when it is on the *meridian,* the imaginary line through the north and south celestial poles and the zenith. From such a location, it follows that the farther south the declination of a constellation, the lower its position in the sky. For example, Leo is never as high as Ursa Major, and Orion (which straddles the celestial equator) is never as high as Leo. Capricornus, at around −15° declination, is lower still, and we eventually reach the stage where constellations are so far south in declination that they never rise for northern observers at higher latitudes. Thus Crux, the Southern Cross, can never be seen from the UK or much of the continental US. The reverse is true, of course, for southern observers viewing northern-hemisphere constellations. It is appropriate to point out here that the constellations are line-of-sight effects as viewed from Earth, and are not groupings of stars that are genuinely associated.

N ow, having explained in outline about the apparent movement of the stars and their positions in the sky, neither of which change in essence from century to century, let us introduce the Sun into the scheme of things. Here there are two effects to consider: what happens as the Earth orbits the Sun in a period of a little over 365 days, and what happens as a result of the Earth's daily rotation on its axis. For the time being we shall ignore the other planets.

The Sun

As the Earth orbits the Sun during the year, the latter appears to pursue a path against the background of the stars – although it is of course too bright to permit us to see them – and this path is called the *ecliptic*. Unfortunately, the ecliptic does not run neatly along the celestial equator, because the Earth's axis is tilted at an angle of 23.5° to the perpendicular to the plane in which it orbits the Sun. This tilt causes the Sun's apparent path to appear as in Figure 1.2. (This inclination of the Earth's axis is the cause of the seasons, which have nothing to do with the Earth moving any closer to or farther from the Sun. But we need to limit ourselves here to the more astronomical aspects.) The Sun reaches its farthest point north (declination +23.5°) on about June 21, when it is overhead on the Tropic of Cancer (latitude 23.5°N), and its farthest point south around December 22, when it is similarly located over the Tropic of Capricorn (latitude 23.5°S). The Sun appears to remain at about the same altitude for a few days, hence the name given to these events: *solstices*, meaning "standing still of the Sun." The June date represents midsummer in the northern hemisphere and midwinter in the southern. The December date represents northern midwinter and southern midsummer.

It is quite straightforward to work out the noontime altitude or elevation of the Sun above the horizon from any position on Earth if we know its declination. Let us take June 21 as an example. The Sun's declination is then +23.5°. At latitude 51°N (the south coast of England, to be parochial) the altitude of the celestial equator is $90° - 51° = 39°$ to the south. Add 23.5 to 39, and we establish that the highest the Sun will ever be along the south coast of England is 62.5°. The altitude of the Sun for the same location at midwinter is just 15.5°.

June 21 and December 22 represent midsummer in the two respective hemispheres. The dates on which the Sun crosses the celestial equator on its apparent annual journey (March 21 and September 23) are called the *vernal* or *spring equinox* and the *autumnal equinox*, respectively. On these dates day and night are the same length; the word "equinox" means "equal night." We can refer back now to the apparently arbitrary position at which right ascension commences to be measured: it is at the spring equinox, when the Sun is in the constellation Pisces, as can be verified from Figure 1.2.

In the last section, we imagined the movement of the stars across the sky for 24 hours without the Sun. Now that we have reintroduced the Sun, Figure 1.2 enables us to see, without the need to consult any

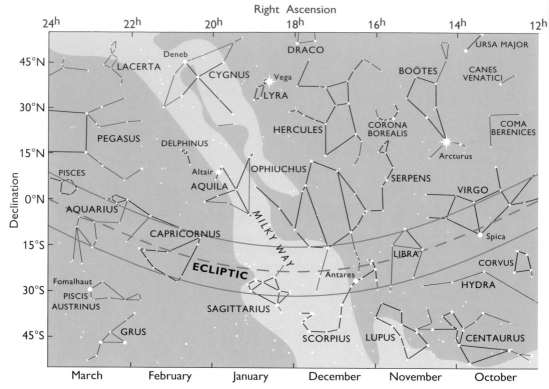

Figure 1.2 *The ecliptic, the path that the Sun appears to follow against the background of the stars over the course of the year. In fact, it is the movement of the Earth about the Sun that creates this effect. Because the Earth's axis is tilted at an angle of 23½°, the ecliptic traces the dashed sinusoidal curve shown on this starchart. The solid lines on either side are the boundaries beyond which the major planets, whose orbits are all slightly inclined to the ecliptic, do not stray as seen from the Earth. (The exception is the small and distant Pluto, whose orbit is more steeply inclined.) The diagram shows why constellations are best seen in certain months of the year. For example, in January, when the Sun is in Sagittarius (RA 19h), the constellation Gemini, 12 RA hours away on the opposite side of the celestial sphere, is high in the sky at midnight in northern latitudes. (The months below the chart indicate when the Sun is in that part of the sky.)*

other document (or even to check the sky), which constellations will be visible at night and which will be lost in the glare of the Sun at any time of the year. On January 5, for example, the Sun is in Sagittarius (RA 19h), so that constellation cannot be seen. But constellations twelve RA hours away (at RA 7h), for example Auriga, Gemini, Taurus, and Orion, are well seen in winter skies at midnight. Chapter 15 shows how a record of the Sun's apparent movement in the sky over the course of an entire year, which forms a figure of eight and is called an analemma, can be made on photographic film.

Now we can consider the matter of the Earth's rotation. Relative to the stars, the Earth completes its daily revolution in a little over 23 hours 56 minutes. That is known as the *sidereal day*. However, the

Earth moves about 1° a day in its orbit around the Sun (although, of course, as seen from the Earth it is the Sun that appears to move by that amount). Therefore the Earth has to rotate not 360° but 361° in order to complete a *solar day*, the extra degree representing 4 minutes in time which gives the solar day of 24 hours.

The difference between the solar and sidereal days means that the stars rise (and set) 4 minutes earlier every day. Thus, for an observer at a particular location, stars which are just rising at 22.00 local time on September 1 will be rising at 20.00 on October 1 (30 × 4 minutes = 2 hours). Moreover, this will occur year in, year out. Winter constellations remain winter constellations! This 4-minute daily gain by the stars is one way of explaining why they gradually "move" into daytime, and then back again into nighttime. Also, it is simple to project the rising or setting times backwards or forwards several months. Thus, to continue the example above, the stars rising at 22.00 on September 1 were rising at around midnight on August 1 and 02.00 on July 1. Moving the other way, they will be rising at 18.00 on November 1 and, say, about 14.00 on January 1. By the way, astronomers usually express all 24-hour clock times in terms of Universal Time (UT), which equates to Greenwich Mean Time (GMT). Universal Time is commonly written with a colon, as in 12:00.

One point about the RA/dec system may confuse newcomers, at least briefly. A location identified by latitude and longitude coordinates on the Earth does not move (unless viewed by an observer in space). However, in considering RA and dec coordinates we have to remember the effects of the Earth's rotation, which causes any location on the celestial sphere to appear to move. Thus the star Spica (RA 13h 25m, dec −11° 10') in the constellation Virgo obviously rises, passes through the meridian, and sets. A major value of the RA/dec system is that it permanently establishes the positions of the stars and other deep-sky objects relative to one another.

Many individual stars in the constellations have names, mostly Arabic in origin. They are also identified by Greek letters, a system introduced in the seventeenth century by the German astronomer Johann Bayer. A hundred of so of the most prominent nebulae, star clusters, and galaxies are known by their Messier numbers (for example, M31 is the Andromeda Galaxy), so called because the French astronomer Charles Messier listed them in the eighteenth century. To add a little confusion, these Messier objects are also known by their NGC numbers, from the *New General Catalogue of Clusters and Nebulae* published in the late nineteenth century, which listed several thousand more.

The planets

Table 1.1 gives some useful information about all nine planets of the Solar System. The planets orbit the Sun in broadly the same plane, but all have slightly different *inclinations* – the amounts by which their orbits are inclined to the plane of the ecliptic. Pluto has an inclination of more than 17°, but the others do not stray far from the ecliptic as seen from Earth, the second biggest inclination being that of Mercury at 7°. This fact gives additional meaning to Figure 1.2, which shows a belt 7 or 8° on either side of the ecliptic. This belt is known as the *zodiac*. It stretches all around the sky, and is the region where the Sun, the Moon, and all the planets, again with the exception of Pluto, are always found. (The belt runs through the twelve zodiacal constellations, and through parts of several others which are not granted the honour of that name.) Thus, a planet will never be found in Ursa Major or Hercules in the northern sky, nor in Centaurus or Grus in the southern sky.

Table 1.1 *The major planets of the Solar System.*

	Average distance from Sun (millions of kilometres)	Equatorial diameter (kilometres)	Period of revolution	Rotation period	Inclination of orbit to ecliptic (degrees)
Mercury	57.9	4,880	88d	59d	7
Venus	108.2	12,104	224.7d	243d R	3.4
Earth	149.6	12,756	365.26d	23h 56m 4s	0
Mars	227.9	6,787	687d	24h 37m 23s	1.9
Jupiter	778.3	143,900	11.86y	9h 55m 30s	1.3
Saturn	1,427	120,540	29.46y	10h 39m 20s	2.5
Uranus	2,869	51,100	84.01y	17.24h R	0.8
Neptune	4,496	50,540	164.1y	16.1h	1.8
Pluto	5,900	2,324	247.7y	6d 9h 18m R	17.2

R indicates retrograde rotation: these planets spin in the opposite direction to the others.

Mercury and Venus are known as *inferior planets*, as their orbits lie inside that of the Earth. Because of this, they show dramatically varying phases as they orbit the Sun. With angular distances from the Sun of never more than 28° for Mercury and 47° for Venus, they are essentially evening or dawn objects for naked-eye viewing. It follows that they can never be seen all through the night. The planets with orbits beyond that of the Earth are known as *superior planets*.

Earth and Mars, like Mercury and Venus, are essentially rocky planets, but beyond Mars and the asteroid belt lie the gas giants – Jupiter, Saturn, Uranus, and Neptune – all with deep, dense atmospheres. The slower-moving superior planets take longer to traverse a given area of the sky: if Mars travels through a constellation in two months, Saturn will take about two and a half years and Neptune over fourteen years. One useful result of this is that once one of these planets is in our night sky, it will remain visible for some years (or months in the case of Mars).

All the planets proceed at their varying speeds in an easterly direction, but one line-of-sight effect (which occurs most dramatically in the case of Mars) may puzzle newcomers. Occasionally Mars checks in its easterly movement, appears to move west for a short while, and then resumes its eastward journey. This is called *retrograde* motion. This happens because the Earth moves faster than Mars: the Earth's year is not far off half that of the Red Planet. Periodically the two bodies are in relative positions on the same side of the Sun whereby the Earth catches up with Mars and passes it. To observers on the Earth, Mars appears to stop and perform what is called a retrograde loop, after which its normal apparent motion is restored (see Chapter 15).

Since the planets are all in orbit about the Sun, it will be evident that, unlike the stars, their positions in the sky cannot be represented on an unchanging map. Still, the normal and quite logical method of showing their positions month by month is to superimpose them on a background chart of the stars.

The Moon

The Moon can dominate the sky on many nights, particularly when it is full or *gibbous* (between half and full). It shines, like the planets, by reflecting light from the Sun. It appears so bright because it is in a largely dark sky and there is nothing to rival it, but in fact its dark surface reflects only 7 percent of the incident sunlight. In this respect it is markedly inferior to Venus, for example, but from the Earth there is a lot more of it in the sky!

The Moon moves eastwards in its elliptical orbit at the rate of about one diameter per hour, or 13° in 24 hours, against the celestial background. This accounts for the fact that it rises later each night, by about 45 or 50 minutes on average. But this time lag can be much shorter. When the angle of the ecliptic to the horizon is very shallow, and from one night to the next the Moon's eastward motion places it only a short distance beneath the horizon, the retardation can be as little as 20 minutes. The opposite occurs when the ecliptic slopes more steeply to the horizon, when the retardation can be over 1 hour.

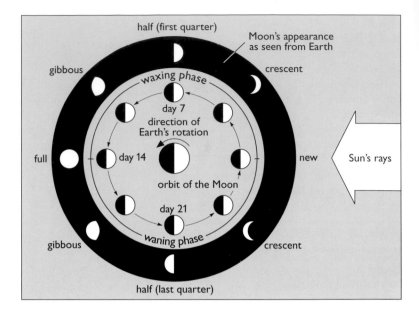

Figure 1.3 *The phases of the Moon. As the Moon moves in its orbit, the proportion of its illuminated side that is visible from the Earth changes. At new Moon, the sunlit hemisphere is turned away from us, and we see only the nightside. As it moves from new to full, the Moon is said to be waxing as it passes through the crescent, half, and gibbous phases. The waning Moon passes through the same sequence but in reverse. The two half phases are often called first and last quarter.*

The Moon's *sidereal month*, the time it takes to return to the same point in its orbit as seen against the background stars, is completed in about 27.3 days. This is also the period taken by the Moon to spin once on its axis, so we see broadly the same hemisphere all the time from Earth. (The far side was not seen until the coming of the space era.) What is called the *synodic month* – the period between successive alignments of Earth, Moon, and Sun – is approximately 29.5 days, and this is therefore the period between one new Moon (or one full Moon) and the next.

The phases of the Moon are illustrated in Figure 1.3. This shows that a waxing crescent Moon of a few days is always an early evening object in a dark sky, while its waning counterpart can rise only shortly before dawn. Similarly, a full Moon must rise in the east as the Sun sets in the west. Artistic licence – or ignorance – in paintings and composite photographs leads all too often to the Moon being depicted in a manner which is physically impossible.

One interesting fact is that, as seen from the Moon, the Earth is in the complementary phase. For example, at times when a waxing crescent Moon is in our skies, a Moon-based observer would see a waning gibbous Earth. While this can be inferred from Figure 1.3, the Apollo lunar missions supplied tangible photographic proof. The lunar landings required a relatively low Sun angle so that the astronauts would have optimum shadow detail. This would give them the clearest view of the surface, essential in making last-minute decisions during the final approach to touchdown. The desired angle was 10°. The first lunar landing mission, Apollo 11, was scheduled to land in the southwestern corner of the Sea of Tranquillity in July 1969. New Moon was on July 14, and a 10° phase angle would occur at the landing site on only one day that month – the 20th. All other mission details (such as the launch from Florida on July 16) were shaped to this one end. As the crew entered lunar orbit on July 19, they took pictures from above a 5-day waxing crescent Moon of a noticeably gibbous waning Earth. When the lunar module *Eagle* redocked with the command module *Columbia* late on July 21 after the momentous landing, the Earth was photographed at last quarter, just as the Moon was at first quarter.

Eclipses

One final point about the phases of the Moon needs explaining. From Figure 1.3, it would be quite logical to assume that solar eclipses occur every time the Moon is new, and lunar eclipses every time the Moon is full. In fact, both sorts of eclipse are relatively infrequent. The Moon's orbit is inclined at about 5° to the ecliptic. When the Moon passes between the Earth and the Sun, it is usually above or below the plane of the ecliptic. It is only when the Moon is at one of the *nodes* of its orbit (the two points at which its orbit intersects the ecliptic) at the time of new Moon or full Moon that the three bodies are aligned, producing a solar or lunar eclipse. Partial eclipses take place if the alignment is not quite perfect. We owe the existence of the beauty of a total solar eclipse to the sheer coincidence that, as seen from the Earth, the two other bodies are about the same angular size.

This chapter has concentrated on explaining the general scheme of things. Other bodies of the Solar System, such as comets, meteoroids, and interplanetary dust, are discussed in later chapters.

CHAPTER 2

Another world

Many forms of photography are difficult or demanding, and sometimes even dangerous, particularly in professional practice. As far as the amateur is concerned, astrophotography makes demands of a technical kind as well as on personal attitudes. The technical demands, moreover, involve some features which will be new even to experienced "everyday" photographers. Astrophotography may be described, indeed, as another world.

Location and exposures

Before anything can be done, the astrophotographer has to search for the subject – a task which most other photographers do not face. When the subject is the Moon the exercise is usually very easy (the note of caution is sounded because how many readers have attempted to locate a newly risen, totally eclipsed Moon?), but most other targets are more difficult. Locating a constellation and checking that it is all within the field of view of the chosen lens requires some elementary astronomical knowledge. And, as the subjects become fainter and the powers of magnification higher, the search becomes harder. This leads to consideration of the low light levels encountered by the astrophotographer, and the resulting lengthy exposures. The classic everyday exposure of 1/125 of a second at f/11 may well be suitable for photographing a full Moon with a film of moderate speed. But, as one moves to other subjects such as stars or meteors, exposures lengthen considerably. For example, an exposure not of 1/125 of a second but of 125 seconds, which many everyday photographers will never have used in their lives, would be regarded as quite short for some subjects. And, as one progresses to more demanding subjects, exposures of many minutes become the order of the day (or, rather, of the night).

There is a corollary to this consideration of low light levels. A keen everyday photographer fully realizes the importance of focusing accurately (many cameras now accomplish this automatically, of course) and will make this an important albeit obvious part of technique. Usually such a procedure is easy. Life is not quite so easy for the astrophotographer. This may sound very surprising, because a moment's thought will indicate that only one focusing distance is needed in astrophotography – infinity. However, while virtually all shorter focal length lenses have a fixed infinity setting, some top-quality telephoto lenses of modest focal length, around 200 mm or more, can be focused beyond the nominal infinity setting to compensate for temperature changes. And this is also true of most catadioptric, or mirror-reflex, photographic lenses (as well as telescopes). If the target is a dim celestial object, focusing is far from easy, and the availability of special, bright viewing screens in the more advanced camera systems is a valuable asset.

When we start out in everyday photography, a major concern is to learn the correct exposure for various subjects. As we gain experience, we learn that the matter is not quite so clear cut. Somebody who, for example, likes a contrasty black-and-white negative to print from may well give a different exposure than another photographer despite using a film of the same speed. The non-existence of what might be called universally correct exposures for a range of subjects is very much part of the experienced astrophotographer's knowledge. Any exposure aimed at achieving high quality is the product of weighing up a complex combination of factors involving equipment, film, subject, procedures, and conditions, and can vary greatly. A straightforward example is that of the Moon photographed at different times after it rises. An exposure made as it comes into view over the horizon, and shines through the maximum thickness of atmosphere, could easily differ by a full stop (see page 21) from one made when the Moon is at its maximum altitude, on the meridian, and shining through the minimum thickness of atmosphere. Similarly, some stars (those called, appropriately enough, variables) and the planets (as orbital motion takes them farther from or closer to us) show variations in brightness quite separate from the effects of the atmospheric conditions under which we view them. Calculating exposures will be dealt with at greater length later, but it is appropriate here to stress the need to allow for variations. In practice, this means making a number of exposures, some shorter and some longer than an exposure time indicated by calculation and/or experience. This is known as *bracketing*.

This is a major reason why it is so important for the astrophotographer to get into the habit from the beginning of keeping detailed notes – something the everyday photographer does not normally need to do. Such notes should include information about the equipment/film combination used, as well as the local viewing conditions and other relevant factors upon which no distant "expert" can meaningfully advise. It is on the basis of these notes that subjects can be returned to and tackled with more confidence, new ones approached with greater insight and, in general, experience gained and progress made.

A**lthough** it will be dealt with later in more detail, there is a major difference concerning photographic theory and practice between astrophotography and many other forms of photography. This difference is fundamental and needs to be understood clearly by the newcomer. To the everyday photographer, the measure of the speed of a lens is its *focal ratio*, known otherwise as its *f-number*. The focal ratio is one vital factor in the calculation of a photographic exposure (the other three being shutter speed, film sensitivity, and the brightness of the subject). It is a value derived by dividing the *focal length* of the lens

Focal ratio and focal length

by its diameter. Focal length is the property of the lens that controls the scale of the image: the longer the focal length, the larger the image. Thus a 25-mm diameter lens with a focal length of 50 mm is referred to as an *f/2* lens.

The focal length of a lens has a direct bearing on the image size of a subject. For a particular lens diameter, a longer focal length will spread the image of a subject – formed from the same amount of light – over a greater area of the film. The lens is then said to be *slower*, because it will take a longer exposure to build up an image of a particular density. Similarly, a lens of shorter focal length (but of the same diameter) will concentrate the image into a smaller area of film, so that a shorter exposure will produce an image of comparable density. Such a lens is said to be *faster*. If we double the focal length the area of the image is four times greater, for it is proportional to the square of the focal length. So, if we double the focal length of a 50-mm focal length *f/2* lens of 25 mm diameter, we have a 100 mm/25 mm = *f/4* focal ratio lens. The everyday photographer understands the importance of *f*-number in exposure calculations, but in astronomy a new situation is confronted.

When we photograph the Moon, or a comet, or an aurora, the size of the image on the film relates directly to the focal length of the lens we use, just as it does when we photograph everyday subjects. The Moon, which is quite a reasonably sized disk when recorded on the film frame of a 35-mm camera fitted with a 250-mm focal length lens, doubles in size when a 500-mm focal length lens is used instead. Astronomical subjects of this kind behave just like those photographed by the everyday hobbyist, and astronomers and astrophotographers refer to them as *extended objects*. Now to the major difference. The stars are so far away that, to all intents and purposes, no matter how great the focal length of the lens, they can be rendered only as point sources. They are not extended objects, and the measure of how fast or slow a lens is in recording them is judged instead by its diameter, not by its focal ratio. The same applies to the planets, up to the point at which (since they are not so far away) we reach a focal length sufficient to record a particular planet as something more than a point of light. That planet then becomes an extended object, and once again focal ratio becomes a major concern in calculating exposures.

This point has been stressed early in the book because it is a potential source of confusion, even to quite experienced photographers. If you asked them to choose the faster of two lenses, a 35-mm *f/1.4* and a 180-mm *f/2.8*, quite understandably they would choose the former, and they would be correct for extended objects. But for photographing the stars they would be wrong, for the former has a lens diameter of 25 mm (35 mm/1.4), whereas the latter has a diameter of over 64 mm (180 mm/2.8). Hence, when using the same film, a camera fitted with the 180-mm lens would record a considerably greater number of fainter stars over a given period of time than would a 50-mm lens.

While we are considering definitions, there is one other potential source of confusion, between astronomers and photographers this time, that needs to be highlighted. It arises from the manner in which the two groups refer to telescopes and lenses. The figures "35 mm," "180 mm," "250 mm," and so on have already been used here in referring to lenses. All photographers will immediately recognize these to be an indication of the focal length of the lenses, and thereby of the relative size of images produced on the film. However, when such figures are used by astronomers they refer to the diameter or *aperture* of a telescope objective or lens. Their main concern is the light-gathering capability of their telescopes (just as the above references to lens diameters concern the speed of the lens in capturing stars as point sources). Throughout this book such figures will be used in the photographic sense of focal length; if the diameter of a lens is being considered it will be referred to quite specifically as such. Fortunately, focal ratio has the same meaning for both astronomers and photographers!

A question of history, and squaring

Many terms from the early years of photography continue to be used. For example, *f*-numbers or focal ratios are often referred to as *stops*. This word dates from the time when the full diameter of a lens was made smaller by placing in front of it a metal plate containing a series of circular holes of different diameters. The exposure was modified according to the stop placed in front of the lens. Aperture is another term used loosely to mean stop or *f*-number. Nowadays, the focal ratio is altered by an iris diaphragm, consisting of a number of blades which close in from the edge of the lens or open out when a ring on the lens is rotated.

It is reasonably easy to understand how an *f*-number is the result of dividing the focal length of a lens by its absolute diameter. And it follows quite straightforwardly that, the lower the *f*-number, the faster the lens – in much the same way that, the lower a golfer's handicap, the better the golfer, and the lower a star's magnitude, the brighter the star (see Chapter 1). But the apparently haphazard sequence of the actual *f*-numbers, with values such as $f/1.4$ and $f/5.6$, needs some explanation. The amount of light a lens transmits is proportional to its area, which in turn is proportional to the square of its effective diameter. Although some rounding off has to take place, squaring the *f*-numbers gives a far more understandable relationship, as shown in Table 2.1.

Thus, in order to halve or double the amount of light transmitted by the lens, the photographer changes the *f*-number one stop higher or lower, respectively. There is a similar relationship for shutter speeds. As a result, an exposure (that is, the amount of light reaching the film, which is governed by *f*-number and shutter speed) can be held constant while the shutter speed and aperture are altered in a complementary fashion to meet the demands of a particular situation, such as subject movement.

Table 2.1 *The sequence of f-numbers and their squares.*

f-number	1.4	2	2.8	4	5.6	8	11	16	22
Squared value	2	4	8	16	32	64	128	256	512

To give an example: an exposure of *f*/8 at 1/125 of a second is equivalent to one of *f*/11 (one stop less light) at 1/60 of a second (one shutter speed more time), and also to one of *f*/5.6 (one stop more light) at 1/250 of a second (one shutter speed less time). This straightforward relationship (which is valid in astrophotography except for lengthy exposures, see Chapter 4) enables most of the target exposures given in this book to be extrapolated to give different shutter speeds and apertures provided the mathematical relationship at the starting-point is maintained.

Numerous problems

Astrophotography is set apart from other forms of photography by natural and human factors which have nothing to do with purely photographic matters. So far as nature is concerned, the everyday photographer often seeks ideal circumstances but can usually make do without. But how do you photograph the stars through clouds? Further, although clouds may not be present, the photographic or observing quality of the atmosphere can vary greatly (astronomers usually call it the *seeing*). It may surprise the newcomer to learn that a seemingly beautiful night with a clear sky full of twinkling stars is often a sign of considerable atmospheric turbulence, and therefore of bad seeing. On the other hand, nights ostensibly less clear and suggestive of a little high haze can be much better because the haze results from less disturbed conditions in the atmosphere. Only experience and results on film can provide the key. Sometimes even the major subjects in astrophotography can conspire against us. All too often the Moon will be strong when we want to photograph meteors – all but the brightest of which are thus rendered invisible.

Obviously, by definition the astrophotographer will most often operate at night. Whether early or late, the delights of, say, the British climate or that in many parts of the US can create problems not faced in some other parts of the world. Condensation will form once the temperature of the front element of a lens falls significantly below that of the surrounding air. (It is significant that astronomers use the term "dew cap" for what photographers call a "lens hood.") The problem can be dealt with, but it does demonstrate the greater challenge to the astrophotographer posed by cold temperatures. There is a serious need to dress warmly and not be dissuaded by any comments from our family or friends about looking as though we are going to the Arctic. And on very cold nights we may feel like moving around, stamping our feet or beating our arms to help the circulation – but not during a lengthy time exposure, because of the resulting vibration.

We humans compound natural problems. Urban areas of many countries are swamped by *light pollution* which makes astronomical observing difficult if not impossible, and astrophotography often even more so. As citizens ourselves we understand the need for much of this lighting. But as astronomers we may be forgiven for looking quizzically at the bulk of streetlights, which are designed in such a way that they direct almost as much light upwards (and uselessly) as they do downwards, where it is wanted. There are many other contributors to light pollution: the bright neon advertisements which are seen by few human eyes during the small hours; floodlighting of sports grounds, buildings, and car parks; lighting at shopping precincts, industrial plant, and filling stations; lights left on in offices overnight; and security lighting, on both commercial and domestic premises. In towns we no longer have a dark sky – it is all too often an orange–grey. Attention has been drawn to the inefficiency and waste of energy resulting from badly designed lighting, as well as to its damaging effect on astronomy, by such organizations as the International Dark-Sky Association. Significant gains have been made in some cases, but it is a hard struggle. In the short term, we may have to be prepared to travel to find a dark sky.

Even in our own gardens and backyards we cannot be apart no matter how we try. As we endeavour to photograph an intriguing conjunction of Mars and Jupiter, we may wonder why the image suddenly begins to dance and break up. Then we realize that the Earth's rotation has brought the two planets directly above the chimney or flue of a nearby house. Perhaps we are in the middle of a lengthy time exposure when a neighbour opens the kitchen door and a bright light imperils both the exposure and the dark adaptation of our eyes. And who can blame the neighbour's dog, on its final inspection tour of the garden, for reacting noisily to the suspiciously muted sounds being made by the astrophotographer on the other side of the fence?

Eventually the sounds of the day's activities begin to fade. Perhaps a cat is delighted to find that somebody is in the garden at an unlikely hour, and comes over to enjoy a pat. Later, one may hear the unmistakable shrieking barks of a fox, or a faint snuffling sound which is puzzling until a family of hedgehogs is located by torchlight/flashlight. Of course, there is need to concentrate on the work in hand but the small hours are a time for philosophizing, too, particularly if one is alone and not working with a companion or group (not an occupation for the nervous, perhaps). One might deliberate on the apparent superficiality of civilization, and on how easily the sounds and semblance of everyday life disappear as the night gets deeper.

Astrophotography is not for those who cannot resist the comfort of retiring to a warm bed, nor for those unprepared to rise from one during the course of the night. These are the disciplinary demands of the calling: if an astronomical event occurs in the early hours then the staunch astrophotographer must be up and about to record the event – unless, for the lucky few, automated equipment is left on patrol. Similarly, in areas where the weather is fickle we must strive to be resolute and photograph an object of interest as soon as the weather allows. To put it off because there is something of interest on TV reveals that we are not made of the "right stuff."

Yes, astrophotography and some philosophizing go hand in hand, and we realize our vulnerability to Murphy's law, which is usually referred to by astronomers as Spode's law. This states not only that if something can go wrong it shall, but also that it shall go wrong in the worst possible circumstances. Thus a lengthy time exposure will be ruined by a cat knocking the tripod (or the astrophotographer sneezing and hitting it with an arm), not at the beginning of an exposure but just before the end so that the maximum amount of time is wasted. Similarly, if due care is not being taken, it will be at the end and not the beginning of a session that the astrophotographer will discover an equipment malfunction.

When this slightly tongue-in-cheek account of the astrophotographer's world is read by likely recruits, there is a chance that they might be dissuaded from attempting to enter it. (It could have been even worse: the saying that the average success rate in astrophotography is perhaps one in twelve or twenty-four exposures if the photographer is very good, or lucky, has not been mentioned!) This would be a great pity. It is true that to do reasonably well and to progress, even in the early stages of astrophotography, requires application and a systematic approach – qualities not be found in the casually interested or those who wish a subject to be "easy." But what enjoyment is there, and what sense of achievement, in practising what is easy?

For those willing to make the effort, to learn from mistakes, and to suffer the inevitable consequences of Spode's law with fortitude and a sense of humour, the rewards and enjoyment are great. There is above us a magnificent panorama, and to seek to capture parts of it on film is a task of endless challenge which makes the successes all the sweeter. This book is intended to help you if you wish to take up that challenge. If you are a photographer already your experience will be of some help, even though astrophotography is "another world." Read on ...

CHAPTER 3

Equipment

It is as well to state the bad news first. Compact cameras, which have been so successful in recent years, are totally unsuitable for astrophotography. This is because they have no B shutter setting to permit the manually controlled time exposures that are such an essential part of astrophotography. (The B stands for "bulb," the pressure device with which the shutter was originally controlled.) This sweeping statement is slightly unfair, in that it is possible to use a compact camera loaded with fast film to photograph a pictorial sky scene at twilight, featuring perhaps clouds with the Moon and very bright planets. But this is the extent of their capability, and they cannot be regarded as of sufficient importance to warrant inclusion in an analysis of suitable cameras.

The camera

Today's ordinary, keen photographer has three basic types of camera from which to choose. In the *single-lens reflex*, the subject is viewed through the lens itself by means of a mirror, which is flipped out of the way at the moment of exposure. In the *twin-lens reflex*, one lens is used to expose the film, while the photographer views the scene via a second lens, usually located above the first. With both these types the photographer sees the image focused onto a large glass viewfinder screen. With the third type, the *rangefinder* or non-reflex camera, the photographer views the scene not via a lens but directly through a viewfinder frame. The second and third types were introduced long before the single-lens reflex became available.

Now, as far as astrophotography is concerned, the rangefinder camera can be employed at least for star photography. Similarly, a twin-lens reflex would be suitable for photographing constellations, and its right-angle viewing system would have the added advantage of making things more comfortable for the photographer (see page 27). However, a basic limitation of both types (with one or two exceptions such as the Leica rangefinder cameras) is their inability to accept interchangeable lenses. It is this feature that over the past decades has led to the overwhelming popularity of the single-lens reflex, commonly known as the SLR. In some ways this name is inappropriate because the camera's major feature of accepting interchangeable lenses really makes it a multiple-lens reflex.

Important too is the ability of a camera to take interchangeable lenses, so that, for example, the photographer can record very extensive constellations at one extreme, and high-quality close-ups of the Moon at the other. This may not be as essential as the B shutter setting, but it does enable most areas of astrophotography to be explored. Moreover, the versatility of the SLR and the fact that the best models are the basis of an entire system of photography that can accommodate the increasing skill and interest of the enthusiast make them the optimum choice for the astrophotographer. Medium-format SLRs (cameras using a 120-mm or 70-mm size roll) are available as well as 35-mm models, but since they are regarded for the most part as cameras for professional use, this discussion will concentrate on 35-mm models.

It may be that some readers of this book are considering buying a camera. There are at least three options, depending on how much money is available. The first is to purchase as new one of the lower-priced SLR models offering a reasonable number of the features that are available on the more expensive models. Such cameras are usually robustly built and may be regarded as the next step for the developing photographer. Various models in the Zenith range and the somewhat higher-priced Pentax K1000 are current examples. The second option is to purchase a used model of one of the leading makes from a reputable dealer. There is a need to select carefully, but in this way an excellent camera providing most of the features required, plus an extensive range of lenses and other items, may be purchased at a cost considerably below new.

The third possibility, of course, is to buy as new one of the latest models from a leading manufacturer such as Nikon, Minolta, Canon, Pentax, Olympus, or Leica. Apart from price, an important difference between the first option on the one hand and the other two is the increased number of features and therefore the greater versatility that the purchaser may expect. Clearly there will be differences of quality between the cheaper and more expensive models too, although this may not always be readily apparent to the newcomer. The choice is one for the individual, and must reflect personal circumstances. There is, however, one encouraging aspect, whatever choice is made. Although the purchaser may have astrophotography very much in mind, these cameras are suitable for most forms of photography and so are likely to be used extensively. And, should the individual regrettably decide to give up astrophotography or photography altogether, the appeal of the cameras is such that a ready market should be found for them.

Many of today's cameras have automatic exposure systems, but, while possible uses here and there are mentioned occasionally in this book, effectively they play no part in astrophotography. The nature of most astronomical objects is such that automatic exposure systems, although extremely sophisticated in dealing with the great variety of everyday subjects, cannot cope. (Hence the reference above to the suitability of older and, by definition, manually operated cameras.) One other feature of many current cameras is a dependence to a greater or lesser degree on battery power to perform various functions, especially to operate the shutter. This is an important consideration for the astrophotographer, since long exposures will often be employed, and continual use of the B shutter setting drains batteries faster than normal shutter speeds. Some very advanced and successful makes of camera – Minolta, for example – are totally dependent on battery power for all functions.

Such dependence on batteries creates a phobia in the minds of some photographers about the total failure of a camera at a critical moment (Spode's law again). This fear seems somewhat exaggerated, for all that is required is care in ensuring that spare batteries of the right type are always carried. (A more serious problem is the possible drop in battery power caused by low temperatures.) In any case, some models offer a flexibility in shutter operation. Thus the Canon F1N has a hybrid electromechanical shutter mechanism in which the B setting can be mechanically operated without battery power, and the Nikon F3 has a mechanical shutter release which also provides a time exposure capability. The Pentax LX is somewhat different. It has a hybrid system offering a choice of either electromagnetic or mechanical shutter operation, but while B is mechanically set and can be used without battery power, if the battery is present in the camera it is under drain while the shutter is open.

Clearly, a detailed review of this subject is not possible here, but it is a point for consideration by those contemplating a camera with astrophotography principally in mind. The above reference to the mechanical or non-battery operation of the B setting should not be confused with the manual operation of a camera's exposure controls – that is, the ability to switch from an automatic exposure mode. Most moderate to expensive 35-mm SLRs have this facility, which, as already stated, is essential for astrophotography.

There are a number of other features of a camera which, although not essential, are highly desirable. In everyday photography, the 35-mm SLR is typically used at eye level, the subject being framed through the camera's viewfinder. In general this is a comfortable position for the photographer and involves no strain. An important item of equipment for the astrophotographer is a tripod, upon which the camera is mounted and may then be pointed at varying angles towards the sky. However, tripods usually extend to no more than about a metre, so the photographer has to bend to view the scene through the finder, the more so if the camera is aimed at or near the zenith. This is more troublesome for tall people and those with any back problems. Some means of viewing the sky by looking down towards the camera (as an astronomer uses a star diagonal at the telescope) will therefore be a great advantage for all astrophotographers.

What is possible will depend on the particular camera system in use. On some cameras from which the standard viewfinder cannot be removed, a right-angle finder can be fitted. This has an inevitable effect on the amount of light being transmitted to the eye. More preferable is to use a camera with a removable viewfinder, and to replace it with one of the various forms of *right-angle viewer* that are available (see Figure 3.1). These can be as relatively simple as what is normally called a waist-level finder, where one looks down at the camera viewing screen via a small magnifier which facilitates focusing, to more complex units

Figure 3.1 *The single-lens reflex (SLR), besides being an admirable general-purpose camera, is well suited for astrophotography. The more advanced camera systems have features which, although not essential, are desirable. The camera on the left, for example, is fitted with the normal, eye-level viewing prism: when the camera is being used on a tripod for astrophotography this can result in the photographer having to bend a great deal to see what is in the viewfinder. A right-angle, high-magnification viewfinder — as in the camera on the right — is much more convenient although by no means inexpensive.*

affording greater magnification with individual eyesight adjustment. The system chosen must depend on camera type and the individual's purse, but both back and eyes benefit from the use of such a viewer and the results achieved can only be better. One feature of many right-angle viewers that may be disconcerting at first is that they reverse a scene from left to right. This can make the task of newcomers, trying to find their way among the constellations, just that little more difficult.

Also desirable is the facility to change from the normal viewing screen supplied with an SLR to one more suitable for astrophotography. Focusing at very low light levels can be difficult, particularly when long lenses are in use, and in photography through a telescope. The screen pattern and central rangefinder disk on many everyday viewing screens serve no purpose in astrophotography. Two interchangeable screens are of value. When starting out, constellations and stars will be the most frequent subjects and an uninterrupted, fine-ground matte screen is the most suitable. In tackling subjects like the Moon or the planets at high magnifications, a screen with a central clear spot and a cross-hair for use in parallax focusing is an advantage. In parallax focusing the eye is moved very slightly from right to left and back again, and if the cross-hair stays in the same position relative to the subject then the latter is in focus. It is a technique that takes some getting used to, but is most effective when developed.

Two other camera features are valuable when working at slow shutter speeds. Exposures longer than a few seconds present no problem if the black card technique (see Chapter 5) is used. However, between such lengthy exposures and very fast ones is a no-man's-land where the results are highly vulnerable to camera shake and vibration. In these cases, the ability to lock up the SLR mirror, which always creates some vibration when it flips out of the light path before the shutter is opened, is most useful. The self-timer (or delayed action release), which enables the shutter to be fired after a period of a few seconds, is also of value in that its use removes the possibility of actions by the photographer causing the camera to shake, even when a cable release is used.

Such features may appear somewhat esoteric, but they can play a definite part in the quality of results. Most are present on top-quality cameras, and it is appropriate that anybody planning a purchase with astrophotography in mind should be aware of the possibilities, though personal budgets may well limit the options. There are other features too. Many cameras now offer slower, manually set shutter speeds from 1 to 8 seconds, several going up to 30 seconds. This reduces the emphasis on using the B setting. A few cameras, such as the Nikon F3 and F4, have a T setting (the T stands for "time"), which performs the same function as B but does not require the use of a cable release. Instead, the shutter is fired and stays open until the shutter speed ring is rotated to another value. Other cameras have a switch enabling the double-exposure prevention device to be overridden, which is helpful when you are making multi-exposure images of the Moon and Sun. *Data backs*, which print the date, exposure data, or reference numbers on or between frames are growing steadily more popular. And, while normally costing a little extra, the choice of a totally black finish to the camera is well worthwhile because it helps to suppress reflections, whether one is engaged in photography at night or perhaps the subsequent photographic copying of originals.

Photographers tend to take a great interest in the technical explanation of how photographs were obtained. In this book, therefore, considerable detail is given about equipment and films. I have for many years been a user of Nikon SLR camera systems, and have found that they meet virtually all my demands. Nikon is a leader in SLR photography, but there are a number of cameras from other manufacturers that are capable of yielding similar results. A review of pictures published in the astronomical press will give information on what cameras are used. Ultimately, it is a matter of individual choice.

Lenses

Just as it is possible to give only limited guidance on camera choice, so it is for lenses. In the final count it is the picture a lens helps to create that is the crucial test, and that test involves a combination of other factors – film, exposure, conditions, and so on – which can either enhance or limit the performance of any lens. With that in mind, it is possible to offer some general observations on the lens in astrophotography.

First and foremost is the fact that astrophotography presents what is arguably the most severe test possible for a lens. All lens systems have potential aberrations which designers endeavour to limit by means of compromises that vary according to the type of lens. Astrophotography tends to press these compromises to the limit. During our first attempts at photographing the stars, we endeavour to "snatch" pictures by using a very fast film with a fast lens set at its maximum aperture. When an everyday photographer uses a lens in this way it may well be to capture a nighttime or available-light scene containing varying blocks of light and shade, and probably "busy" subject matter, to draw the eye. Lens aberrations will be scarcely noticed.

In a constellation image, however, there is only a dark sky with points of light, and any distortions will be revealed very clearly. When a fast lens is used for star photography there is almost certain to be some *coma*, in which points of light are spread into pear-shapes, and possibly *vignetting*, a darkening of the image towards the edges of the field of view. In the same way, most lenses in everyday photography yield their best performance when stopped down two or three stops from full aperture, whereas the astrophotographer often wants maximum speed. One or two lenses, such as Nikon's 58-mm *f*/1.2 Noct-Nikkor, have been designed for optimum correction of coma, but they are very expensive. So, for the most part, we have to make the best of what are often excellent products used in the most disadvantageous way. Various ways of endeavouring to do this appear in the pages of this book.

A second observation is a corollary of the first. In reviews of a lens, it may be stated that laboratory tests showed the lens to be capable of resolving so many lines per millimetre – one of the recognized performance standards. That information is worth knowing, but we must remember that for astrophotography the lens is not going to be used in optimum circumstances, and certainly not in a laboratory. We need to know about such factors as flare (internal reflections) and edge definition when the lens is used at maximum aperture, not in an "empty" performance under ideal conditions – although all these factors may point to the same conclusion.

The Japanese in particular have developed a flourishing industry of independent lens manufacturers as distinct from camera manufacturers making their own products. Newcomers to photography always ask for advice about this matter since the independents' prices are usually lower. Generalizing is difficult, but I feel that in the main we get the lenses that we pay for, though the differences may not be readily apparent. Thus, in general use a lens designed and made by a leading camera manufacturer and one made by an independent may not seem to differ in optical performance. But it is more than likely that the mechanical strength of the former's lens will be superior, enabling it to withstand rougher treatment, and that optically it will have the edge when used under the most demanding circumstances – which certainly occur in astrophotography.

More specific suggestions can be made about the most suitable focal lengths for use in astrophotography. For recording the constellations, a normal 50-mm focal length lens, which the everyday photographer is likely to have already, is perfectly satisfactory, though a somewhat

Figure 3.2 *At two extremes: the astrophotographer has need of lenses with greatly differing focal lengths. The 35-mm f/1.4 on the right, weighing about 400 g (1 lb), has a picture angle of 62° and is often used for photographing the constellations. The 1000-mm f/11 catadioptric or mirror-reflex lens, weighing 2000 g (4¹/₂ lb), has a picture angle of only 2° 30', and is an admirable lens for photographing the Moon and Sun (the latter through a special filter).*

wider-angle lens of around 35 mm will be needed for more extensive constellations (see Figure 3.2). Notwithstanding the potential aberrations, the lenses should be as fast as possible. At the other extreme, photography of the Moon and Sun really demands longer focal lengths, and a 500-mm mirror-reflex lens, which is smaller and lighter than conventional designs, is an admirable starting-point, even if it is of fixed aperture.

While there are many bargains available, our pockets are not limitless, and perhaps three lenses will be the most that many of us can afford. In that event, a strong case can be made for the third lens being a moderate focal length zoom lens, say from 35 to 105 mm. These lenses have improved greatly in quality in recent years. While not as fast as standard lenses, they are by no means slow. They provide a flexibility, when used with high-speed films, which is valuable when photographing what might be described as the more pictorial scenes, such as the Moon and planets at twilight with interesting foreground detail.

As with cameras, the use of these and other lenses is not limited to astrophotography. The wide-angle, fast lens may be used for "slice of life" candid photographs, while the long lens can be used for bird or sports photography. There is no need for the lenses to be idle between sessions of astrophotography!

Accessories

There is an old saying in photography that a camera should never be hand-held at a shutter speed slower than the reciprocal of the focal length of the lens in use. This is a rather involved way of stating that if you are using, for example, a 200-mm focal length lens, you should place it on a tripod for any shutter speed slower than 1/250 of a second (the nearest to 1/200). This sound advice, well supported by experience, indicates that in astrophotography a tripod should always be used.

It is not a question of any tripod. The lengthy time exposures often called for, and the risk of camera shake and vibration from various sources, necessitate a solid tripod whose legs can be firmly locked in position and which displays the minimum of whip or movement (see Figure 3.3). Modern lightweight tripods are convenient for carrying around and are satisfactory for meeting the demands of everyday photography. With extreme care they may be used for constellation photography (with short focal length lenses), but for longer focal lengths and the "in between" shutter speeds to which reference has already been made (see page 29), a heavier tripod is essential. While it cannot be regarded as a portable item, if an old-fashioned, professional tripod of great weight can be found at a reasonable price then it should be purchased immediately as a valuable investment in quality.

One detail in particular should be checked when buying a tripod, whether old or new. When the camera is fixed to the tripod, is it possible to angle the camera platform so that the lens points directly upwards? This facility will be needed from time to time, and various handles and other projections on some designs of tripod make it very difficult or impossible to aim the camera at an elevation of 90°. If a tripod is otherwise satisfactory, the problem can be overcome by attaching a heavy-duty ball-and-socket head, but it is obviously an advantage if this further item is not required.

Various types of cable release are available. (As already noted, one is not required if the camera has a T shutter setting.) They differ chiefly in the manner in which the cable is locked, the size of the plunger head, and their length. The release is one item which is essential for the astrophotographer but yet is not costly – a pleasant change.

The everyday photographer, particularly if an enthusiast, is likely to use filters quite frequently. It is my experience, however, that they play a far more limited role in the early stages of astrophotography, although they come into greater prominence later. Early on, it is sound policy to regard a filter as constituting two more surfaces through which an already limited amount of light has to pass, and therefore as something to be dispensed with. (Every time a light beam encounters a surface, it becomes a little weaker.) An exception might well be a deep-red filter to reduce the effects of light pollution when using black-and-white film.

There is one final observation to be made. It does not concern astrophotography only – indeed, it concerns all photography – but it is still worth making in this context. Manufacturers of cameras, accessories, and films publish instruction booklets and leaflets. They have an obvious, commercial incentive for customers to derive the greatest value from their products. Usually the instructions are extensive and extremely helpful in using, and exploring the potential of, the products to the full. All too frequently, however, photographers pay scant attention to the information supplied with what can be a very

Figure 3.3 *The fixed camera and a firm, 4-kg (9-lb) tripod. Many popular tripods are too flimsy to satisfy the exacting demands of astrophotography. A lightweight unit may be attractive because it is easy to pack and carry, but the astrophotographer frequently uses much longer time exposures than other photographers and such exposures demand a very firm and steady (and therefore usually heavy) tripod – which is also more stable in windy conditions.*

expensive purchase. This is short-sighted, and limits the development of the individual's skill. Get out the instruction booklet for your camera again (can you put your hand on it immediately?), and read it. It will be very surprising if you can say that you know it all.

In the early years of photography there was no sophisticated shutter mechanism. The sensitized paper or plate was so slow that the "artist" used a hat or lens cap to uncover the lens for an exposure that ran into many seconds. For lengthy time exposures the astrophotographer imitates the early pioneers by using a large black card, which may be cut from a box in which photographic paper is supplied, or something similar. The technique is elaborated in Chapter 5.

A white-light torch/flashlight is useful for checking the observing site for obstructions before a session, and to make sure nothing is being left

Non-photographic Items

behind afterwards. The provision of a red-light torch needs a little more explanation. Our eyes' capability of adapting to darkness has already been explained, in Chapter 1. In working around our camera, altering its controls and making notes, we need some light. However, the light from an ordinary torch would appear blindingly bright to our eyes and, of course, ruin our dark adaptation, which it will take time to regain. It so happens, however, that the dark-adapted eye is least sensitive to red light. So, while a red light is sufficient for the astronomer's or astrophotographer's needs, it does not affect dark adaptation, or at least does so only minimally. Specialist astronomical stores sell red-light torches/flashlights, but it is easy enough to locate a piece of dark red plastic about the house or toolshed. Bicycle rear lights are not recommended: they are efficient for their intended use, but tend to be far too powerful for our purpose.

The provision of an electronic timer (as opposed to the use of a watch) for carefully timing long exposures is a matter of personal choice. The advantages of the countdown timer of the type used in kitchens or photographic darkrooms are that the (usually) LCD time display is easily set by buttons or some other means, and an alarm sounds at time zero. A watch is smaller and therefore more difficult to operate, particularly when fingers are beginning to get cold.

Finally there are the notepad and pen, which are regarded so highly by astrophotographers. No guidance is needed on the former, but some of the generally available ballpoint and other pens deal poorly with the task of writing on paper that is becoming damp in the night air. A plastic cover could be used to prevent this, but I have found that the Fisher pressurized cartridge pens that were used for many years by flight crews in the US space programme write satisfactorily on damp paper. Doubtless there are other types. You may choose to avoid the dampness problem by using a small tape recorder instead.

CHAPTER 4

Films

Today the amateur has a very wide range of high-quality colour transparency, colour negative–positive, and black-and-white films from which to choose. In this chapter, only colour transparency and black-and-white films are dealt with as they are the most suitable for the newcomer to astrophotography. This may seem a little strange because negative films yielding colour prints are the almost universal choice of the typical amateur, with transparency film trailing a long way behind. The reason lies in the nature of the subjects that the budding astrophotographer will be photographing. The typical photo-shop lab offers a good service in processing and printing films of conventional scenes. But a night sky with stars, an aurora, or a meteor trail crossing a starscape are not conventional subjects. What we are asking the lab to do is make a colour print from a masked (orange) negative without knowing even the approximate colour of the original subject. This is a difficult task, and the risk of disappointment is high. Thus, although colour negative–positive films (called negative films for short) are of excellent quality and yield good results, even when underexposed or, in particular, overexposed (their *latitude*, as it is called, is better than that of transparency films), my advice is to stay with transparency films until experience has been gained. Advanced astrophotographers make more use of negative colour film because of the options it offers them for subsequent darkroom manipulation, but in the early days it is best to use a film that yields a positive colour image once processing has been completed, without any further demands being made on photographer or darkroom worker.

In Chapter 2 the point was stressed that astrophotography is "another world" – and nowhere is this more so than with films. Almost without exception, the films used by the amateur astrophotographer have been designed for normal use and for the reproduction of typical, everyday scenes such as flowers in the garden or people's faces, though obviously the faster films are meant for occasions when the light level is lower. The films are not manufactured so as to produce their best results in recording the frequently exotic objects that are the astrophotographer's target. One important aspect of this difference is the way in which the films are tailored to be used at shutter speeds between about 1/10 and 1/1000 of a second. Some astronomical subjects can be photographed at such speeds, but most cannot, and this introduces an important

**Colour
transparency films**

problem (known as reciprocity failure) that will be discussed below, and mentioned quite frequently thereafter.

In choosing films for use in astrophotography there is a constant temptation to select materials that are very sensitive to light – fast films. Often such films are a necessity, for example when photographing constellations with a fixed camera. However, for subjects that do not require very fast films in the ISO 1000 range, a slower material should be selected. (ISO stands for the International Standards Organization, which devised the present system for rating film speeds: the higher the number, the faster the speed. The values are essentially the same as the older ASA ratings.) The reason is a simple one: all other things being equal, slower films yield better quality than faster films, and pictures exposed on them will be of higher definition and less grainy. While some photographers use fast films as a form of "one-upmanship," their results illustrate the truth of the photographic adage that we never get something for nothing. Fast films should be used with discretion.

The principal film manufacturers – including such names as Agfa, Fuji, Ilford, 3M (Scotch), Kodak, and Konica – offer an extensive range of products. Films rated at up to ISO 100 in speed can be described as slow, characterized by very high quality, good colour saturation, and lively contrast (the difference in density between the shadows and the high-lights). Their use in astrophotography is limited to subjects where light is abundant, chiefly the Sun and the full Moon. Films between ISO 100 and 400 are now described as of medium speed, and are used where light is at rather more of a premium (for example, when photographing the crescent Moon). The quality of these films is still high, but, because of their increased speed, the images are grainier, and of lower resolution and contrast. The third group of films, introduced in relatively recent years, attain claimed speeds of ISO 1000, 1600, and even 3200. Their far greater sensitivity to light results in yet lower resolution and contrast and higher graininess, as well as what might be described as "background noise" ("fog," in photographic terminology, which is the inherent density found in an unexposed but developed film). Typically, these are the films that newcomers to astrophotography will use with a fixed camera to capture images of the constellations that are free from star trailing caused by the rotation of the Earth (see Chapter 8).

In general, the slow- and medium-speed films are exposed using shutter speeds not too dissimilar from those of everyday photography. But when they and the ISO 1000-plus films are exposed for periods longer than 1 second, then *reciprocity failure* must be allowed for. Theoretically, similar amounts of light should affect a film in the same way, whether the light arrives over a short or a long period of time. For instance, half the amount of light for twice the time should have the same effect as twice the amount of light for half the time. This is an example of what is known as a linear effect. Unfortunately, it does not work like this with photographic film. Because of low-intensity reciprocity failure (we need not worry here about the high-intensity form), lengthy expo-sures have to be far lengthier. The reason for this is complex, but can be explained by an analogy. In a normal person-to-person conversation in a room, each participant will have little problem in comprehending and remembering what is being said. However, if they are at opposite ends of a hall, and one is speaking very quietly and only at infrequent intervals, it will be difficult for the other person to hear what is being said and to maintain a high degree of attention for very long. In this case, the message will take longer to get through and to register.

Manufacturers tend to supply more data about reciprocity failure for their black-and-white materials than for colour, but these data nonetheless give a useful indication of the effect. Thus Kodak recommends no compensation for shutter speeds of up to 1/10 of a second for a wide range of its black-and-white films, but longer exposures have to be compensated for. In the case of an indicated exposure time of 100 seconds, either the aperture should be opened by three stops, or the duration of the exposure increased to 1200 seconds – from less than 2 minutes to 20 minutes.

Colour film suffers from a major additional difficulty with lengthy time exposures in that it basically consists of three layers sensitive to the three primary colours – red, blue, and green. These layers are carefully configured so as to provide a natural colour balance over the normal exposure range. However, once that range is exceeded the balance can break down and the colours produced in a final transparency go wildly astray. This is why manufacturers do not recommend the use of most of their colour products for exposures in excess of 1 or at most 10 seconds. Out of necessity, astrophotographers take little notice of the advice!

This may begin to sound very forbidding. In practice, though, at least some of the films perform well, and indeed far better than we have any right to expect, when subjected to circumstances for which they were not designed. The exposures likely to suffer from the effects of reciprocity failure are, as indicated by the figures above, those of a few seconds – shots of lunar eclipses or aurorae, for example – up to constellation photography lasting many seconds or, when using a manual guider (see Chapter 8), some minutes. Lunar eclipses and aurorae are likely to be less frequent subjects for the newcomer's camera, and reliance can be placed on bracketing to achieve a satisfactory result, but constellation photography is another matter. For this you should test the leading high-speed films to see how they perform against one another. Take care to see that tests are soundly based. Factors over which you have control should remain constant: for example, use identical photographic equipment and operating procedures. But other factors, such as the seeing, can vary considerably, even over a short period of time. As far as possible, like must be compared with like.

The test programme may be shaped according to the exposure times indicated in Chapter 8: stepped from, say, 10 seconds, through 20 and 30 seconds, to 1, 5, 10, 15, and 30 minutes. For exposures of this length there is little published information on reciprocity failure, and we have to find out for ourselves how a film performs under our particular conditions. To unravel apparent differences in film speed from the differing reciprocity characteristics is time-consuming, but in fact is unnecessary since in the end it is the films' overall performance that we are judging one against the other. Colour quality is largely a matter of subjective opinion at this early stage, although as experience is gained one's opinions on how well a particular film renders astronomical objects becomes better informed.

A critical element in colour acceptability for the astrophotographer is the appearance of a film's maximum density. This is normally referred to as *D-Max* for short. Strictly speaking, D-max is the density produced in those areas of a developed film which have been totally unaffected by light: the borders of images and the ends of the film roll. However, for our purposes a film's D-max characteristics will have an effect on those areas of a picture that have received very little light.

Now, when designing a colour film, photo scientists are concerned mainly with achieving the best possible rendering of the individual colours. When combined together in a processed image, the colours may not integrate to a neutral black D-Max. This does not matter much in everyday pictures, because we are not very interested in shadows and do not look at them closely. But in a constellation picture exposed over a relatively short period of some seconds, and with a good-quality dark sky unaffected by light pollution, the maximum density will appear over a large area as the sky between the stars. Any marked colour bias in a film's D-Max will then be obtrusive and even objectionable.

Four of the leading ISO 1000-plus colour transparency films currently available are Kodak Ektachrome P1600 Professional, Fuji-chrome P1600D Professional, Agfachrome 1000RS Professional, and Scotch (3M) 1000. The first two are basically slower-speed films customized for push-processing (see below) to high speeds. The other two are normally processed for the speeds indicated. One problem is that films, and even the names of basically the same films, seem to change so rapidly that it is difficult keeping up.

I have not had extensive experience with the Fuji material, but my results have revealed no serious problems, and many speak highly of it. The Scotch film (a very early leader in the high-speed colour field) I have found to be extremely fast with standard processing, but it has a greenish D-Max which I consider unacceptable. The Ektachrome film has a pleasant blue-black D-Max but, although rated at ISO 1600, it is noticeably slower than the Agfachrome, although the latter is rated at a nominal ISO 1000. A significant consideration here is that Kodak itself does not recommend Ektachrome P1600 for exposures any longer than 1 second, presumably because of poor reciprocity characteristics. The Agfachrome's D-Max is an acceptable brown-black; the film is rated at the nominal ISO 1000 and processed normally. I must stress that it is for the individual to undertake tests and to make a personal choice on the basis of those tests, not my opinions!

Push-processing is much in vogue in colour slide photography generally, and astrophotographers are among its keenest proponents. An outline of colour film processing is given in Chapter 13; suffice it to say here that for transparency film an effective speed increase can be secured by extending the first stage of development (which develops the silver image). This is because reversal material is processed first to a negative and then to a positive. In a reasonably exposed transparency the shadow densities are considerably less dense than the D-Max, and the full density potential of the material is not used because when projected the picture would appear too dark. However, if the film is exposed at double the nominal rating, more shadow detail (that is, a higher density) is recorded. Because it is a reversal film, if the first development stage is then extended, all the exposed areas (including the shadow areas) are lightened – not darkened, as happens with negative film. So an effective speed increase results. This is not the case with traditional black-and-white films, as will be discussed a little later.

Once again there is a price to pay: graininess increases and the colour balance can shift. Nonetheless, push-processing is a technique that can be used to advantage in reducing lengthy exposure times. You may find in certain cases that quality seems very little affected. The film's characteristics have now altered, but I remember an occasion some years ago when I wished to use an ISO 400 rated film. Instead, I used ISO 200 Ektachrome in preference to the ISO 400 equivalent, and push-processed to achieve the higher speed rating. I considered the resulting transparencies to be of better quality than those produced by the higher-speed film.

Newcomers to astrophotography are well advised to weigh up for themselves the various films available in the different speed ranges. Reviews in astronomy magazines are of value, particularly as new and improved or modified films seem to be introduced with astonishing frequency, and can serve to reduce the list of films to be tested. But in the final count there is no substitute for direct experience. In general, frequently changing from one film to another is not wise since it will usually mean that the full potential of any single film is never properly established.

Sometimes, however, new developments can affect choice, both positively and negatively. For many decades Kodachrome transparency films tended to be the high-quality standard against which all other colour transparency films were judged (although the speed rating was always low). The appearance some years ago of an ISO 200 version immediately made it a candidate for some astronomical uses previously denied this type of film. Then again, at one time Fuji ISO 400 colour transparency film was extremely popular with experienced astrophotographers, but the colour balance of the film was subsequently altered by the manufacturers in a way which was doubtless an improvement for normal photography, but which was generally condemned by astrophotographers. I mentioned earlier that I did not like the greenish D-Max of 3M's original ISO 1000 transparency film. Subsequently, however, the company introduced a new Scotchchrome family of films which have totally different characteristics. The ISO 400 and 800/3200 P versions have an extended red sensitivity which I find excellent for photographing such objects as emission nebulae.

In considering the performance of colour films, there is one further point that needs to be made. When photographed, some astronomical objects appear very different to how they look to the eye. A classic example is the Orion Nebula (M42). The light from emission nebulae of this type is confined largely to two narrow wavebands. One of these is near the peak sensitivity of the human eye, which sees the nebula as a whitish or light bluish green. This waveband falls between the peaks of the blue- and green-sensitive layers of colour film, but the other band, which is not seen well by the eye, records strongly on the red-sensitive layer. Hence the apparent discrepancy; we may choose which we prefer.

Black-and-white films

While colour transparency film will doubtless appeal to many newcomers to astrophotography, black-and-white film has much to offer. Since the Moon is a monochromatic object it is best suited to black and white, and extremely high-quality results can be obtained. On the grounds of cost, black-and-white film is a sensible choice for meteor patrol work and recording the passage of artificial satellites, for which large numbers of exposures are necessary, and trails are measured direct from the negatives. It is also a good choice for early attempts at constellation photography, for there is no need to print the negative in order to assess one's progress.

What has been said about speed ratings for colour transparency films applies also to black and white. Inherently an ISO 100 film will yield finer grain, higher resolution and contrast, and lower fog than an ISO 400 film. However, it is the latter speed of film that will be most used by the budding astrophotographer. As a result of new grain technology introduced by Kodak in the 1980s, it is necessary to identify two general groups of film.

Until the new-technology films were introduced, the workhorse ISO 400 films of professional and amateur photographers alike were Kodak Tri-X and Ilford HP5 (the latter is now designated HP5 Plus). These were, and are, high-quality versatile films with excellent exposure latitude. In astrophotography and other uses the films can be push-processed, with adherents frequently claiming considerable speed gains. In fact, no speed gain is possible. The ISO speed of films of this type is fixed at the time of manufacture, and no amount of manipulation of exposure or development can alter it. The only leeway is the one-third-of-a-stop safety factor that most films incorporate, but this has so insignificant an effect as to be scarcely noticeable.

What has happened when a photographer claims to have increased the speed of a film such as Tri-X is that details in the shadow areas of a picture have been sacrificed, either because they were not considered to be important or because the contrast of the original scene was so low (for example, under fluorescent lighting) that there were virtually no shadows anyhow. But that does not constitute a genuine increase in film speed, and push-processing results in increased graininess, contrast, and density overall, with overdeveloped highlights.

The reciprocity characteristics of Tri-X film are of obvious importance when one is contemplating lengthy exposures, and considerable increases in exposure time are needed. Kodak recommends that an indicated exposure of 10 seconds should be extended to 50 seconds, or two stops more, and one of 100 seconds to 1200 seconds – that is, 20 minutes – or three stops more.

Kodak introduced its family of T-Max films in 1986. These undoubtedly represented a revolution in black-and-white photography, and were quickly followed up by other manufacturers such as Ilford with its Delta film technology. The T-Max films are based on the tabular grain concept that Kodak first introduced with its colour films. By providing a much larger surface area than conventional grains of the same mass, T-grains are able to "capture" more light and adsorb large amounts of sensitizing dyes and other chemicals. The result is fast films with the grain and resolution of medium-speed films, and medium-speed films with the image qualities of very slow films. Additional advantages for the astrophotographer are that the contrast of the T-Max films is considerably higher than that of Tri-X, the fog level is lower, and the reciprocity characteristics are much better. With T-Max 400, for example, a nominal 100-second exposure need be increased only to 300 seconds (one-quarter of the Tri-X exposure time) or the aperture opened by one and a half stops (compared with three stops). With T-Max 100, the recommendation is 200 seconds and one stop.

However, it is in push-processing that the new-technology films may be claimed to have had their greatest impact. The old photographic adage that you can't get something for nothing – that you cannot increase a film's apparent speed without losing quality somewhere else – is still strictly true. However, when it is used with dedicated compensating developers the quality loss in T-Max is so limited that the effective speed can be said to have been altered. This is why Kodak and most of the other manufacturers do not quote ISO values (which are unalterable international standards) for the new-technology films, but *exposure index* (EI) values. When subjected to push-processing, the films do not build up extreme contrast or grain as do the older, conventional films. It is the development of photographic fog (density introduced by developing chemicals) that limits how far these films can be pushed, but fog does not set in before significant gains in speed have been made. Thus EI 100 films can take a three-stop push to a value of EI 800, and EI 400 films similarly to EI 3200, while the high-speed T-Max P3200 can be pushed to a startling EI 25,000 and, some claim, even further.

It has been necessary to describe the differences between the traditional and new-technology films at some length. But we should not be carried away by considerations of speed and push-processing. When photographing a full or gibbous Moon, for example, EI or ISO 100 films will be quite fast enough – as will 200 or 400 speed films for the crescent phases of the Moon. With fast lenses it is doubtful whether a speed of more than 400 or 800 will be needed for early attempts at star photography. The important thing is to take matters slowly and carefully: with (conventionally processed) films of up to EI or ISO 3200 available, you may well see no point in following the enthusiasts of push-processing. Start out at ISO 100 or 400 for your chosen subject or subjects, and move up in speed only if the need appears.

What you will find is that the enthusiasts, in astrophotography as well as elsewhere, are so dedicated to their own favourite film and processing technique that any albeit innocent questioning or criticism is likely to be strongly rebutted. Nowhere will this be more so than in comparing the performance of the older, conventional films with the new!

Kodak Technical Pan 2415 Film is widely used by astrophotographers, but mainly for deep-sky photography of dim objects and for solar photography through the telescope, which are largely beyond the scope of this book. A brief reference to the film, however, is made in Chapters 6 and 16.

Finally, while I have no direct experience of its use, some readers may wish to test Ilford's ISO 400 XP2 film (the Moon is a suitable subject). XP2 is basically a colour negative material which yields a final dye image for black-and-white printing. It is generally agreed that in terms of grain, resolution, and tonal scale the film is superior to any other in the same speed group when used optimally. Since, however, liberties are frequently taken with films in astrophotography, and the special processing of this film as well as the making of prints from it is best placed in the hands of specialist laboratories (although it can be processed in standard colour negative–positive C41 chemistry), the potential for the beginner would appear to be limited.

It is appropriate to end this somewhat wide-ranging review with two pieces of practical advice. First, when colour transparency film is sent for commercial processing, it is vital to remember that laboratories have little experience of astrophotographs and their appearance. Constellation shots cause particular difficulty for operators trying to locate the dividing line between two frames, and your hard-won images may be returned inadvertently cut in two. Two policies are recommended: either request that the film be returned uncut and unmounted (and carry out this operation personally), or shoot one or two everyday scenes at the beginning of the film so that the cutting and mounting machine may be set up correctly.

Second, while subjects such as eclipses require a large number of photographs to be taken over a very short period, the new astrophotographer is likely to take only a relatively small number of images (perhaps ten at the most) at any one time. Most transparency films are 24 or 36 exposures long. So, to avoid having to wait for the entire film to be used up before seeing the results, you can cut the film carefully into two or three sections and store them in plastic reloadable cassettes available from photographic stores. It is easy enough to do this if you have access to a darkroom or changing bag; if not, a specialist dealer (for a small fee), or a keen and well-equipped photographer friend, might oblige. Of course, unless you process your own films this will increase the cost of processing.

A twelve-exposure length of film with leader is around 55 cm (22 inches) in length, and an eighteen-exposure film around 80 cm (31 inches). Make sure that you load the film in the correct way: with the long end of the spool facing you, the film should be wound around it in a clockwise direction.

CHAPTER 5

Procedures

The chapters that follow this one concentrate on the photography of specific celestial objects. The manner in which a photographic session is planned and then conducted does not differ greatly according to subject, so to minimize possible repetition in later chapters, outline guidance is given here. Some of the comments may seem elementary but, taken as a whole, they constitute a sound basis upon which the inexperienced can conduct a session with good chances of success.

No vast amount of setting up is required in the initial stages of astrophotography, so we may quite frequently take a chance on the weather. Scattered fair-weather cumulus cloud, for example, should not dissuade us from attempting a programme of Moon photography or, depending on the extent of the cloud, constellation photography. However, it is prudent to be aware of likely developments. If the local forecast predicts a warm front moving in, and a glance at the sky reveals extensive cirrus cloud already developing into cirro-stratus towards the horizon, then it would be sensible to postpone any astrophotography.

Similarly, one must be realistic about the potential effect of wind speed on attempts to photograph some targets. Long focal length lenses present a large area to the wind. When they are being used to photograph the Moon, for example – especially at the slower shutter speeds used for crescent phases or, even worse, during lunar eclipses – and it is windy, results are likely to be poor even with the camera mounted on a firm tripod. Quite moderate focal lengths can be affected over long time exposures, and it is a sound general rule to regard windy conditions as being unsuitable for most forms of astrophotography. You might, though, be able to shelter the camera and tripod in some way. Of course, the decision is shaped by events: few astrophotographers would put their cameras away during a major event such as a solar eclipse simply because a strong wind was blowing!

Astrophotography during the summer months can be a great pleasure (even if night scarcely falls at all), but winter returns all too quickly. No programme of astrophotography or observing can be carried out well if you are feeling very cold, so there is an obvious need to dress for the conditions. We are fortunate that cold-weather clothing has greatly improved in recent years. Wear numerous, light layers of clothes so as to trap air for maximum warmth. Thermal underwear should be high on the list of presents for astrophotographers.

Combatting the cold

Remember the need to cover your head, through which a disproportionate amount of body heat escapes, as well as making sure that your footwear has thick soles to combat the effect of standing on a cold surface for long periods of time. Lightweight padded snow boots (even though there may be no snow) are an excellent choice. Ordinary gloves will spend as much time off cold hands as on them when a camera is being operated, so wear the sort that combines open-ended fingers with a mitten-like cover which can be pulled up over the fingers. Of course, a flask of hot drink is very welcome during lengthy sessions in cold weather.

Dressing for cold weather is part of everyday life in many parts of the world, so there is no need to elaborate on it here. But the point needs to be made strongly for the benefit of newcomers to astrophotography that any idea of just slipping out for a few minutes to dash off one or two exposures is a prescription for misery and therefore failure. It will not be a few minutes, and as the ill-dressed photographer gets colder so the chances of any success plummet.

Preparations

For your first sessions in astrophotography it is a good idea to have an outline programme, even if it is just a mental one or headings on a scrap of paper. Perhaps the aim is to photograph ten constellations over a couple of hours as they move close to the zenith, or to experiment with various exposures of the Moon on black-and-white film and compare the results. This is another facet of the systematic approach which has been highlighted already. It is wise, however, not to make the plan too complex or ambitious. Assume that things will always take longer than you think, and plan ten exposures rather than fifteen or twenty. Have a reserve of targets so that more can be tackled if things go well.

The planning should include consideration of the most efficient way of operating. For example, if the aim is to record a number of constellations with two lenses of different focal lengths, it is easier to record each constellation using the two lenses before moving on to the next, rather than photographing all the selected constellations with one lens mounted, and then having to repeat the series of camera movements for the second sequence.

With photography scheduled, it is sound to check that the equipment is in working order while there is still time to take corrective action – for example, when shops are still open. It is annoying to commence a session only to discover that the battery of the red-light torch/flashlight is exhausted and that there is no spare. The situation is even worse if it is a battery-powered camera that is affected. The most sensible policy is to maintain reserves of expendable items such as batteries and bulbs, and to purchase replacements on a routine basis as soon as a replacement item starts to be used.

Whether the location initially chosen for astrophotography is in the garden or further afield, check on an earlier night that no lights will shine directly and continually into the camera lens. During sessions, ban all matches, lighters, and white-light torches other than your own from the area. Finally, when you come to the actual photography, follow good, sound everyday photographic practice. Make sure the lenses are clean, because you need to capture as much light as possible from your faint targets. If you keep film in the freezer (so as to minimize the chemical changes that inevitably occur as the sensitized film ages), allow several hours for it to come up to room temperature before putting it in the camera. And make sure that, when loaded, the film is being taken up by the film wind (if it is, you should see the rewind crank arm rotating). An ultraviolet filter is often left on the front of a lens not so much for its filtration value, but as protection for the lens's front element. In astrophotography, a filter means two more surfaces through which light from a faint target has to pass, so any UV filter should be removed.

So, the evening is fair, the targets are chosen, and the spirit is enthused. Make a checklist of the items you need for the session. This may sound quite unnecessary, but if your site is some way from home and you arrive there without an important piece of equipment, you will wish you had taken such a precaution.

Equipment checklist

1. Loaded camera, with one or two everyday pictures already exposed at the beginning of the film; lens(es); lens hood; cable release.
2. Tripod.
3. Planisphere/star maps. These will not be needed during photography of the Moon, for example, but are useful to have for identifying objects in the sky that you do not recognize.
4. Timer; black card.
5. Red-light torch; white-light torch.
6. Pen; notebook, with notes on intended targets.
7. Reserves of expendables, such as batteries. Take a second film in case the work goes extremely well, the evening continues fair, and you are inspired.
8. Although not essential, a small picnic table or broad-topped stool is useful as a surface on which to place items not in continual use and too large for pockets: black card, planisphere, lenses (be careful!), and so on. A light-coloured surface facilitates finding the objects in the dark.

Before setting up any equipment on the chosen site, sweep the area (whether it is in the garden or elsewhere) with the white-light torch for any obstructions which in the dark could prove dangerous, or at least ruin an exposure as you trip and knock the tripod over. The white-light torch should not be used again until the session is concluded. Full dark adaptation of the eyes can take as much as an hour or so.

The procedure to be followed during a series of exposures is much the same whatever the target, apart from the extremes of shutter speed that can be used. In the checklist that follows, it is assumed that a fast film is being used for constellation photography with a standard shutter speed of, say, 20 seconds.

The procedure itself

Procedure checklist

1. Set the shutter to B. Set the aperture to maximum. Focus the lens on infinity (some people tape it at this position to prevent any accidental alteration). Check that the camera/tripod combination is firm and locked. Set the timer to a chosen duration (20 seconds).

2. Locate the object visually. Frame it in the viewfinder. (Remember that if a right-angle viewer is in use, the image is often reversed left to right, which can take some getting used to when trying to frame constellations.)

3. Place the black card in front of the lens but not touching it. Fire the shutter with the cable plunger and lock it. Wait 2 or 3 seconds for vibrations to dampen, and then remove the card carefully without touching the lens. Simultaneously start the timer. (Locking or unlocking the cable release while holding the card requires dexterity. Some cables make locking easier by using, in place of a threaded nut, a disk which is rotated in advance in one direction so that when the plunger is pressed the cable locks automatically. This still leaves the problem of unlocking the cable, an action requiring two hands, while holding the card in front of the lens. For relatively short exposures such as the 20 seconds assumed here, you can try firing the cable release and holding the plunger down rather than locking it. There is a risk of camera movement if the cable has no slack, but with care this technique can be made to work. Experiment, and judge the technique by the results you get. If the camera has a T setting, a cable release is not required – an obvious advantage.)

4. Hold the card in readiness well to one side of the lens as you observe the area of sky you are photographing.

5. When the timer sounds, place the card in front of the lens immediately. Unlock the cable release to end the exposure, and place the card to one side. Cut the timer alarm and reset it to 20 seconds, using the red-light torch if the timer does not have an LED display. Wind the film on.

6. Make additional notes on the exposure. Most will have been written in advance, but any changes should be carefully recorded, as well as observations made during the exposure of, for example, any aircraft, meteor, or satellite. (With a programme such as this there is no need to cover up the lens during the passage of an aircraft and recalculate the exposure time; it is simpler just to repeat the exposure.)

7. Check the front of the lens for condensation (see page 50). Take care not to breathe when close to the viewfinder or lens, otherwise condensation will form immediately.

8. Check that the aperture setting is as required, that the shutter is still set to B, and that the focusing distance is infinity.

9. Return to step 2 and repeat the sequence.

The procedure checklist can be modified for shorter exposures. It may also require adaptation according to the features of the camera in use. If you feel the need, you can draw up your own list.

The 20-second exposure time for star images assumed in the checklist above is long enough for the black-card technique to be used without it causing problems. But the technique cannot be used with the faster shutter speeds required in photography of the full Moon or Sun. The ideal here is to be using a camera in which the mirror can be locked in position so as to remove another source of vibration, and a self-timer that releases the shutter after a delay, thereby reducing any slight camera movement created by operating the shutter release cable. The delay introduced by the self-timer is several seconds, so the timer should not be used if we are trying to take advantage of a brief period of excellent seeing, which is likely to happen only in advanced astrophotography. If the camera does not have one or both of these features, then there is still a very good chance of getting satisfactory exposures with shutter speeds of, say 1/250 of a second or faster, even with long focal length lenses.

The risk of camera shake and vibrations causing "smeared" images is greatest with shutter speeds ranging from about 1/60 of a second to 1 second or so. These are the speeds used for the crescent Moon, eclipses, and some conjunctions, and the problem is compounded when long focal length lenses are selected. Our reactions are nowhere near quick enough for us to use the black card at the faster end of this range, and it is unlikely that its use will prove very satisfactory at the slower end (our actions occupy too great a proportion of the brief exposure), even though it must be attempted. One small advantage here, however, is that locking the cable is clearly not necessary (nor possible).

Once again, there is little fear of vibration when using a sophisticated camera that features not only a mirror lock but also a self-timer. Such cameras will usually have preset shutter speeds of 1, 2, 4, and 8 seconds (if no higher), so the shutter may be set to these values without using the B setting. It is a different matter for cameras without these features. In the absence of a mirror lock and a self-timer, the use of a bulb (or pneumatic) shutter release cable should be considered because it subjects the camera to less physical movement than a conventional cable does. Ensuring that the tripod is rock steady, choosing wider apertures to get faster shutter speeds, and possibly choosing a faster film (with somewhat inferior grain characteristics) to achieve even faster shutter speeds will all help to reduce vibration or its effects. If you need to use a shutter speed of 1 or 2 seconds and it is not available as a preset speed on your camera, then you will have to practise with the black card to gain as much proficiency as possible. It is impossible to generalize and there are no simple solutions, but something will have been achieved if you become alert to the problems of working in this speed range, especially with long focal length lenses, which exaggerate any image smear. A sound policy is to experiment and to establish the best results that can be achieved with various procedures.

The problem of movement

At the end of the session there is continuing need for care. Check that the final exposure has been terminated and that notes have been completed. Never trust to memory! Although you may not have been using the camera's exposure meter system (if it has one), it may

The end of the session

have become activated. If it does not cut out automatically after a set period, switch it off now. At this stage the dark adaptation of your eyes ceases to be important. Switch on the white-light torch and gather together all the items of equipment. Whether you are outside your own house or miles away, sweep the site with the torch and make sure nothing is being left behind.

The everyday photographer will not use the B shutter speed very much, and after the last exposure it is very easy to forget to unlock the cable release, thereby fogging the shot (and possibly one or two adjacent frames too) as soon as the camera is taken into a brightly lit room. So do that, and check that the film has been rewound. How many of us, at some time in our photographic careers, have opened a camera back without checking that the film has been rewound? This is sad at any time, but doubly so when the pictures that are ruined represent minutes or even hours of effort in less than comfortable conditions.

When equipment is taken from cold, outside temperatures into a warm room, condensation immediately forms on all exposed surfaces. (Notepaper will have dampened anyway during the session; at home lay the sheets out separately so that they do not stick together as they dry.) It is best not to wipe the surfaces of equipment, but to leave them to dry in their own time overnight. The condensation probably does no harm, but it is natural to feel a little unhappy about expensive cameras and lenses being left in this condition. There is, however, a straightforward way of preventing it. What is needed is a large, clear plastic bag with a ribbed seal along the top, or even a plastic lunchbox, that will take the camera and lenses. Before you come indoors, place the camera with lens still fitted in the bag or box, and seal it. Indoors, condensation will immediately form on the outside of the container, but not on the equipment inside it. It takes some time for the temperatures to balance, and unless there is extreme urgency about the results it seems sensible to leave the camera and lens inside the container until the morning. As to when you remove the film from the camera, get into a set routine. Rewind the film (trying, if you are doing it manually, not to rewind all of the leader – see Chapter 13) immediately after ending the last exposure, extract it from the camera, and place it in a film can. Alternatively, after rewinding carefully, leave the film in the camera until the morning, and unload it when the camera is removed from the plastic container.

The next day, or as soon as possible, all equipment should be checked and non-optical surfaces wiped over with a soft, clean cloth. Use a lens brush or an air puffer to remove any dust from the inside of the camera. Alternatively, use an aerosol can of air – but be very careful to hold it upright, and do not direct a powerful blast of air from a short distance straight at the focal plane shutter.

Most important of all, check the back and front elements of the lenses that were used during the previous night's session. Since the back element is protected by the camera body when the lens is fitted, it should rarely need attention, but dust, dirt, and fingerprints can all too easily affect the front element. First of all, hold the lens upside down and use a lens brush or puffer to remove as much dust as possible. Take a lens tissue (not a spectacle-cleaning tissue, which usually contains silicone and can damage the surface and coatings of photographic lenses), fold it in half several times, and apply one or two drops of lens-cleaning fluid to the centre of the pad. Starting at the centre of the lens and, holding the tissue at the edges, wipe in a circular motion outwards. You may need to repeat this with a new tissue, but never apply lens-cleaning fluid direct since it could seep around the edges of the lens and into the lens barrel. As a test of how clean the lens element is, breathe on it. If the condensation evaporates evenly as a gradually diminishing circle, the lens is clean; if patches or spots show up in the condensation, start again. When all is well, replace the UV filter (if you have one) and the rear and front lens caps. All is then ready for next time.

Notes: learning from experience

The manner in which notes are made for a photographic session is a matter of personal choice. Figure 5.1 shows how the essential information could be recorded on the page. You may prefer instead to use a small tape recorder for your notes. If you do, it would be wise to keep handy a copy of the note headings shown in Figure 5.1 because it is easy to forget to record some of the details. An advantage of the tape recorder, of course, is that you will not suffer from damp paper; on the other hand, electrical devices and cold and damp conditions often do not go well together. It's up to you.

How the notes are used once the film has been processed and the results have been checked is also a matter of personal choice. I usually transfer as much information as possible to individual transparency mounts. I record subjects, camera, film, and exposure information, together with date, on a plain piece of paper which acts as the cover of

Figure 5.1 *A set of headings for recording notes for a photographic session. Some of the main headings can be made into column headings if, for example, different lenses or f-numbers are being used. Also, if you do your astrophotography from more than one site, you should note the location. The 'Exposure begun' column is useful if, in the absence of a data back recording the time (see page 29), an unexpected (and unobserved) event is recorded on the film.*

Date:	Camera:	Lens:	Stop:	Film:
Subject		Exposure begun	Shutter speed	Comments

a plastic slide wallet, and keep the original notes in the wallet behind the title sheet. Filing by subjects is another approach. It really does not matter what system is chosen, nor how informal it is, provided information on previous successes and failures is readily accessible when you need it for planning another session.

Should "failed" images be thrown away? If they are utter failures (such as completely fogged frames), there is no point in keeping them. But if the images are just not very satisfactory, and indeed if they contain any information at all, keep them on file, at least for a few years. Every now and then unexpected celestial events take place and it could be that you were taking a picture of just the right area of the sky at just the right time. Spode's law decrees that this is the very frame you might be tempted to throw away. So think before you discard anything, because you might be able to demonstrate that the law does not always operate!

Combatting dew

When air cools and reaches the critical temperature known as the dew point, water droplets condense on any surface at or below that temperature. All too often, despite the use of a lens hood, this surface seems to be the front element of a lens. A lens tissue can be used to remove the condensation but it will quickly re-form. A hair dryer used gently from a safe distance at intervals is effective, even during exposures, provided you and the dryer keep out of the field of view of the lens. But most hair dryers are powered from mains electricity/line current, which may not be available. A battery-powered lens heater is an efficient way of providing just enough warmth to keep the temperature of the front element of the lens slightly higher than that of the surrounding air.

Figure 5.2 shows a heater I have used. The minimum amount of heat required was estimated at 2 watts, powered by 6 volts, and the resistance was calculated at 18 ohms, according to the formula resistance equals voltage squared divided by wattage. The heater consists of

Figure 5.2 *A six-resistor lens heater with battery pack and battery charger. The resistors are mounted inside a dedicated lens hood which fits all lenses with a standard 52-mm front thread. The unit is switched on by simply joining the heater wire to the battery wire by a connector.*

a string of six $\frac{1}{2}$-watt, 3-ohm resistors in series to distribute the heat equally around the edges of the lens. A small hole is drilled through the side of a dedicated lens hood to take the wire from the power supply, and the resistors are positioned at intervals around the inside of the lens hood, and held in place by short strips of electrical tape.

From Ohm's law, according to which current equals voltage divided by resistance, the current passing through an 18-ohm resistance operating at 6 volts is 0.333 amps, or 333 milliamps. Various types of power supply can be considered, but rechargeable nickel–cadmium batteries provide a safe and easily portable solution. A set of four C-type rechargeable batteries (nominally 1.2 volts) has been found to operate the heater for approximately 6 hours before recharging is required.

Materials
- C-type battery holder with snap-on leads
- Four C-type rechargeable nickel–cadmium batteries
- Universal battery charger
- About 2 metres (6 feet) of electrical wire, 16/0.2 gauge or similar, which is long enough to allow the battery pack to be placed beneath a tripod out of the way; it is joined to about 20 cm (8 inches) of wire from the resistors by a connector
- Six $\frac{1}{2}$-watt, 2-ohm resistors
- Soldering iron and solder
- Electrical tape

CHAPTER 6

The Moon

In terms of the exposures required, the Moon presents the easiest task of all for the newcomer to astrophotography since it is a body reflecting light from the Sun – just as the Earth does. (The Moon does it very poorly, reflecting only 7 percent of the Sun's light, whereas the Earth reflects 36 percent, but the situation is directly comparable.) Photographing the Moon is thus no different in principle to photographing a sunlit terrestrial scene. Newcomers will therefore feel very much at home with "lunar" exposures such as 1/250 of a second at $f/11$. It is natural to think of using colour film when photographing the Moon, but the lunar surface is essentially grey. This makes it a prime target for black-and-white film, which also affords an opportunity to deal with some of the problems caused by extremes of lighting contrast on the atmosphereless Moon. Colour, however, does come into its own during lunar eclipses.

Although the exposure times can be similar to those for everyday shots on Earth, the focal lengths required for meaningful photography of the Moon are very different. The Moon is one of the Solar System's larger satellites, with a diameter of 3476 km (2160 miles), and it orbits at a mean distance of 384,000 km (239,000 miles). From Earth it has an angular size of a little over $1/2°$, much the same as the Sun's apparent size. In terms of capturing it on film, this size is demanding. There is a useful formula for the approximate image size of the Moon produced by a lens mounted on a 35-mm camera:

Image size = Focal length/100

(The denominator is actually 110, but 100 simplifies the mathematics and is good enough.) This means that every 100 mm of focal length will yield about 1 mm of Moon on the film. So our "normal" 50-mm lens will produce an image 0.5 mm in diameter!

The result of using different lenses

The effect of this is illustrated in Figure 6.1. Pictures of the Moon were taken with 50-mm, 180-mm, 500-mm, 1000-mm, and 2000-mm lenses, and here the full frames of the resulting images have been enlarged by the same factor. While the Moon's image as recorded with the 50-mm lens is extremely small, even with enlargement, some of the dark lunar maria can be distinguished. These details are much clearer in the image obtained using the 180-mm lens, in which larger craters such as Tycho in the southern hemisphere are discernible. Numerous craters are apparent in the 500-mm lens image and there are obvious, further gains with the two longest lenses.

The lens, as I have stressed, is only one factor in producing an image, and film is another, major component. Thus if we enlarge a 5-mm diameter Moon image five times and a 10-mm diameter image five times so that there is a fair comparison of lenses, it will be evident that the latter appears to be sharper because the grain structure of the film is less obtrusive.

However, a major reason why lenses of longer focal length give better results is their greater light-gathering capability, so we are back again considering lens diameters. If we limit the consideration entirely to the theoretical resolving power of the lenses, we can calculate their performances in arc seconds from the formula

Resolving power $= 114/d$

where d is the diameter in millimetres. A 50-mm $f/1.8$ lens has a diameter of almost 28 mm, with an optimum resolving power therefore of 4 arc seconds. The 180-mm $f/2.8$ lens can resolve 1.78 arc seconds, the 500-mm $f/8$ mirror lens 1.82 arc seconds, the 1000-mm $f/11$ mirror lens 1.25 arc seconds, and the 2000-mm $f/11$ mirror lens 0.63 arc seconds. Notice, incidentally, that it is not simply a question of focal length *per se*. The fast 180-mm $f/2.8$ lens has a diameter of over 64 mm, and so has a better resolving power than the 500-mm $f/8$ lens with a diameter of 62.5 mm. It is a question of lens diameter and light grasp.

Notwithstanding this, for good photography of the Moon there is no substitute for focal length (though time-lapse photography, producing multiple images on a single frame, can be made with shorter focal length lenses). With careful exposure and processing, a 200-mm focal length lens will produce a worthwhile image. If, however, a focal length of 500 mm can be used, then, all things being equal, the gain in quality will be significant. Increasingly, everyday photographers are applying their hobby to sports, birdwatching, and similar activities in which there is a premium on focal length, and the compact 500-mm mirror lens is becoming particularly popular. The power of shorter focal length lenses may be boosted, of course, by the use of *teleconverters*, though there is then a loss of speed.

Once again, it has to be said that in using our long focal length lenses we are not getting something for nothing. As seen from the Earth, the Moon moves in its orbit from west to east, but because of the Earth's rotation, each night it appears to move in the opposite direction, from east to west. The varying orbital velocity of the Moon complicates any calculations, but on average it is moving eastwards in its orbit at about one lunar diameter (3476 km/2160 miles), or around half a degree, per hour. The Moon's apparent movement in the opposite direction as a result of the Earth's rotation is much faster: a little under 15 seconds of arc per second of time.

(a)

(b)

(c)

(d)

(e)

Figure 6.1 *Sufficient focal length is critical in obtaining satisfactory photographs of the Moon. The full 35-mm film frame has been enlarged to the same degree in each of these five images to demonstrate the results obtained by using (a) 50-mm, (b) 180-mm, (c) 500-mm, (d) 1000-mm, and (e) 2000-mm lenses. Film and processing were standard throughout, but the last two frames were taken during a different lunation (the sequence of phases from one new Moon to the next).*

Without going into too much detail, the formula that is elaborated in Chapter 8 for securing essentially trail-free images of the stars is also valid for the Moon. Divide 700 (or 500 if we are being hypercritical; see page 82) by the focal length of the lens, and the resulting figure is the maximum exposure in seconds that will result in virtually no image movement with a fixed camera. So this threshold exposure is (being hypercritical) 1 second with a 500-mm focal length lens, and only ¼ of a second with a 2000-mm focal length lens. How feasible are such shutter speeds?

(a)

Figure 6.2 *The effect of film choice and developer is well demonstrated in these two images of the full Moon. For the first image (a), Kodak Technical Pan 2415 film was used, rated at ISO 100. The exposure was 1/60 of a second through a 2000-mm, f/11 Nikkor mirror-reflex lens. The film was developed in HC-110 (dilution D). Technical Pan is a high-contrast, high-resolution film which helps to compensate for the blandness of the full Moon. The second image (b) was taken on T-Max 400 film using the same lens, but with an exposure time of 1/125 of a second. The film was developed conventionally in HC-110 (dilution B). Although T-Max has a lively contrast, this print obviously has a shallower contrast gradient than the first image. Printing skills are very important in making comparisons of this kind, and it could be argued that the Technical Pan image should have been printed on a paper that was one grade softer (less contrasty). Of the two original prints the Tech Pan image may appeal because of its greater liveliness, but careful study reveals the T-Max image to have a higher information content.*

The two images were taken some five years apart. By chance they enable us to distinguish the effects of lunar libration, the wobbling of the Moon on its axis (see page 65). Compare how close the Mare Crisium (the dark circular feature at top right of the disk) is to the limb (edge) in the two images. The difference is not enormous, but we can see more of the trailing edge of the Moon in (b). Similarly, study of the dark crater Grimaldi, close to the leading (left) limb of the Moon just beneath centre, reveals that it too is closer to the limb in (b).

**Exposures –
and the need
to bracket**

The Moon is an extended object whose visibility through the Earth's atmosphere varies considerably. Such variation has been constantly mentioned throughout this book, and is another reminder of how necessary it is to use suggested exposures only as a basis for experimentation. With the Moon we also have the variation in exposure necessitated by the Sun's changing phase angle. For example, during the early lunar "morning" (or late "evening"), when the Moon appears to us as a slender crescent, a longer exposure is required than when the Sun is overhead, at lunar noon, when we see the Moon as full. These conditions, fortunately, are generally more predictable than the state of the Earth's atmosphere.

(b)

The exposures given in Table 6.1 are a guide for your first attempts. It is essential to follow the good photographic practice that has already been stressed, particularly when the uncomfortable, in-between shutter speeds are indicated. And do bracket your exposures. Take one exposure that is one stop (or shutter speed) more, and another that is less by the same amount. For good measure take two more exposures, one two stops more and the other two stops less.

The two film speeds in Table 6.1 are the most suitable for black-and-white work, but it is somewhat tedious to have to extrapolate the information to other films and/or other focal ratios. Fortunately, there is a convenient formula into which chosen film speed and focal ratio may be inserted to give approximate shutter speeds in seconds:

$$t = f^2/sB$$

where t is the time, f is the focal ratio, s is the film speed, and B is a brightness value for the phase of the Moon. Values for B, which you may refine as you gain experience, are: crescent 20 (try 10 for a very slender crescent); quarter 40, gibbous 80, and full 200. Again, these values are provided to enable the newcomer to make a meaningful start so that film will not be wasted because of wildly inappropriate exposures. But there are no universally correct answers – only those that work for the individual

Table 6.1 *Guide exposures for different lunar phases.*		
Moon's phase	ISO 400 film	ISO 100 film
Crescent	1/125: *f*/8	1/30: *f*/8
Quarter	1/250: *f*/8	1/60: *f*/8
Gibbous	1/500: *f*/8	1/125: *f*/8
Full	1/1000: *f*/8	1/250: *f*/8

These suggested values can be extrapolated for other focal ratios: e.g. the exposure for photographing the crescent Moon with an *f*/11 lens on ISO 400 film would be 1/60 of a second.

astrophotographer's particular set of circumstances: equipment, film, and processing, and atmospheric and lighting conditions.

It was suggested at the beginning of this chapter that the Moon is a subject for the black-and-white worker, but this is not to the complete exclusion of colour. Colour transparency film can be used to record the various phases of the Moon. One interesting experiment is to photograph it when low on the horizon, and then follow it up to its highest point, taking photographs using the same exposure, and compare the colour reproduction. Near the horizon the Moon is usually more orange, a result of the far greater thickness of atmosphere through which light from the Moon has had to pass.

Dealing with contrast

Nonetheless, black-and-white film provides us with some flexibility in dealing with the contrast problems inherent in photographing the Moon. When the Moon is full, it is the high noon of the Moon's month-long day-and-night cycle. As on Earth, shadows are extremely short and it is difficult to discriminate objects. For the photographer the full Moon is a bland object, and there is a need to enhance what contrast does exist. Within limits, we can pursue a policy which will be familiar to the experienced black-and-white worker. Contrast in a negative is controlled by development, so if we underexpose the Moon and overdevelop we should produce greater contrast and therefore a livelier image. About half a stop of underexposure and one-third of overdevelopment should be the limit, otherwise increased grain resulting from the overdevelopment will become obtrusive in the older types of film. The more versatile new-technology films will also repay experimentation. But there is another film, which I use much of the time, which is a favourite of many experienced astrophotographers.

Kodak 2415 Technical Pan is a fine-grain film with extended red sensitivity that is used widely in astrophotography. Its value here is that whereas it can be exposed at a rating of up to ISO 64 to yield negatives with a normal contrast index (a standard measure of contrast in a developed image) of up to about 0.70, it can be rated as high as ISO 200 and then deliver a contrast index which has been claimed to be as high as 2.50. This is a top-quality film which is well worth experimenting with in lunar photography (see Figure 6.2), as well as elsewhere.

With the crescent moon the contrast problem is reversed. The subject is extremely contrasty, and the chances of getting totally dark blacks and featureless bright areas are high. Normally a higher-speed film is used to photograph the crescent Moon and this helps since faster films tend to be less contrasty than slower ones. The wider latitude of a higher-speed film also helps in the attempt to record detail in shadows and yet not lose detail entirely in the bright areas. The technique here is the opposite of that used when dealing with the full Moon: a degree of overexposure, and then of underdevelopment to limit contrast (see Figure 6.3), both by the same proportions as indicated for the full Moon. In both cases choice and manipulation of the most suitable printing papers contribute to an optimum result. A project to photograph the day-old crescent Moon is described in Chapter 15.

(a)   (b)

Figure 6.3 *Adjustments to the exposure and development times can help with the control of contrast in photographing the crescent Moon. The first image (a) was exposed on Kodak Tri-X film for 1/30 of a second through a Nikkor 2000-mm mirror-reflex lens. It is a satisfactory image, but the surface towards the limb becomes steadily more "washed out." The film was developed conventionally in D76 diluted 1 : 1. The second image (b) was taken on T-Max 400, but whereas the exposure of 1/60 of a second was standard the development time in D76 diluted 1 : 1 was cut by 25 percent. This caused the detail along the terminator (the border between lunar day and night) to be less well delineated, but the bright areas towards the limb have not developed so much and more detail is discernible. This was a useful experiment, but remember that if you are comparing films the tests should be conducted under absolutely equivalent conditions.*

Lunar eclipses

While a lunar eclipse does not have the drama of a solar eclipse, it is a fascinating experience to watch as the Moon declines from its normal brightness, acquiring an orange-red or coppery hue at the height of the eclipse. Fascinating it may be, but the astrophotographer is set a sterner test than when recording normal lunar images.

Figure 6.4 shows broadly what happens in a lunar eclipse. The period from when the Moon first touches the outer edge of the *penumbra* to when it moves completely out of the penumbra on the other side can last for around 6 hours. The period of totality, when the Moon is wholly within the *umbra* of the Earth's shadow, is much shorter, up to about 1¾ hours. When the Moon first moves into the penumbra it looks hardly any different from when it is normally lit by direct sunlight, but

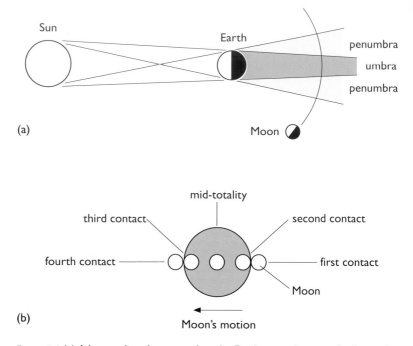

Figure 6.4 *(a) A lunar eclipse happens when the Earth moves between the Sun and the Moon. The three bodies are roughly in this alignment once a month (at the time of full Moon) but, because the Moon is inclined at about 5° to the ecliptic, exact alignment – and hence an eclipse – is much less frequent. (This diagram is not to scale.) (b) The various stages of a lunar eclipse as the Moon moves through the Earth's shadow. The size of the shadow helps to explain why a lunar eclipse lasts much longer than a solar eclipse, which occurs when the much smaller Moon passes between the Earth and the Sun.*

imperceptibly this begins to change. At *first contact* a broad line of shadow begins to move across the lunar surface, and has covered the Moon by *second contact*. For photographs of the Moon partly in the umbra and partly in the penumbra, exposure has to be for one or the other since the film cannot handle both extremes of lighting at the same time. Deepest darkness occurs quite logically at mid-totality. At *third contact* the Moon's leading limb begins to move out of the umbra. *Fourth contact* is when the Moon's trailing limb is just about to pass out of the umbra, and then the final penumbral stage begins.

Photography of the various stages of a lunar eclipse is complicated by the relative brightness or darkness of the Moon during totality, its position in the sky, and atmospheric conditions at the photographer's location – all of which could affect exposure times significantly. Although the Earth totally blocks off all direct sunlight from the Moon during totality, the lunar surface is illuminated by sunlight refracted, and reddened, by the Earth's atmosphere. The totally eclipsed Moon is therefore not black but a hue which may be orange or red or a muted copper, depending on the state of the Earth's atmosphere. Several recent eclipses, for example, have been very dark because of the massive eruption of Mount Pinatubo in the Philippines in 1991 (see Figure 6.5).

(a) (b)

Figure 6.5 *Almost three years separate these two pictures, but the main difference results largely from a major volcanic eruption, that of Mount Pinatubo in the Philippines, in the intervening period. Picture (a) is of a light, almost rose-coloured, fully eclipsed Moon despite the existence of thin cloud cover. The eclipse took place on 1990 February 9 and was recorded on Agfachrome 1000RS Professional film loaded in a Nikon F4S camera that was fitted to an f/10 telescope with a focal length of 2000 mm. The exposure was for 20 seconds. Picture (b) was taken on 1992 December 9 during an eclipse of the Moon that was generally agreed to have been one of the darkest in living memory – the result of the enormous quantity of ash injected into the atmosphere in 1991 by the volcano. The picture was taken with a 1000-mm f/11 Nikkor mirror-reflex lens on Scotchchrome 800/3200P transparency film. The exposure was 1 minute, and for an exposure this long it was vital that the camera mount tracked at the correct lunar rate. The lighter area at the bottom right of the lunar disk in (a) and at the top in (b) indicates that the Moon's track through the umbra of the Earth's shadow was well to the south and the north, respectively, in the two eclipses. (All full dates in this book are given according to standard astronomical practice in the form "year, month, day.")*

Table 6.2 provides a basic guide to exposures for the eclipsed Moon. Often, longer focal length lenses will not be available in the fast focal ratios given in Table 6.2 for exposures within totality. Approximate

Table 6.2 *Guide exposures for the eclipsed Moon.*

Eclipse phase	Film speed (ISO)					
	64	100	200	400	1000	1600
Deep in penumbra	1/60 s at f/8	1/60 s at f/11	1/60 s at f/16	1/125 s at f/16	1/250 s at f/16	1/500 s at f/16
Whole Moon within umbra	1 s at f/2	1 s at f/2.8	1 s at f/4	1/4 s at f/2.8	1/8 s at f/2.8	1/15 s at f/2.8
Mid-totality	4 s at f/2	2 s at f/2	2 s at f/2.8	1 s at f/2.8	1/2 s at f/2.8	1/4 s at f/2.8

Table 6.3 *Guide exposures for total lunar eclipse at slower f-numbers.*

Eclipse phase	Film speed (ISO)		
	400	1000	1600
Whole Moon within umbra	2 s at f/8 or	1 s at f/8 or	1/2 s at f/8 or
	1 s at f/5.6	1/4 s at f/5.6	1/4 s at f/5.6
Mid-totality	8 s at f/8 or	4 s at f/8 or	2 s at f/8 or
	4 s at f/5.6	2 s at f/5.6	1 s at f/5.6

exposures with slower focal ratios for three films are given in Table 6.3. Yet again, it must be stressed that these exposures are to be used as a basic guide only: experiment to see what suits your equipment and conditions.

Table 6.4 *Total lunar eclipses to AD 2010.*

Date	Areas witnessing entire eclipse	Time of mid-totality (UT)
1996 April 4	Europe, most of Africa, extreme east of South America	00:09
1996 September 27	Central and South America, eastern half of US, UK and most of Europe, West Africa	02:54
1997 September 16	East Africa, Eastern Europe, India, western Asia and Western Australia	18:46
2000 January 21	North and South America, UK and Western Europe	04:43
2000 July 16	Eastern Asia, Australia, New Zealand, islands of the western Pacific	13:55
2001 January 9	Most of Africa, Europe, India, and western Asia	20:20
2003 May 16	Eastern North America, Central and South America	03:40
2003 November 9	Europe, Western Africa, eastern South America, northeastern North America	01:18
2004 May 4	Western Asia, Central and Western Africa	20:30
2004 October 28	Western Europe and Africa, South America, most of US	03:04
2007 March 3	Europe and Africa	23:20
2007 August 28	Central Pacific	10:37
2008 February 21	West Africa, Wetern Europe, South America, Central and Eastern US	03:25
2010 December 21	All of North America, Central America	08:17

Source: Fred Espenak, *Fifty Year Canon of Lunar Eclipses: 1986–2035*, NASA Reference Publication 1216, 1989; available from Sky Publishing Corp.

The problem of the Moon's movement during an exposure must be considered. A 500-mm $f/8$ mirror lens should yield a good image with the fastest films when the Moon is wholly within the umbra, and a reasonable image during mid-totality (even though, if the exposures indicated in the tables are accurate, the totally eclipsed Moon requires a 2-second exposure, as against a target of only 1 second from the formula 500/focal length). For the best results during totality, lenses of even longer focal length must be mounted on a camera drive or on a telescope tracking at the lunar rate. However, since the eclipsed Moon is a relatively indistinct object it will still be worth experimenting with a fixed camera and long lenses. Incidentally, it is at a time like this that focusing by the parallax method with a bright screen (see Chapter 3) is a great advantage.

A lunar eclipse lasts much longer than a solar eclipse and, unlike a solar eclipse, it is not a spectacle that is restricted to a very limited path across the Earth's surface for a brief time – it may be seen anywhere in the world where the Moon is up (and skies are clear!). Table 6.4 lists forthcoming total lunar eclipses and the locations from where the Moon is in the sky for the entire sequence of events.

A phenomenon much more frequent than a lunar eclipse but one which is intriguing in its own right and a good test of developing photographic skills is earthshine. When the Moon is at crescent phase, the dark part of its disk is sometimes faintly visible. Traditionally called "the old Moon in the new Moon's arms" (although it should depend essentially on whether a waxing or waning Moon is being talked about), the almost ghostly glow is caused by the reflection of daylight from Earth onto the night areas of the lunar surface. The cause is not fully explained in most books, and is interesting.

Earthshine

It must be remembered first of all that the phase of the Moon is the complement of the Earth's phase as it would be seen from the Moon. Thus, an observer on a one- or two-day-old waxing crescent Moon would see a waning, gibbous Earth just past full. When the waxing crescent is no more than a day or so old, the earthshine effect is difficult to see because the Moon is in a relatively bright sky. But as it ages to two and three days, it is still quite high as dusk falls and it faces an Earth which is still only two or three days past full. The disk of Earth looms thirteen times larger (in area) in the Moon's sky than the Moon does in ours, and this coupled with the Earth's greater reflectivity makes it forty times brighter. Earthshine is the result. The effect can still be seen at four days or so, but by then the Earth is waning quite appreciably as seen from the Moon, and the encroaching glare from the rapidly growing daylight area of the Moon overpowers any lingering earthshine (and stops down the iris of our eyes for good measure). The effect is reversed as the Moon wanes to a crescent.

One may theorize that earthshine should be brighter during the Earth's northern-hemisphere winter. Then the Arctic icecap is at its most extensive, and large cloud systems occur frequently. At that time too it is summer in the Antarctic, and the southern icecap will be prominent from the Moon. Ice, snow, and cloud are more reflective than the Earth's landmasses and oceans, and should make earthshine brighter. This would make a fascinating, in-depth study (see also Chapter 15).

Photographing earthshine is much like photographing an eclipse. Using 500-mm $f/8$, 1000-mm $f/11$, and 2000-mm $f/11$ lenses and ISO 400 film, I typically bracket from the optimum 1/60 or 1/30 of a second for the correctly exposed crescent itself, jumping to a series of exposures of ½, 1, 2, 4, and 8 seconds. Good though naturally varying results for the earthshine usually come from the longer exposures in the sequence. Movement of the Moon during this period must be taken into consideration, but earthshine is only a very low light level, and any movement is difficult to discern. So, as with a lunar eclipse, those without access to a camera mount or drive should not be dissuaded from trying. In my experience, no attempt should be made to photograph earthshine once the Moon is more than three days old. The daylit crescent is then so bright that the shutter speeds selected for the earthshine result in gross overexposure of the crescent, irradiation (the scattering of light through the silver halide crystals in the film) causing light to spread far beyond the crescent itself.

Multi-image frames

Effective images and good instructional material result from a sequence of exposures of the Moon on a single frame (see Figure 6.6). The technique is very straightforward. If your camera has no special switch to disable the double-exposure prevention device, it may be overriden by depressing the film rewind button in the bottom plate of the camera. Then, when the the film lever wind is operated, the film will not be wound on. In a sequence of exposures of this kind, with an interval of some minutes between each pair, it is imperative to remember to operate the override procedure and tension the shutter immediately an exposure has been finished. This must be done as a matter of routine. The work of many tens of minutes can be ruined by leaving this operation until an exposure is due and then forgetting to operate the override. Spode's law strikes again!

We have seen that the image of the Moon recorded on film through a 50-mm lens is very small: 0.5 mm at maximum. However, the attraction of the 27° vertical and 40° horizontal field of view of this lens is that a large part of a lunar eclipse can be encompassed within it. When enlarged five times, the overall image is by no means insignificant, and if enlarged still further it could make quite an impressive record. Obviously settings for the individual exposures have to be modified according to what stage the eclipse has reached. Longer lenses can be used, but the increased diameter of each Moon image, along with the blank space that has to be left between each pair of images, results in a shorter time sequence of the eclipse being recorded. The same technique may be used simply to demonstrate how the Moon's apparent colour changes with growing elevation from the horizon. Multi-image frames of lunar events are discussed in more detail in Chapter 15.

Figure 6.6 *The Moon rising and coming out of eclipse on 1982 December 30. This is an excellent example of how well dynamic events can be portrayed on one frame of film. Using a home-built 4 × 5 inch sheet film camera with a 400-mm f/4.5 lens, Akira Fujii made exposures at 5-minute intervals. The original was shot on Ektachrome 64 film, with exposures varying from $1/2$ a second at f/5.6 for the thin crescent to 1/125 of a second at f/11 for the nearly full Moon.*

Libration

Multi-image frames are a form of what we might call time-lapse photography, although that technique is normally presented in a moving form. An even longer form of time-lapse photography, with images separated by months or even years, can be used to demonstrate the Moon's libration (from the Latin for "to balance"). This is the apparent wobbling of the Moon on its axis, deriving from at least three causes. It is libration that enables us to see, at one time or another, 59 percent of the Moon's surface rather than the 50 percent we might expect from the Moon keeping the same hemisphere facing the Earth.

There are several types of libration. *Libration in longitude* results from the Moon's orbit being elliptical. The Moon's speed varies according to its position in its orbit, but its speed of rotation remains constant. As a result of this mismatch, the face the Moon presents to us oscillates slightly from left to right, and we can see areas further round its east or west limb. *Libration in latitude* results from the plane of the Moon's orbit around the Earth being inclined by 5° to the plane of the Earth's orbit around the Sun. There are times when, because of this, we can see more of the Moon's north or south polar region. *Diurnal libration* enables us to see slightly "over the top" of the Moon when it is rising and "under the bottom" when it is setting. This is because the greater radius of the Earth gives the observer several thousand kilometres in height advantage when the Moon is on the horizon.

Careful scrutiny of pictures such as those in Figure 6.2 can reveal differences on the limb and polar regions caused by libration. Libration in longitude has the greatest effect, accounting for 8 of the extra 9 percent of the Moon's surface the various librations bring into view.

CHAPTER 7

The Sun

The beginning of this chapter is undoubtedly the most controversial part of the book. Many astronomy authors and other experienced observers are categorical in stating that there is only one safe way of looking at the Sun: to project the Sun's image through a telescope onto a white card which is shaded from the surrounding daylight by some form of curtaining or box, or by a large card through which the telescope pokes. The reason for the warning is obvious. Figures for the amount of solar energy falling on the Earth's surface include so many zeros that our minds cannot grasp the physical facts. However, we can appreciate the calculation that the Sun's surface is well over a quarter of a million times brighter than a sunlit scene on Earth. And even more directly, we know the extreme discomfort (to say the least) we experience when we glance inadvertently at the Sun. Add to this the fact that optical instruments gather far more light and energy than the human eye, as demonstrated when a magnifying glass or lens is used to set fire to paper, and the concern about photographing the Sun will be fully understood.

Safety, and filters

But these few facts are not all. The public interest in looking at the Sun is concentrated almost entirely at solar eclipses, especially a total eclipse. At these times various allegedly safe viewing filters go on sale. But many of them, while offering deceptively comfortable viewing of the uneclipsed portions of the Sun's disk, are likely to transmit infrared and ultraviolet radiation that can damage the retina without the user suffering pain or distress at the time of viewing. This is because the retina, like the lens of the eye, has no pain receptors. (Although the danger of retinal burns from infrared radiation has always been stressed, recent research has established that there is an even greater danger from UV radiation, resulting in what is called photochemical damage, than from infrared.) Smoked glass is a typical example of an unreliable and therefore dangerous "filter." The behaviour of individuals compounds the problem: stories abound of people at responsibly organized eclipse viewing sessions suggesting piercing a hole in a safe filter "to see the Sun more clearly." To be frank, there is little evidence on the incidence of damage to people's eyes on such occasions. But, given the apparent lack of wisdom of some members of the general public, the considerable concern felt about direct viewing of the Sun must be appreciated.

The fact remains that there are perfectly safe filters for observing and photographing the Sun available at modest cost to the newcomer to astrophotography. A safety drill does have to be observed, but it is assumed that anybody reading this book will realize the vital importance of following the correct procedure. It should be quite clear which filters are safe and which procedures should be followed, but you can always fall back on good sense and the maxim, "if in doubt, *don't.*" In passing, while the health of our eyes must take obvious precedence over possible damage to equipment, it is worth repeating a further word of warning. One of the world's biggest telescope manufacturers categorically advises against using a telescope to project the Sun's image onto a white card because of the potential damage resulting from the build-up of intense heat within a telescope focused on the Sun.

Specialist filters used for viewing and photographing the Sun (see Chapter 16) reduce the level of solar radiation by a factor of 100,000 – that is, they transmit just 0.001 percent and block 99.999 percent. The same effect can be achieved by the newcomer to astrophotography, but as a two-stage process: reducing the sunlight that falls on the film, and protecting the eye when aiming the camera.

Any part (no matter how small) of the Sun's visible surface, the photosphere, can be photographed through *neutral density filters* (ND filters) with a density level of 5.0. This does not mean a 5× filter as everyday photographers understand it. There the 5 refers to the factor by which the filter reduces the light, and hence the factor by which a normal unfiltered exposure must be increased to achieve a comparable result when using the filter. A neutral density value of 5.0 in fact represents a filter factor of 100,000 (i.e. 10^5) – the amount required for photographing the Sun. (This figure of 5.0 should not be confused with that of an ND filter with a density level of 0.5, which has a filter factor of a mere 3×!)

Gelatine ND filters are available, but since there is no single filter with a density of 5.0, two must be combined: a 4.0 with a 1.0 or a 3.0 with a 2.0. The use of two filters rather than one has no significant effect on image sharpness. The filters must be handled carefully, and a gelatine filter holder is a wise purchase to help protect the filters in use. (Glass ND filters are available in various countries, but since their prices in diameters up to 122 mm are comparable to those of the specialized solar filters already referred to, they are unlikely to be purchased by newcomers and are not discussed further here.) These filters are used at the front of the lens; their use at the rear would allow solar radiation into the lens with the possibility of damage from the build-up of heat. The drawback with the ND filters is that they block only the visible spectrum by the required amount, and not the potentially dangerous infrared and UV wavelengths. So additional protection is required for visual observing and, more to the point, for aiming and focusing a camera.

This is provided by black-and-white film of the sort used in ordinary photography. When such a film is fully exposed by unrolling or extracting it from a cassette in bright light and then developed normally, instead of the variety of tones seen in a typical negative the film consists of a dense layer of metallic silver. It has been established that film thus

(a)

Figure 7.1 *(a) An annular eclipse of the Sun seen from California on the late evening of 1992 January 4. The picture was shot on Ektachrome ISO 100 film loaded in a Nikon F4S camera fitted with a lens/teleconverter combination which yielded a focal length of 450 mm and a focal ratio of between f/5.6 and f/8. This is one of five autobracketed exposures made at the time of an attractive scene showing Sun, (rapidly thickening) clouds, hot air balloon, and glitter path across the Pacific. The exposure was for 1/2000 of a second. (b) Some minutes later, the complete annulus has been formed although it was not perfectly symmetrical. The cloud of an approaching front has thickened appreciably, but the exposure on ISO 400 colour transparency film at between f/5.6 and f/8 was still 1/3000 of a second, in an autobracketing sequence extending over five frames.*

(b)

exposed and developed can be formed into a filter with an ND value of 6.0, which provides good protection for the eyes. This density can be obtained by sandwiching two thicknesses of film together (with both the duller, emulsion sides facing inwards). 120 size film will provide a reasonable area for comfortable and safe viewing, and 4 × 5 inch film even more so. The film can be mounted in a suitable frame. One medical opinion is that such a filter should be looked through for no longer than 30 seconds at any one time, so as to allow the physiological processes that operate within the eye time to conduct heat away from the retina.

Filtering the Sun's light for photography is thus a two-stage operation. The camera is aimed to frame the Sun, and focusing is accomplished with the home-made viewing filter held over the lens of an SLR camera. Then the viewing filter is removed and the two-layer photographic ND filter screwed into position before exposures are made. At no time when using an SLR should the eye be applied to the viewfinder without the viewing filter in position. It must also be stressed that only viewing filters made from black-and-white film are safe and effective. Colour films, whether of the transparency or negative–positive type, are totally unsuitable because they contain very little or no silver when exposed and processed, and it is the metallic silver that protects the eyes. Polarizing filters, too, are unsuitable. The viewing filter itself should not be used for photography, incidentally, because the metallic silver in it scatters light and makes the image slightly less sharp.

Finally, you need to remember good, basic photographic practice if you are engaged in a lengthy period of photography of the Sun, as during an eclipse. The camera (and the film inside it) should be kept shaded while photography is not taking place. Moreover, since the photographic ND filters do not absorb infrared wavelengths, the camera should not be pointed at the Sun continuously unless either a totally opaque card or the viewing filter is held in front of the lens. The danger to the lens and camera components from the build-up of heat is a real one.

(a)

Figure 7.2 *One of the most dramatic total solar eclipses of recent years was that of 1991 July 11 which lasted for just under 6 minutes 30 seconds as seen from La Paz in Baja California Sur in Mexico. (a) This picture is from a colour original on ISO 200 film exposed through a Nikkor 1000-mm focal length f/11 lens for 1/15 of a second. It was one of a series of progressively longer exposures aimed at recording the extent of the solar corona. (b) As totality ended, the beautiful diamond ring effect was seen for perhaps one second. The picture was shot on an ISO 400 colour negative film. The exposure was 1/500 of a second. Very noticeable during totality was a large prominence on the western limb of the Sun resembling the famous Horsehead Nebula; it can be seen just below the glare of the diamond ring effect. No filter was needed for these exposures.*

Solar eclipses

Despite the Sun's diameter being over four hundred times greater than that of the Moon, the two bodies have approximately the same angular diameter as seen from the Earth. An eclipse of the Sun occurs when a new Moon lies precisely between it and the Earth. If at the time of the line-up the Moon is closest to the Earth in its elliptical orbit, at a point called perigee, then the size of the totally shadowed area (the *umbra*) it creates on the Earth is at its largest possible diameter of about 270 km (170 miles). Then, for observers in the optimum position totality can last for the maximum possible time – somewhat over 7 minutes. Often the umbra is smaller, and therefore the period of totality is considerably shorter. If the line-up happens when the Moon at its farthest point from the Earth (apogee), its disk does not cover all of the Sun, the umbra does not reach the surface of the Earth, and in

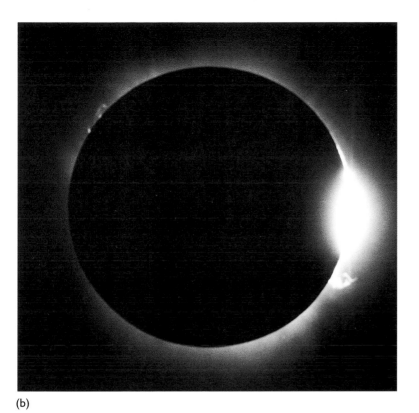

(b)

mid-eclipse a narrow ring of the solar photosphere outlines the Moon. This is called an *annular eclipse* (see Figure 7.1), and tends to attract less interest than the dramatic spectacle of a total eclipse. (An annular eclipse must be photographed using ND filters, even though the ring of sunlight, the annulus, is very narrow.)

As the Sun and Moon keep pace with each other for two hours or so, a path of totality sweeps over the surface of the Earth at a speed, depending on the elevation of Sun and Moon, of as much as 8000 km/h (5000 mile/h). Along the centreline of the path, totality lasts the longest. Observers outside the path but within the *penumbra* of the Moon's shadow see only a partial eclipse. Solar eclipses and paths of totality are predicted well in advance, and one published list gives details to the year 2510! It is calculated that the average period between eclipse paths crossing the same location on the Earth's surface is about 400 years. Solar eclipses up to the year 2010 are listed in Table 7.1.

First contact is the name given to the moment when the Moon's disk first begins to pass in front of the Sun. A chip out of the Sun appears and grows steadily until only a slender crescent is left beyond the Moon's leading edge. This too disappears at *second contact*, when totality begins. *Third contact* occurs when the Moon's trailing limb coincides with that of the Sun, following which the first sunlight reappears. *Fourth* or *last contact* is the moment when the Moon's disk parts company with the Sun's.

As the slender crescent of the photosphere diminishes and the shadow of totality rushes towards observers, the last remnants of

Table 7.1 *Total solar eclipses to* AD *2010.*

Date	Path of totality	Maximum duration of totality
1995 October 24	Iran, Afghanistan, Pakistan, India, Bangladesh, Burma, Thailand, Cambodia, Vietnam, Malaysia (Sabah), Pacific	2m 10s
1997 March 9	Mongolia, northern China, Siberia	2m 50s
1998 February 26	Pacific, Panama, Colombia, Venezuela, West Indies, Atlantic	4m 09s
1999 August 11	Atlantic, southwest England, France, Germany, Austria, Hungary, Romania, Bulgaria, Turkey, northern Iraq, Iran, Pakistan, India	2m 23s
2001 June 21	South Atlantic, Angola, Zambia, Zimbabwe, Mozambique, Madagascar	4m 57s
2002 December 4	Angola, Zimbabwe, Botswana, South Africa, Mozambique, Indian Ocean, southern Australia	2m 04s
2003 November 23	Antarctica only	1m 57s
2005 April 8	Total eclipse over central Pacific; annular eclipse over Panama, Colombia, Venezuela	0m 42s
2006 March 29	Brazil, Atlantic, Ghana, Togo, Benin, Nigeria, Niger, Chad, Libya, Egypt, Turkey, Kazakhstan, Russia	4m 07s
2008 August 1	Northern Canada, Greenland, Russia, Mongolia, China	2m 27s
2009 July 22	India, Nepal, Bangladesh, Bhutan, China, Ryukyu Islands, Pacific	6m 39s
2010 July 11	South Pacific, southern Chile, Argentina	5m 20s

Source: Fred Espenak, *Fifty Year Canon of Solar Eclipses: 1986–2035,* NASA Reference Publication 1178, Revised 1987; available from Sky Publishing Corp.

sunlight shine through valleys between mountains on the Moon's leading limb as *Baily's beads*. The last flash of light from the Sun's limb creates what is graphically called the *diamond ring effect*. As this disappears, the gases of the chromosphere are seen for a brief period as a red rim, and prominences – sheets of hot gas or plasma writhing from the Sun's surface for tens of thousands of kilometres into space, spring into view. The beautiful, pearly hue of the corona (see Figure 7.2(a)) develops as totality progresses. On the Earth, a pseudo-night falls and planets, stars, and sometimes previously undetected Sungrazing comets are seen clearly. But all too soon the Moon's trailing limb moves on. The sequence of diamond ring (see Figure 7.2(b)), Baily's beads, and crescent Sun is repeated, now in reverse order.

There is a natural tendency simply to watch what is one of nature's greatest displays, but for the photographer there is a need to concentrate on a plan. There are two distinct phases of photographing an eclipse. During the short minutes of totality, when the photosphere is hidden in its entirety by the lunar disk, both viewing and photographic ND filters may be lowered or removed from lenses. At all other times both sets of filters *must* be used. Photographic exposures of the Sun's disk using the 5.0 ND filter remain the same whether the Sun is "full" or only the slenderest of crescents is showing. The following formulas give the basis for calculating exposures during these "phases" of the Sun (remember that the Sun is an extended object):

$$(\text{Focal ratio})^2 = \text{Film speed} \times \text{Shutter speed} \times 100$$

or

$$\text{Shutter speed} = \frac{(\text{Focal ratio})^2}{\text{Film speed} \times 100}$$

As an example, for an ISO 200 film and a focal ratio of $f/11$, the second formula gives:

$$\text{Shutter speed} = \frac{11 \times 11}{200 \times 100} = \frac{121}{20,000} = \frac{1}{165}$$

There is no shutter speed of exactly this value, so we would choose 1/125 or 1/250 of a second as the basis for bracketing the exposures.

Exposures for the various stages of a solar eclipse are largely a matter of experience, but Table 7.2 gives some guidance for the features of totality and for the partial phases. I stress once again that exposures should be bracketed, although pre-eclipse tests of exposures using the ND filters can be carried out (at approximately the same time of day as the eclipse will occur) to get more precise exposure values for photographic coverage either side of the period of totality. High-resolution black-and-white film is normally used in advanced studies of the Sun, but certainly for the amateur only colour film can do justice to the glorious sights of totality.

Exposure times are but one of the considerations facing you during the eclipse. As with photography of the Moon, focal length is important and the same approximate formula (focal length/100 = diameter of the disk on the film) applies. We must consider also the subject movement

Table 7.2 *Guide exposures for solar eclipses.*

Film speed (ISO)	Partial phases (5.0 ND filter)	Totality (no filter)				
		Baily's beads	Diamond ring	Prominences	Inner corona	Outer corona
25	1/125 s at f/5.6	1/125 s at f/11	1/60 s at f/8	1/125 s at f/4	1/30 s at f/2.8	1/4 s at f/2.8
50/64	1/125 s at f/8	1/250 s at f/11	1/125 s at f/8	1/125 s at f/5.6	1/30 s at f/4	1/4 s at f/4
100/125	1/125 s at f/11	1/500 s at f/11	1/250 s at f/8	1/125 s at f/8	1/30 s at f/5.6	1/4 s at f/5.6
200	1/125 s at f/16	1/500 s at f/16	1/500 s at f/8	1/125 s at f/11	1/30 s at f/8	1/4 s at f/8
400	1/250 s at f/16	1/1000 s at f/16	1/500 s at f/11	1/125 s at f/16	1/60 s at f/8	1/8 s at f/8
1000	1/500 s at f/16	1/1000 s at f/22	1/500 s at f/16	1/250 s at f/16	1/125 s at f/8	1/15 s at f/8

threshold for exposure time, given by 500/focal length. There is a third, more mundane matter, at least for those of us in some countries. The largest size of modestly priced gelatine ND filter of the densest value readily available in the UK and US is 75 mm square. This obviously limits the lenses of long focal length that can be used to those with a front element diameter of effectively 72 mm – in practice, a moderate telephoto lens of up to 500 mm focal length. As we have already seen in the case of the Moon, such a lens gives an image some 5 mm in diameter on the 35-mm film frame, which is satisfactory, and its 5° angle of view also allows adequate space for recording the solar corona.

Table 7.2 should be reviewed, together with the tentative choice of lens, so that a careful choice of film speed can be made. The best possible film quality is important, and in general a slower or medium-speed film should be selected. There is then a penalty in that faster focal ratios or slower shutter speeds have to be used, but the values indicated in the table are by no means too daunting.

Once again, good photographic practice can help. Your programme of photography should not be too complex – quite apart from any other reason, you ought to have some time to enjoy the spectacle. As already suggested, experiments should be conducted in advance to establish accurate exposures when using ND filters, and a careful if brief plan of exposures to be made during totality should be drawn up. These exposures should be rehearsed at twilight, using a red-light torch/flash-light to alter shutter speed/*f*-number controls, as you may well need to do this during a particularly dark eclipse. With slower shutter speeds, precise and careful discipline is required along the lines detailed in Chapter 5. Ensure that the tripod is as firm as possible. Resist the natural temptation to rush exposures during totality: allow a few seconds at least to elapse between them so that vibrations induced by firing the shutter and winding on the film have time to dampen out. Make sure, too, that ample film is available for the planned number of exposures during the few minutes of totality. Better to load a new film (possibly of a faster speed) in good time for totality than to run out. Make sure it is loaded correctly and is winding on before the great moment arrives. If you do reload, the period immediately afterwards would be a good time to remove the filters and check that focusing, shutter speed, and focal ratio are as required.

An alternative to taking a series of individual pictures is to expose a series of images on one frame (by overriding the double-exposure prevention device), as explained when discussing photography of the Moon. A 50-mm focal length lens has an angle of view, in terms of its diagonal, of 46°. The Sun and Moon move at about 15° per hour, so this is a convenient size for encompassing the entire 2-hour sequence of an eclipse. However, the image size of the Sun will be extremely small. A 200-mm focal length lens cannot be used to record the entire eclipse, but does give an impressive solar disk, its angle of view of more than 12° allowing approximately ten exposures with pauses of 3 or 4 minutes in between each exposure on the 35-mm frame. For the most attractive result, the predicted times for the period of totality should be obtained

Figure 7.3 *After a solar eclipse begins, light passing through the leaves of a tree projects images of the partially covered solar disk. Photographing the multiple images is straightforward.*

and an attempt made to commence the first exposure at a time which allows the exposure made at totality to appear in the middle of the frame. This totality exposure will be the only one exposed without the ND filters in place and the shutter speed/focal ratio will need to be altered accordingly. Multi-image solar eclipse photography is discussed further in Chapter 15.

Outside totality itself, the pressures are not too intense. If you have a second camera available, you can use it to photograph some of the associated phenomena. Once the Moon has started to pass across the face of the Sun, sunlight passing through foliage forms multiple images of the Sun's phase on the ground (see Figure 7.3). The exposure details will be quite conventional for photographs of this effect. During totality the eerie light along the horizon is an intriguing subject: try an exposure of $f/2.8$ at around 1/60 of a second with ISO 400 film, or just go with your meter. Certainly the most elusive subject for the camera is *shadow bands*, alternating light and dark bands which ripple quickly across the ground and other surfaces, sometimes seen just before or after totality. Their cause is not completely understood, but is thought to be irregular refraction of the crescent Sun (see e.g. *Sky & Telescope*, May 1991, page 482). Photographing them, even on a specially prepared light-coloured surface, is made difficult by their speed of movement and low contrast, and few successful shadow band pictures have been published. Try an exposure of about 1/250 of a second at $f/1.4$ with ISO 400 film.

Any attempt at capturing these secondary phenomena is best left to a companion: the eclipse itself must take precedence for you. During the partial phases of an eclipse, and particularly if you are using a lens of relatively short focal length, do not hesitate to take unashamedly pictorial photographs of the scene (see Figures 7.1(a) and 7.4). On the other hand, since the appearance of the Sun is quite unmistakable

Figure 7.4 *Those with a technical interest want totally clear skies for eclipse photography of the Sun. However, the presence of some cloud can make for intriguing images. Seen from the UK, there was a partial eclipse of the Sun late in the evening of 1982 July 20. Scattered cloud lay near the western horizon, with quite thick stratus blanketing the bottom of the Sun and thin layers of cloud making the rest of the disk appear almost Jupiter-like. Small flocks of birds flying in front of the Sun are easily seen in the original picture. A sequence of colour images was exposed through a 1000-mm f/11 Nikkor lens during the partial eclipse, some with exposures based on the solar disk only (as here) and others based on a reading of the sky.*

and if you are shooting with a lens of long focal length, you may choose to ignore my earlier advice about using transparency film and try a negative colour film. Any minilab operator, especially if told what the subject is, should be able to produce good-quality prints and enlargements for you.

Relatively few of us are fortunate enough to see a total eclipse of the Sun. This is one of the prime reasons for joining an astronomical party going abroad (see Chapter 14). There is fascinating, more advanced photographic work to be done in studying the Sun (see Chapters 15 and 16), but in terms of emotion there is nothing to rival your first eclipse. Good luck!

CHAPTER 8

The stars

The constellations are a natural subject for the newcomer to astrophotography, for identifying and photographing them is an enjoyable and instructive method of exploring the night sky. They may be photographed in black and white or colour. Using black-and-white film is an economical way of testing techniques and skills, for you need proceed no further than a black-and-white negative. This can be studied under a magnifier, projected, or used to produce a paper print or positive transparency. But colour has a greater drama and appeal. Moreover, colour photographs obtained with the minimum of equipment and experience can demonstrate features of the stars which are beyond the capability of the human eye to perceive.

The lenses used to record the constellations are of relatively short focal length, and the best way of finding out which are the most suitable is by practice. Go out with a camera and lenses on a good, clear night, and look through them at constellations that are well placed. The highest in the sky are the most suitable. A star map will help you to locate the constellations in advance, and to appreciate their relative sizes in the sky. Some books give figures for these sizes in "square degrees." These are quite useful and, without opening a star map or even looking at the sky, you will realize that Pegasus at over 1100 square degrees is very much larger than Lyra at under 300. But that does not take us very far because, while we can easily work out the area of sky covered by one of our lenses, constellations come in all sorts of shapes as well as sizes, and can refuse to fit neatly into the rectangular shape of our picture frame. So we need to check at first hand, and the first time out it makes sense not to expose any film, but just to look and learn.

Many of the constellations will fit into the 27° (vertical) by 40° (horizontal) field of view of the standard 50-mm focal length lens. With it, we can comfortably photograph Auriga or Gemini or Cassiopeia in the northern winter sky. It will also cover the whole of Orion or Perseus, but only if the camera is angled so that the long axis of the field of view accommodates the greater "length" of the constellations compared with their "width." Some of the constellations are much smaller – Lyra, for example, fits comfortably into the field of view of an 85-mm focal length lens – while others need the greater coverage (38° by 55°) of a 35-mm wide-angle lens. Ursa Major, Leo, Taurus, and Hercules come into the latter category. I should point out that these references are to the full extent of the constellations: the familiar bright stars of Ursa Major or

Leo, for example, fit into the field of view of a 50-mm focal length lens, but the entire constellations, out as far as their official boundaries, are far bigger. The so-called Summer Triangle, the beautiful multi-constellation feature formed by Vega in Lyra, Altair in Aquila, and Deneb in Cygnus, also requires a 35-mm lens. Some constellations are even bigger and demand a full 24-mm wide-angle lens. Hydra, the largest constellation in the sky, falls into this category. For those who like a little mathematics, another way of working out this information is to establish the size that a given astronomical object will occupy on a 35-mm film frame. This can be worked out from the formula

$$\text{Image size} = a \times f/57.3$$

where a is the size of the object in degrees of arc and f is the focal length of the lens. As an example, the distance from Dubhe to Alkaid at the extreme ends of Ursa Major is 26°, so if we use a 50-mm lens the size of the image is

$$26 \times 50/57.3 = \text{almost } 23 \text{ mm}$$

which will fit comfortably into the nominal 23×34 mm picture size of a mounted 35-mm slide.

This introduction points the way, but you should set out to gain practical experience of fitting different focal lengths to various constellations. If the ultimate purpose is to prepare a set of constellation slides for teaching, you might consider choosing a single focal length so that the size of the field of view does not alter between slides, as this would confuse students. Similarly, a standard might be established whereby the celestial equator is always parallel to the long axis of the picture frame. The 35-mm wide-angle lens is in many ways suitable, but the inclusion of the larger constellations would call for a 28- or 24-mm focal length lens (despite other drawbacks, discussed later).

Star trails

Before you get into the detail of theory and technicalities, I suggest that you find a sky as far away as possible from city lights, load your camera with a medium-speed colour film (ISO 200 or 400, no faster), set a 50-mm lens at $f/2.8$ (also no faster, even if it does open up to $f/1.8$ or more), select a number of constellations, and shoot 10-minute time exposures of each. If the sky is reasonably dark, make one exposure lasting about 30 minutes of the Ursa Minor region, preferably with Polaris centred in the frame. Then, turn the camera to the south, identify from the star atlas the constellations on view through which the celestial equator runs, and photograph that region too, also with a 30-minute exposure.

When the film has been processed, not only will the 10-minute exposures record the stars as trails, thereby demonstrating the 15° per hour rotation of the Earth during the exposure, but the trails will vary considerably in colour. Exposures made with a driven camera aimed at recording the stars as points of light are often long enough for the brighter stars to overexpose and therefore appear whitish in colour. With photographs of trails, the light from the individual stars slowly moves across the film, so the degree of exposure of each part of the film the trails cross is much less, and so more colour is present. The whites, light blues, yellows, oranges, and reds in your photographs are not scientifically accurate records of the colours of the stars, since a number of variables are involved, including how well the different colour-sensitive layers in the film have been balanced by the manufacturer.

Nonetheless, the colours are usually a good approximation, and photographic film has a greater ability to distinguish (and record) the hues than do our dark-adapted eyes. So in photographs we see white Castor next to yellow Pollux in Gemini; the massive, orange-red Betelgeuse in Orion compared with the brilliant white Rigel, which is 60,000 times more luminous than our Sun (see Figure 8.1); and the blueness of Vega in Lyra contrasting with the light orange of Arcturus in Boötes. The different colours of the stars revealed by such straightforward exposures are actually indications of their different surface temperatures. This is the basis of stellar spectroscopy. By studying a star's spectrum, much can be discovered about its physical condition and composition. Spectroscopists classify stars according to their spectral type: from the very hot O-type stars, down through B (hot and

Figure 8.1 *The shape of the constellation Orion is unmistakable, even though the stars are trailed. This 10-minute exposure through a Noct-Nikkor 58-mm lens (specially designed for night photography) at f/2.8 was on relatively slow film, ISO 200 Agfachrome Professional, to limit the effect of any light pollution or airglow (see pages 86 and 87). On faster film, light pollution or airglow would quickly build up a background "fog." The orange of Betelgeuse contrasts sharply with the brilliant white of Rigel and the varying shades of blue of the other bright stars. The Orion Nebula (M42), just below Orion's belt, appears lilac on this film; other films render it slightly more reddish. As it is a dim, diffuse object moving across the film, the saturation is never very strong. Pictures like this are a useful general representation of the colours of the stars.*

white, like Rigel), A (cooler white stars such as Sirius, the brightest star in the night sky), F, and G (yellow like our Sun), to K (orange like Arcturus) and M (orange-red like Betelgeuse).

The picture centred on Polaris (see Figure 8.2) will also show different colours. However, its greatest interest is that it demonstrates how Polaris lies very close to the celestial north pole, because it only just shows a trail in photographs taken with a wide-angle or normal lens. The trails of the stars around it increase in length (despite them all having been recorded for the same amount of time) the farther they are from the pole: as their declination decreases, they appear to travel farther (or move faster, to put it another way). This intriguing demonstration of celestial geometry is matched by that in the picture of the celestial equator (see Figure 8.3). Here the stars right on the equator appear to be travelling in straight lines and for the greatest distance, while those to the north record increasingly curved (but shorter) trails the farther they are from the equator, and the stars to the south behave similarly, although the curve is in the opposite direction, that of the south celestial pole. Both pictures are quite simple to obtain, yet they suggest extremely well, within the inevitable limits of a flat surface, the three-dimensional nature of the celestial sphere above our heads.

Figure 8.2 *Star trails around the celestial pole are among the simplest yet most dramatic images that can be taken with a fixed camera. This is a 30-minute exposure on ISO 200 Ektachrome Professional film using a 35–105-mm Nikkor zoom lens set to 50 mm focal length and the maximum aperture of f/3.5. The saguaro cactus and foreground rocks of the Arizona landscape are dimly lit by security lights at a nearby resort complex. Polaris, at the top left, scarcely moved during the exposure, but the stars of Cassiopeia, towards the right edge of the frame, show quite long trails.*

Figure 8.3 *A 10-minute exposure is long enough to demonstrate clearly the apparent paths of stars at the celestial equator. The region shown here is between Leo and Virgo, and the equator is about two-thirds of the way up the frame. At top and bottom of the image it is clear that the star trails arch in opposite directions, towards the north and south celestial poles, respectively. A 50-mm f/1.4 lens was used for this picture, and the original was on Agfachrome 1000RS Professional film.*

As with many other pictures, the addition of pictorial elements in the foreground can heighten impact – a mountain or castle beneath Polaris or a constellation angled close to the horizon and reflected in water. But the main reason for suggesting starting with the simplest exercises in star photography is that, notwithstanding the simplicity, sound knowledge is derived from the results.

While photographing star trails is an encouraging and instructive beginning, it will be only a matter of time before the newcomer wishes to record the stars as they appear to the eye. As the approach of this book is to consider astrophotography using essentially photographic rather than astronomical equipment, the major question is how to overcome the effects of the Earth's rotation within this limitation.

The stars as "points of light"

In Chapter 2 reference was made to the focal length of lenses, and to the fact that the stars (which may be described as point sources as opposed to extended objects) are so far away that their image size on film is not related to focal length. While we may talk loosely about their images on film as being points of light, this is not in fact accurate. The magnitude of a star, the characteristics of lens and film, the length of exposure, and the state of the atmosphere all affect the end result. A bright star such as Vega, for example, will record on film as a much bigger "point of light" than a fainter star will, and image size will increase with exposure (see Figure 8.4). The concept of the image size of a star on film is important because, if there is some exposure threshold below which a star will record without it trailing as a result of the Earth's rotation, then the goal of taking more realistic pictures is within reach.

Figure 8.4 *When is a point source not a point of light? The answer should perhaps be "always." Lens characteristics (for example, shooting at different f-numbers) as well as overexposure or underexposure can affect the apparent size of a star on film. Here the brilliant star Vega was photographed (together with some nearby companions) using a Noct-Nikkor 58-mm f/1.2 lens. However, the governing factor here is gross exposure. The lens was first opened to its widest aperture of f/1.2, and a 4-second exposure made. After waiting for 2 minutes to allow Vega to move far enough for the next image to be exposed on a different part of the film, another 4-second exposure was made with the aperture at f/2, and so on down to f/8. An ISO 400 black-and-white film was used. This experiment demonstrates how bright stars become overexposed in time exposures calculated to record fainter stars.*

The American lecturer and writer on astrophotography Barry Gordon has devised such a value based on a combination of experience and calculation. He selected 0.05 mm as a trail length which is short enough to be indistinguishable from a point image on the film. From there he calculated that for the fastest-moving stars (those at the celestial equator) any exposure in seconds shorter than $700/F$, where F is the focal length of the lens in use, will yield essentially trail-free images. (For the hypercritical, $500/F$ yields a trail length of 0.036 mm, which is nearing the limits of a film's resolution.) The value for stars away from the equator – which, as our trail pictures have shown, appear to move more slowly – grows more in the photographer's favour, and for stars at declination 50° the maximum exposure time goes up to $1000/F$ seconds. This means, therefore, that if we are using a standard 50-mm focal length lens, exposures of up to $700/50 = 14$ seconds are possible before trailing becomes apparent.

Of course, all the other factors must be such as to allow an exposure of this duration. The main factors are film speed, film latitude, lens speed, star magnitudes, and the condition of the atmosphere (which can attenuate the light from stars drastically). Remember, too, that when photographing point sources it is the absolute diameter of the lens that is important, not the focal ratio. As we have seen, a lens's absolute diameter is calculated quite easily by dividing its focal length by its focal ratio; thus, a 50-mm f/1.8 lens has a diameter of just under 28 mm. Because there are so many variables, guidance on exposures can only be approximate. Table 8.1 gives suggested exposures for stars to just beyond naked eye visibility (approximately magnitude 6) for various lenses when used at maximum diameter or aperture (that is, not stopped down).

Certain features of camera design, for example the need to reduce vignetting (the darkening of an image towards the edges) to a minimum, and for the back of the lens not to foul the reflex mirror, result in many lenses being constructed in such a way that finding their effective diameter is not a matter of performing a simple division sum, as described above. The front diameter in such lenses is in fact larger than the f-number would suggest. The calculations become a little complicated, but the values given in Table 8.1 still provide a good starting-point for experimentation. The wide-angle 24-mm focal length lens would be regarded by the everyday photographer as quite fast, but its diameter is so small compared with the other lenses that relatively lengthy time exposures are required when it is used to photograph the stars. This was why a note of caution was sounded in the previous section when it was suggested on grounds of field of view that a 24-mm focal length lens might be used as the standard focal length for a constellation photography project.

Stopping down a lens inevitably reduces its effective diameter. If the lenses listed in Table 8.1 are stopped down to their next focal ratio value, the diameter too is reduced, to the extent that time exposures on ISO 1000 film have to be increased to those appearing in the ISO 400 film column.

We may now revert to the formula for trail-free star images. Using a 50-mm focal length lens gives us a safe exposure time of around 14 seconds if we assume that we are photographing stars on the celestial equator, but about 20 seconds if our subjects are around 50° declination, say Ursa Major, Perseus, Andromeda, Cygnus, or Auriga. The figures for the 35-mm wide-angle lens are better, at 20 seconds and almost 30 seconds, respectively. The 180-mm focal length lens in these

Table 8.1 *Suggested exposure times for recording star images with a fixed camera.*

Lens and absolute diameter	Film (ISO speed)			
	200	400	1000	1600
24 mm f/2.8, 8.6 mm	15 min	8 min	4 min	2 min
35 mm f/1.4, 25 mm	2 min	1 min	30 s	15 s
50 mm f/1.8, 28 mm	2 min	1 min	30 s	15 s
85 mm f/2.8, 30 mm	2 min	1 min	30 s	15 s
180 mm f/2.8, 64 mm	30 s	15 s	8 s	4 s

(a)

(b)

Figure 8.5 *Two pictures of the Cygnus/Lyra region of the summer sky, which includes the Milky Way. South is at the top. Lyra (with the brilliant star Vega) is towards the left edge of the frames, and the Northern Cross of Cygnus fills much of the middle. Each exposure was for 30 seconds on a fast ISO 1000 black-and-white film through a Nikkor 35-mm f/1.4 lens fitted to a fixed camera. The first (a) was shot at the maximum aperture, while for the second (b) the lens was stopped down to f/2.8. Stars abound in (a), but both Vega and Deneb (towards bottom centre) are badly overexposed, and Vega is also affected by coma. Neither problem appears in (b), although because of the length of the exposure some slight trailing is apparent, despite the use of a short focal length lens.*

two cases yields trail-free time exposures of only about 4 and 6 seconds, but because it has a much bigger diameter it is by no means at a disadvantage. Correlating these figures with those in Table 8.1 indicates that when using high-speed films of ISO 1000 and above in a fixed camera with a fast standard lens fitted, we can secure photographs of stars down to magnitude 6 which are essentially free of trailing.

If we curb our ambitions and aim to record stars only down to magnitude 3, for example, then the exposure times are shortened considerably. With ISO 1000 film and a 50-mm $f/1.8$ or 35-mm $f/1.4$ lens at maximum aperture, the required exposure time is only 4 seconds. Even the 24-mm $f/2.8$ lens yields a more manageable exposure of 30 seconds.

While it is still broadly true that slower films yield higher-quality pictures than faster films, evolving film technology has created not only a revolution in film speeds but has made possible levels of quality quite unheard of just a few years ago. These improvements have affected black-and-white as well as colour film (both transparency and negative). It is these changes that have given the newcomer to astrophotography the chance to photograph the constellations with what is in effect non-astronomical equipment. It is a revelation for people who have been taking astrophotographs for some years to see the way in which exposures of a matter of seconds can in optimum circumstances begin to record diffuse nebulae – objects which previously required exposures of many minutes. It is all extremely encouraging, and it is almost certain that the exposures given in this section will be found to understate the potential of some films: one film may have more latitude, or better reciprocity characteristics, than another and will therefore record stars fainter than the target magnitude 6. Therefore as part of your test programme you should compare different films of nominally similar speed. Colour rendering of the dark sky in particular is another important consideration. Most of the films we purchase are intended for general-purpose photography and, when used in the extreme circumstances of astrophotography, can produce bizarre results.

Despite this optimism, we should be aware that we are pushing at the limits. We are, in effect, "snatching" pictures to combat the rotation of the Earth. To do this we are using fast lenses wide open (here focal ratio and diameter are as one), and once again must recognize that we never get something for nothing. Using lenses in this way exacts penalties. Off-axis coma and other aberrations present problems, and it is an unpalatable truth that wide-angle lenses in particular may perform best at about three stops slower than the maximum (see Figure 8.5). Although not strictly an aberration, vignetting is also likely to take place. We can compensate for these drawbacks to some degree by keeping important objects away from the edges of the field of view whenever possible. But how can this be done with a large constellation which is filling the frame? In some circumstances we may just have to grin and bear it.

Nor do the problems stem only from within the camera and lens. The very fast focal ratio of our lenses, combined with fast films, records extended objects quickly – and there are two such "objects" which can intrude strongly into our pictures: light pollution (see below) and, surprisingly, the night sky itself. A phenomenon called the *airglow*, a faint luminosity caused by solar radiation ionizing atoms and molecules in the upper atmosphere, can be recorded in relatively long exposures. If the sky in such exposures appears to be pale green, it could be airglow because this is the wavelength emitted by atomic oxygen. There should be no problem with exposures of up to a few minutes, but airglow could certainly be recorded in the 10- to 30-minute exposures recommended earlier for star-trail photographs. This is why I have suggested that the focal ratio used should be held to *f*/2.8 and no faster. Although not perhaps so exotic, moonlight has an obvious and even more powerful ability to render the fainter stars invisible. In a long-exposure photograph taken when a full or near-full Moon is up, the sky appears almost as blue as it does during the day. A crescent Moon is

Figure 8.6 *This photograph of much of the same part of the sky as in Figure 8.5 (also with south at the top) shows the effect of a lengthy exposure made possible by mounting the camera on a drive tracking at the sidereal rate. A 24-mm wide-angle lens with an aperture of f/2.8 was used, and the exposure was for 6 minutes on a fast black-and-white film. Vega is towards the lower left, and Deneb is to the left of the data block. The third element of the Summer Triangle, Altair, is at top centre. An exposure of this length captures the images of many more stars, with the result that the main outlines of the constellations are less distinct.*

Figure 8.7 *A Haig mount, placed on a firm base, with clock and red-light torch/ flashlight. The hinge is on the far side, out of view, but clearly seen is the rotating bolt which at one revolution per minute slowly opens the boards, enabling the camera to track the stars. This particular Haig mount was made by Mr Haig himself.*

bearable, but as the phase grows the deep-space astrophotographer admits defeat and turns to tasks such as checking equipment or preparing plans for the future.

Light pollution is a serious problem. In and around large urban areas its effects are obvious. The sky is not black or even dark at all, and only the brightest stars can make themselves visible. The high-pressure sodium streetlights that now predominate in so many localities produce a pall of orange light that covers the sky, and grows brighter the closer our eyes or cameras look towards the horizon. In areas that are lit by mercury streetlights, a greenish blue replaces the orange. At fast focal ratios, colour film rapidly records the predominant colour of the light pollution, and many of the less bright stars are lost to view.

If you cannot get to a site free from light pollution, its impact can be limited by using slower focal ratios. But this also reduces the effective diameter of the lens, so while the light pollution may be curtailed, the fainter stars will also be lost. A more sophisticated remedy is to switch to a lens with the same diameter (and therefore the same starlight-gathering power) but longer focal length, and hence slower focal ratio. The problem then will be whether the longer focal length (taken with other factors) will permit an exposure short enough to avoid star trailing.

While I do not wish to overexaggerate the limitations imposed on the astrophotographer by light-polluted skies, it is an ever-growing problem and something of which the newcomer should be fully aware. Creative use of the lens may help, and when you have more experience you may decide to buy one of the special filters designed to limit the effects of light pollution and at the same time enhance contrast to bring out faint objects like nebulae. The US company Lumicon, for example, has developed a range of such filters for visual observing and photography. These include a Deep-Sky Filter™, a UHC (Ultra High Contrast) Filter™, and an Oxygen-III Filter™. But filters like these are not cheap, and in the end the only effective solution might be to travel to a location with darker skies. Once again, tests should be conducted over a range of time exposures, from say 10 seconds to 10 minutes in a number of steps, and a critical evaluation made of the results.

As experience is gained, star maps or planispheres become easier to read and relate to the sky overhead. To track down fainter objects (and in the absence of a computerized star-finding system of the kind now supplied with some telescopes), the more experienced astronomer or astrophotographer *star-hops* from stars whose locations in the sky are known, via less well known stars located on the star maps, until the target object is located. I have found that if the search area has been previously photographed, then star-hopping with the aid of a black-and-white photographic print is easier. This is probably because the photograph is more realistic than a line drawing on a star map, particularly in its reproduction of star magnitudes. So our early work may well pay practical dividends in later years.

Tracking the stars

A means of breaking away from the restraints imposed by the rotation of the Earth is to fix the camera to a mount that rotates in the opposite direction so as to compensate. The axis of the mount is aligned accurately on the celestial pole, and the platform to which the camera is attached is driven by an electric motor so as to move through right ascension, parallel to the celestial equator. These mounts are therefore known as *equatorial mounts*. The camera can thus track the stars, at a rate equivalent to one revolution in just under 24 hours – the sidereal rate – so that relative to the camera they appear stationary (see Figure 8.6). This is the system used on many telescopes as well as on specially designed camera mounts.

The beginner will probably consider these equatorial mounts a little too advanced, but good results and valuable experience may be gained from a simple manual mount which can be built without too much difficulty. Designed in the mid-1970s by Scottish astronomer George Haig, it is known as the *Haig mount* or (perhaps with due regard for the modest cost incurred in making it) the *Scotch mount* (see Figure 8.7). Astrophotographers in the US often refer to this home-made piece of equipment as a *barn-door* or *tangent-arm drive*, and I understand there are rival US claims for its invention.

Figure 8.8 *A 4-minute exposure of the Taurus area using a Haig mount. Using the mount rather than a fixed camera position enabled the 35-mm wide-angle Nikkor lens to be stopped down from f/1.4 to f/2.8 for better control of off-axis aberrations such as coma. The film was Tri-X, rated at ISO 400 and developed in HC-110 (dilution B). Right of centre are the Pleiades, with the V-shaped Hyades cluster and Aldebaran below to the left. The top of Orion (with Betelgeuse prominent) is at bottom left, Auriga is towards the top left, and part of Perseus lies above the Pleiades.*

The implications of the use of this or any equatorial mount are immediately evident. Longer time exposures are made possible, and film and lens settings can be selected for optimum effect (such as limiting aberrations) rather than being forced by the need to avoid star trailing when a fixed camera is used. One such photograph is shown in Figure 8.8.

As shown in Figure 8.9(a), the main base or "anchor" of the Haig mount is a block of wood about 30 cm (12 inches) or so long, with a cross-section of some 7 × 10 cm (3 × 4 inches). One end is sawn carefully at an angle equal to that of the latitude at which it will be used (for example 34° for Los Angeles or 51° for the south coast of England). A piece of board at least 15 × 30 cm (6 × 12 inches) in area and up to 15 mm (over ½ inch) thick is fixed to the sawn end by glue and/or wood screws. Another board of the same dimensions is attached to it by means of a long hinge (or two hinges very accurately aligned with each other).

A drive screw or bolt is inserted through the fixed board at a distance from the hinges calculated such that one complete revolution of the screw will move the other board by the correct angular rate to track the stars. This depends in turn on the pitch of the screw (see the caption). A tapped bearing for the bolt may be set into the fixed board, but it is quite adequate to make a slightly undersized hole in the fixed board, work the screw through once or twice, and then lubricate the hole with Vaseline or grease before threading the bolt in again and leaving it in position. A slender strip of metal or thin plywood is attached to the head of the screw so that it may be turned by one finger without setting up vibrations in the mount.

The camera bracket, which can be home-made, as shown in Figure 8.9(a), or a shop-bought photographic ball-and-socket head, as shown in Figure 8.9(b), is fixed to the moving board as close to the hinges as possible to achieve maximum rigidity. A retaining bracket, which prevents the hinge boards from flapping open when the mount is being carried, and a carrying handle are two optional extras fitted to the mount shown in Figure 8.7.

While one or two people claim to have been successful, in my view no attempt should be made to fit the mount to a tripod since it could not possibly be fixed firmly enough. The mount should be placed on a level and wide wall top, a steady table, or some similar surface providing convenient access for rotating the drive screw in time with the second hand of a watch or clock. Polar alignment along the hinge line is carried out by using a small mirror, as shown in Figure 8.9(c).

I have found the most convenient operating arrangement to be that shown in Figure 8.7, seating myself to one side of the table, with a small clock clearly in view. After preparing the camera, the lens is covered with a black card and the shutter locked open by a cable release. The clock is already running (illuminated by a discreetly angled red-light torch/flashlight), and at a suitable moment, when the second hand is pointing to 15, 30, 45, or 60, the card is removed and rotation of the drive screw is begun. In tests conducted with lenses up to 50 mm in focal length, I have found it entirely satisfactory to move the drive screw by a quarter-turn at 15-second intervals, although once experience is gained it is quite easy to keep pace with the second hand of the clock in a continuous movement. Doubtless, the ingenious will think of ways to power the mount by a small electric motor capable of rotating the bolt at one revolution per minute.

For developments of the basic Haig mount, see for example *Sky & Telescope*, February 1988, pages 213–14, and April 1989, pages 436–41.

Figure 8.9 (a) *Construction of the Haig equatorial camera mount. Critical dimensions are the angle θ, which must equal the observer's latitude, and the distance D. D is 229 mm for a 6-mm SI or 0 BA screw, with a 1 mm per turn thread; but 291 mm for a $^1/_4$-inch Whitworth screw with 20 turns to the inch. (b) A ball-and-socket head can be used for the camera bracket. (c) Polar alignment is by sighting along the hinge line. The angle of the mirror is not important – it need not be horizontal. (By courtesy of George Y. Haig.)*

(a) wood or metal strip — ¼" Whitworth machine screws

wing nuts

camera

bracket

hinge

PLAN — hinge line

d

drive screw, 1 turn per minute

to north celestial pole

θ

ELEVATION

12 mm plywood 0.3 m x 0.15 m

camera bracket (see detail above)

hinge

wooden 'anchor' block

drive screw, 1 turn per minute

movable board

fixed board

(b)

wing nut

to north celestial pole

(c)

mirror

CHAPTER 9

The planets

Over the last quarter of a century, interplanetary spacecraft such as NASA's Pioneers, Mariners, Vikings, Voyagers, Magellan, and Galileo have sent back to Earth many thousands of pictures which have been not only of great scientific value, but often beautiful and awe-inspiring. We have seen as though we were there the deserts and volcanoes of Mars, the multicoloured belts and zones of Jupiter's atmosphere, the exquisite rings of Saturn, and the exotic surfaces of the moons orbiting the gas giants. Even when it was suffering its initial problems, the Hubble Space Telescope also returned splendid images of the planets. Such pictures may give newcomers to astrophotography high expectations of what can be achieved. It is well to make clear from the outset that planetary photography is one of the most difficult undertakings for even the highly experienced astrophotographer. But all is not lost for the novice. Excellent pictures can be taken, but we have to accept the limitations resulting from the nature of the planets and of our equipment.

Variations in size

Since they are members of the Solar System, the planets are on the Earth's doorstep compared with the stars, but they are still relatively small. Their actual sizes and distances from the Sun are given in Table 1.1 (page 14). Their apparent sizes as seen from the Earth vary according to the positions of the Earth and the planets in their respective orbits (see Table 9.1). At its best, the Earth's nearest planetary neighbour, Venus, is about one-thirtieth the size of the Moon when full. We can work out its size, in millimetres, on a 35-mm film frame from a modification of the formula given in the previous chapter:

Image size = $a \times F/206,280$

where F is the focal length of the lens in millimetres and a is the apparent size of the object in arc seconds. For Venus's maximum size and a powerful lens of 1000 mm, the formula yields an image size of 0.32 mm. This is certainly bigger than the smallest point sources our lenses and films can resolve and record, but is not very exciting, to say the least. Since Venus at the optimum time is the largest of the planets as seen from the Earth, we are faced squarely with a problem of focal length. If 0.1 mm is taken as the image size that is the threshold between an object acting as a point source on the one hand and an extended object on the other, then the focal length required to secure it varies

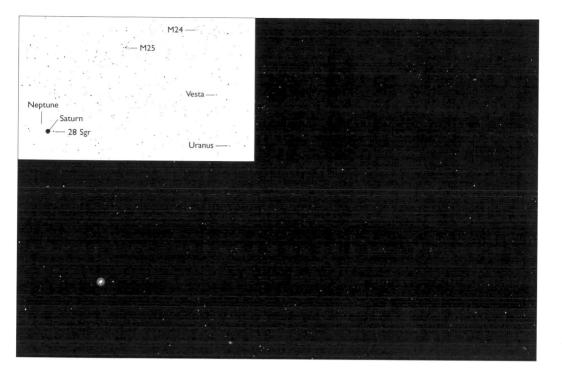

Figure 9.1 *The constellation Sagittarius frequently holds a rich photographic harvest of objects. Included here are the planets Saturn, Neptune, and Uranus, the asteroid Vesta, and a number of Messier objects. The essential requirement for a picture of this kind is a tracking mount, but otherwise all that is needed is care – and a knowledge of this feature-packed area of sky. The exposure was for 25 minutes on hypersensitized 2415 film. The camera was a Nikon F4S with a 180-mm f/2.8 Nikkor lens fitted. A deep red filter was used to combat the light pollution, which was worsened by the low altitude of Sagittarius as seen from the UK. Saturn was inevitably overexposed in such a long exposure, but in no way does this spoil the image.*

from about 500 mm for Venus and Jupiter to not far off 10,000 mm for Neptune. But 0.1 mm is still very insignificant (the dot over an "i" in a very small typeface, perhaps), and to reach image sizes where, all things being equal, some detail can be discerned demands a focal length of around 10,000 mm for Venus and Jupiter and about twice that for Mars and Saturn. This is without considering tiny Mercury on the one extreme and distant Uranus and Neptune on the other. And if those planets are extremely difficult for our purposes (see Figure 9.1), tiny Pluto may be dismissed completely.

Such focal lengths are clearly beyond the newcomer to astrophotography, but fortunately there is much that can be done nonetheless. The magnitudes of the planets vary according to their size and distance from us but, if we strike an average, all the way out to Saturn they are, even at their very worst, on a par with the brighter stars (down to magnitude +1.4 for Saturn at its most distant).

Table 9.1 *Apparent diameters of the planets, in arc seconds.*	
Mercury	5–13
Venus	10–65
Mars	4–25
Jupiter	31–50
Saturn (disk)	15–21
(rings)	35–49
Uranus	3.1–3.7
Neptune	2.0–2.2
Pluto	0.06–0.1

Table 9.2 gives exposures that can be used as a basis for a first exploration of planetary photography, using two lenses of moderate focal length but quite wide diameters. Remember again that, since the planets behave as point sources at these focal lengths, lens speed depends on absolute diameter, not focal ratio. (While Uranus is marginally within the scope of a fixed camera, Neptune certainly requires a driven camera. Both are omitted from consideration for the rest of this chapter.) Although most of these exposures fall within the category of what earlier were termed "no man's land" shutter speeds, that test our technique to the full, they are nonetheless well within the bounds of achievability. The planets may appear to be small, but out to Saturn at least they are quite bright. This has the additional bonus of causing few worries when we apply the severe 500/focal length test for image trailing.

Separated though they are by many tens and even hundreds of millions of kilometres, the planets frequently appear to be close to one another in the sky. These conjunctions are line-of-sight effects which present various types of picture opportunity. In the first instance, the photographer can secure images of planets in the same field of view without too much regard for other objects, such as stars. While a compromise exposure or bracketing will be required if, say Mars and Jupiter are included together in the field of view (as is evident from Table 9.2), the relative brightness of the two is close enough not to result in severe overexposure or underexposure at any reasonable setting. However, beyond satisfying yourself that you can take such a picture, there is little lasting interest in recording two points of light on the same piece of film.

Table 9.2 *Guide exposures for recording the planets on ISO 400 film, for two lenses.*		
Planet	180 mm f/2.8, 64 mm dia.	50 mm f/1.8, 28 mm dia.
Mercury	1/15 s	1/4 s
Venus	1/250 s	1/60 s
Mars	1/8 s	1/2 s
Jupiter	1/60 s	1/15 s
Saturn	1/8 s	1/2 s
Uranus	15 s	1 min
Neptune	2 min	8 min

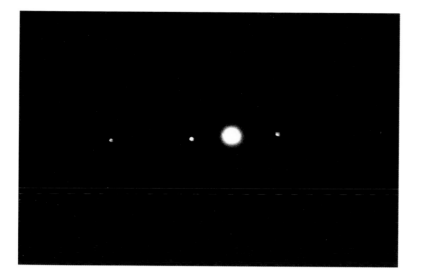

Figure 9.2 *Jupiter and its largest moons can be photographed with long focal length lenses (as well as telescopes). The main problem is that different exposures are needed for Jupiter and for the moons. This is a section of a larger image obtained on Fujichrome ISO 1600 transparency film during a 1-second exposure using an f/11 1000-mm Nikkor mirror-reflex lens. Securing three of the Galilean satellites on film resulted in the disk of Jupiter being overexposed.*

Much more interesting is to photograph Jupiter with one or more of its four major moons – Callisto, Ganymede, Europa, and Io. Ganymede is the largest, with an apparent diameter of 1.5 arc seconds, so endeavouring to photograph it and the others (if not hidden by the planet) is a major test of lens resolution in particular and equipment/photographer capability generally. When Jupiter is closest to the Earth, the moons have magnitudes of between 4.6 and 5.7 compared with Jupiter's −2.7, so in any images of the moons Jupiter is bound to be overexposed. With a 1000-mm $f/11$ mirror lens and ISO 400 film, the moons require an exposure of approximately 2 seconds (where some slight trailing may be expected), whereas Jupiter itself normally requires only about 1/125 of a second. A sequence of exposures between the two is indicated, and Figure 9.2 is an example of what can be obtained.

Lunar occultations of the planets

It is well within the capability of photographic lenses, especially those of longer focal length, to record occultations by the Moon of planets and stars. As a result of the Earth's rotation the Moon appears to move westwards as night progresses, while by virtue of its orbital motion around the Earth it is actually moving eastwards with respect to the background stars and planets at a speed of about 1 km/s (0.6 mile/s), or across a space equal to its own diameter in an hour. Inevitably, therefore, it passes in front of other bodies. Such events, known as occultations, are awaited with some eagerness by enthusiasts since careful timings of the beginning and ending of an occultation can

Figure 9.3 *In a dramatic sky over Houston in Texas, Jupiter is about to be occulted by a waning crescent Moon on the morning of 1990 August 18. Venus can be seen much closer to the horizon. ISO 400 colour transparency film was loaded in a tripod-mounted Nikon F4S fitted with a 180-mm f/2.8 Nikkor lens. The exposure, one of a bracketed sequence, was 1/8 of a second at f/8.*

provide valuable, additional information about the occulted body as well as the Moon's position in its orbit.

The event can be dramatic, too. If the Moon is waxing, the dark lunar limb reaches the star well before the daylit portion and causes it to disappear quite suddenly (demonstrating, incidentally, that the

Figure 9.4 *Oncoming dawn and dark clouds frame the waning crescent Moon and Venus just as well as a foreground of interesting rocks or trees might have. The sky is still dark enough and the phase of the Moon slender enough for earthshine to be recorded clearly. Below Venus is the prominent orange star Aldebaran. A 4-second exposure was given on Ektachrome ISO 200 film using an 85-mm Nikkor lens at f/2.8.*

Moon has no appreciable atmosphere: if it had, the object would fade gradually). If the Moon is waning, the reverse happens and an occulted star will suddenly appear when the Moon's dark lunar limb uncovers it. Of course, there are also appearances and disappearances at the bright limb. The leading edge of a full or waning Moon approaching a star or planet can be watched until the last second. And, knowing the speed of the Moon eastwards in its orbit, and given advance information on the object's path behind the Moon's disk, a watch will give a good indication of when an object will reappear at the bright limb of a full or waxing Moon.

The disappearance of planets tends not to be so sudden, mainly because unlike stars they have an appreciable angular size, but also because they too are usually travelling with the Moon in an easterly direction, although not as quickly as seen from the Earth. Longer lenses are obviously preferable in recording such an event (see Figure 9.3).

Table 9.3 *Guide exposures for recording lunar occultations on ISO 400 film, for two lenses. Venus and Jupiter are treated as extended objects.*

Planet	500 mm f/8, 62 mm dia.	1000 mm f/11, 91 mm dia.
Venus	1/2000 s	1/1000 s
Mars	1/8 s	1/15 s
Jupiter	1/250 s	1/125 s
Saturn	1/8 s	1/15 s

Figure 9.5 *Photographs of planetary conjunctions with the Moon using conventional photographic lenses are enhanced by a colourful sky and an interesting foreground. Both are present in this photograph taken at the Cederberg Observatory in South Africa. A waning crescent Moon and Venus appear in a fiery red dawn sky as seen beyond the outline of one of the domes. The exposure of ¹/₂ a second at f/3.5 on Ektachrome ISO 100 film was based entirely on the sky since it was intended that the dome should be a silhouette only. A 35–105-mm Nikkor zoom lens enabled variations in framing to be tried before choosing the best composition.*

While the Moon is obviously an extended object, at the focal lengths necessary the planets separate into a mixture of extended objects and point sources; however, the differences are manageable. Table 9.3 gives some target exposures. With ISO 400 film, a typical exposure for a crescent Moon could well be 1/60 of a second at $f/11$, and that for a full Moon 1/250 or 1/500 of a second at the same aperture. This clearly demonstrates that for the most part occultations taking place during a waxing or waning crescent phase of the Moon present few exposure balancing problems if Mars or Saturn is the planet that is to be occulted, whereas Venus and Jupiter when treated as extended objects are perfectly compatible with exposures for the full Moon. How to obtain a multi-image photographic record of the progress of a lunar occultation is discussed in Chapter 15.

**Conjunctions –
pictorial
opportunities**

This all seems a little involved, so it is understandable that for many newcomers the most attractive pictures of conjunctions of the planets are the easiest and least demanding in terms of equipment. Unashamedly pictorial views at dusk or dawn may be composed around a very slender crescent Moon and an attractive foreground. This might be composed of trees or buildings, or even clouds – and there is no reason why any of these should not be lit, provided the light source is low level (see Figures 9.4 and 9.5) – and water provides the fascination of reflections. I suggest dusk or dawn photography partly because there may be a chance of capturing Mercury, the elusive planet closest to the Sun (see page 101). But the main reason is that, although the human eye is not sensitive enough to see them, a relatively long photographic exposure can record delightful hues in the sky which are totally missing from the somewhat sterner exercises on the Jovian moons or occultations.

The lens for such shots could well be the normal 50 mm, although I have found a 35–105-mm $f/3.5$ zoom very useful since it gives a flexibility that is well worth the slight disadvantage of speed loss. Table 9.2 gives target exposures for a 50-mm $f/1.8$ lens and ISO 400 film, which is again recommended because the grain structure of ISO 1000 and faster films becomes intrusive in the lighter skies of dusk and dawn (see Figure 9.6). As the lens will be have to be used wide open for the planets, and the values recommended for the Moon are $f/8$ and $f/11$, the Moon is certain to be somewhat overexposed. However, this need not be objectionable with the slender crescent phase. A wide bracketing needs to be attempted, with the longer exposures aimed at securing an

Figure 9.6 *Venus and a waning crescent Moon with earthshine recorded as dawn was breaking on 1987 April 25. The 2-second exposure was made on Agfachrome 1000RS Professional film, although a slower film could have been used to advantage. The lens was a 180-mm f/2.8 Nikkor. As seen from some parts of the world, the Moon occulted Venus that morning.*

Figure 9.7 *The colours in the sky at sunset present both opportunities and challenges to the astrophotographer of conjunctions. In this scene, recorded on 1989 April 25, Jupiter is very bright at the centre, while Mercury can be seen to the lower right, framed by bushes and trees. Mars is at the extreme top left, where in the original picture it appears as a very small but distinctly red point of light. Aldebaran and the Hyades are to the lower left of Jupiter, and one of the horns of Taurus is the bright star to the lower right of Mars. Aircraft light trails (see Chapter 12) are usually a nuisance, but the one here, left by an airliner bound for London's Gatwick Airport, introduces an interesting balance into the composition. It suggests the sort of object that would be seen in the night sky if plans for orbiting advertising platforms ever come to pass! The 2-second exposure at f/2.8 was on ISO 400 Professional Fujichrome film loaded in a tripod-mounted Hasselblad camera.*

attractive sky. I usually employ shutter speeds of 1/60, 1/30, 1/15, 1/4, 1/2, 1, 2, 4, and 8 seconds, with the fastest possible aperture. Although the planets vary a great deal in their brilliance (and none more so than Mars, from magnitude −2.8 to +1.5), bracketing is a rough and ready means of obtaining some satisfaction.

The full Moon and Venus may be photographed in the same frame without problem, but the full Moon should be rigorously excluded from pictorial images that include any of the other planets. The attempt to accommodate their lower brightness by increasing the exposure will result in gross overexposure of the Moon and the likely creation of a ghost image of it. This is a form of lens flare caused by double reflection of the bright light source between the internal surfaces of the front and back components of the lens. Most lenses suffer from it to some degree if a brilliant light source is included in the field of view, the ghost being inverted usually and in the opposite side of the picture to the original. The only way to exorcise the ghost is to diminish its effective brightness by stopping down the lens, or to exclude it from the field of view altogether.

I have omitted Uranus and Neptune from most of this chapter, and ignored Pluto altogether, but what of Mercury? It must be admitted that Mercury is the most difficult subject among the remaining planets. Not only is it very small (its diameter is about one-third greater than the Moon's, although it is much farther away, of course), but it orbits so close to the Sun that it is never seen in a dark sky from temperate latitudes. It is always quite close to the horizon, where it can be masked by atmospheric haze and air pollution (see Figure 9.7). Mars, because of its small size and all too frequent great distance from the Earth, can be difficult, although it does relent from time to time. Venus – the traditional evening or morning star – is by far the most brilliant of the planets, so much so that it creates something of an exposure problem when photographed with its less well endowed companions of the ecliptic.

The final requirement for the newcomer to planetary photography is information about phases of the Moon, and forthcoming conjunctions and occultations. This will be found in the astronomy magazines and some newspapers. Finding two planets within the field of view of a normal focal length lens is quite common; three is by no means unusual, but greater numbers are rarer events. Five planets (Mercury, Venus, Mars, Jupiter, and Saturn) were relatively close together in the constellation Capricornus in February 1962, but Spode's law decreed that they be too close to the Sun to be viewed from the Earth.

CHAPTER 10

The Earth is a planet, too!

The title of this chapter needs some explanation. Few readers will see anything unusual in finding aurorae and noctilucent clouds featured in a book about astronomy, even if most of us do not see them very often. It may come as a surprise, though, to find phenomena such as rainbows, halos, and lightning included here. But should we be surprised? When space artists portray the other planets of the Solar System, what may be called atmospheric and optical phenomena often feature prominently – and quite rightly so, as they lend a sense of reality and help to portray the physical make-up of those planets. I believe that astronomers should go some way along this path in studying the Earth. I realize that some of the subjects dealt with in this chapter might be regarded as "atmospheric physics," but they do portray various aspects of our dynamic Earth. If it were possible for any of us to travel to the surface of Mercury, Venus, or Mars, or to orbit the gas giants, we would spend most of our time studying and photographing the kinds of phenomenon discussed in this chapter. So why don't we do the same with Earth itself? On our imagined trip to other planets we would be taking many photographs of what on Earth would be called "landscapes" (though of an exotically different type), and we should not proceed too far in that direction. But dynamic and frequently beautiful images of the effects the Sun has on the Earth's atmosphere are themes I believe ought to be included in a book devoted to astronomical photography, particularly as good basic equipment can be used to capture many of these sights. First, though, we look at two striking nighttime manifestations of the Sun's influence.

Aurorae

The aurora borealis, or northern lights, is a nighttime display of shifting coloured patterns most commonly seen at high latitudes, such as southern Canada or Scotland ("aurora" is Latin for dawn). The aurora australis is the southern hemisphere equivalent, but studies there have been hindered by the fact that the high southern latitudes contain few land areas. However, research into aurorae has intensified since the coming of the space age, and few who have seen them can have failed to be impressed by the images beamed back to control centres by spacecraft such as NASA's Dynamic Explorers. One such image shows a huge glowing oval about 4500 km (2800 miles) wide astride the geomagnetic pole and running through Siberia, Scandinavia, Greenland, Canada, and Alaska. Whenever possible, the crews of space shuttle orbiters have added to the flow of images. A new view of the aurora, indeed.

The complex interaction between solar activity, the Earth's magnetic field, and the atmosphere that results in the aurora is still being elaborated, and questions remain unanswered. Suffice it to say here that aurorae occur at about 100 km (60 miles) and above in the upper atmosphere, and are linked to solar activity, particularly sunspots and flares. But even for those with scant technical interest, the spectacle of an aurora cannot fail to impress, and it makes a splendid subject for the camera (see Figure 10.1).

Sometimes an aurora is nothing more than a dim glow, not unlike moonlight. At other times we may be privileged to witness an exotic display of arcs, bands, and rays in shades of green and red which sometimes hang motionless in the sky, and then suddenly begin rapid shifts and undulations which seem as though they should be accompanied by suitable, awe-inspiring sounds, but which take place in utter silence.

Aurorae vary greatly in brightness, from very dim to an intensity that can light up the surrounding countryside as though it were twilight. This variation in brightness and the large differences in speed of movement pose problems for the photographer, so bracketing is essential. Using a fixed camera with a 50-mm or wide-angle lens at maximum aperture (aurorae are extended objects) and loaded with ISO 400 or 1000 colour film, exposures of up to 1 minute should be

Figure 10.1 *When holidaying in high northern (or southern) latitudes it is worth keeping a careful watch for aurorae. This picture was taken aboard a Norwegian coastal steamer, which accounts for the slightly crooked star trails recorded over a 5-second exposure as the ship rolled gently. The exposure was delayed deliberately until an aircraft taking off from a nearby airport appeared to be flying through the aurora. The lens was a 50-mm f/1.4 Nikkor, and the film was ISO 1000 3M (Scotch).*

given for relatively dim and inactive aurorae. When they are bright and highly active, a stepped series of exposures of about 2, 5, and 10 seconds should be made. Anything much in excess of this will risk overexposure and therefore desaturation of colour, as well as blurring and merging of the features. Differences between the peak sensitivities of eye and film (and the different UV transmission characteristics of lenses) will not infrequently result in the colours of the film record not according with visual memory.

How often you will have the opportunity to photograph aurorae depends on your geographical location. Most aurorae are confined to high latitudes, although activity moves move further south during periods of maximum sunspot activity. The great display of 1989 March 13/14, for example, was seen as far south as the Caribbean. Figures published by the Aurora Section of the British Astronomical Association (see Table 10.1) demonstrate the relative infrequency of observed aurorae in more southerly latitudes, and their increased frequency at sunspot maximum (1979 and 1989) compared with sunspot minimum (1986) or with the approach of minimum (1993). Nonetheless, the occasional strong display can still be seen at sunspot minimum, as happened in 1986.

Noctilucent clouds

During summer months, aurora enthusiasts can either rest with the coming of night-long twilight and the midnight Sun, or turn their attention to noctilucent clouds. These are clouds that form at an altitude of about 80 km (50 miles), above 99.9 percent of the atmosphere and about 65 km (40 miles) above the region of weather. At this height they remain illuminated by the Sun some time after sunset – their name means "luminous night clouds." Once they were believed to consist of dust particles of extraterrestrial origin that had become coated with ice, but a more favoured view now is that small amounts of water vapour lifted above the stratosphere by the upwelling of cold air from polar regions freezes into ice clouds in the $-75°C$ ($-100°F$) temperatures encountered there. Whatever their origin, when seen edge-on the ice crystals reflect sunlight in white, blue, or gold hues depending on the position of the clouds relative to the horizon, and

Table 10.1 *Numbers of aurorae observed at geomagnetic latitudes of 53 to 63°N in years of sunspot maxima (1979 and 1989) and minima (1986 and 1993).*

Year	Geomagnetic latitude										
	53°N	54°N	55°N	56°N	57°N	58°N	59°N	60°N	61°N	62°N	63°N
1979	8	9	20	23	25	62	90	104	138	140	141
1986	8	8	10	14	15	20	34	44	85	96	113
1989	2	5	8	17	39	44	71	85	146	154	164
1993	0	0	0	7	7	8	30	38	47	67	70

Geomagnetic latitude is measured with respect to the Earth's magnetic axis, and differs slightly from geographic latitude. Thus the geomagnetic latitude of the English Channel is 53°N, compared with its geographic latitude of 50°N.

are so thin that bright stars shine through them. They form bands, veils, whirls, and billows that have been likened to the "waves of a ghostly ocean."

Occurring from around late May to August in the northern hemisphere, the clouds are a splendid subject from latitudes up to about 60° for those lucky enough to witness them. Their movement can be very fast, in excess of 500 km/h (300 mile/h), so shutter speeds also need to be fairly fast. Using ISO 200 or 400 colour film, an exposure sequence of 2, 4, 8, and 12 seconds at $f/2.8$ at least is suggested.

The rest of the phenomena discussed in this chapter are to be seen largely or exclusively in the daytime, and some general remarks need to be made. The equipment recommended for most of the subjects covered in this book – the 35-mm SLR camera, a tripod and cable release when lengthy exposures demand them, and (usually) colour transparency film – should still be used. But there are some additions. Although many of the subjects considered on the following pages are often intrinsically quite bright, compared with their surroundings in the sky they are relatively faint. To deal with this we need to use films which are not unnecessarily fast (remember, the slower the film, the greater its contrast) and which have inherently higher contrast characteristics. This means that whenever possible you should use the excellent ISO 50 films currently available from Kodak, Fuji, and Agfa, with Kodachrome film to take the speed up to ISO 200 if needed.

Daytime targets

Since many of the subjects will be very bright, I need to say a little about how an exposure meter works. It is calibrated on the assumption that a picture has a mixture of light and shade which approximates to an overall medium grey of 18 percent. Confronted with a very light picture, be it a sky, a beach, or a snow-covered glacier, the meter endeavours to render it a medium grey, and a disappointing underexposure is the consequence. A rough-and-ready way of overcoming this difficulty is to increase the exposure by one half-stop or a full stop for such scenes. Alternatively, you can take a reading off your hand, or indeed from an 18 percent grey card, which are sold for this precise purpose.

The variety of subjects will also make additional demands on lenses. For some, like rainbows, you will need a wide-angle lens and one of at least 24 or 28 mm focal length. If you have a very-wide-angle lens of 18 mm, so much the better. At the same time, you may wish to concentrate on particular phenomena, such as parhelia (see page 109), for which a zoom lens would be an advantage. If you have one of the ever more popular shorter zooms of 35–105 or 35–135 mm focal length, this will prove useful – particularly if you can extend its range by adding a ×2 teleconverter, though there is then a penalty to be paid in loss of lens speed. An 80–200-mm zoom would also be valuable. The reason I have recommended the zooms is that the search for some of the phenomena described in this chapter may take you on long journeys, and anything that cuts down the amount of equipment to be carried is worthwhile.

If your camera does not have a built-in exposure meter you will need to get a separate one, because a meter is used a great deal in calculating

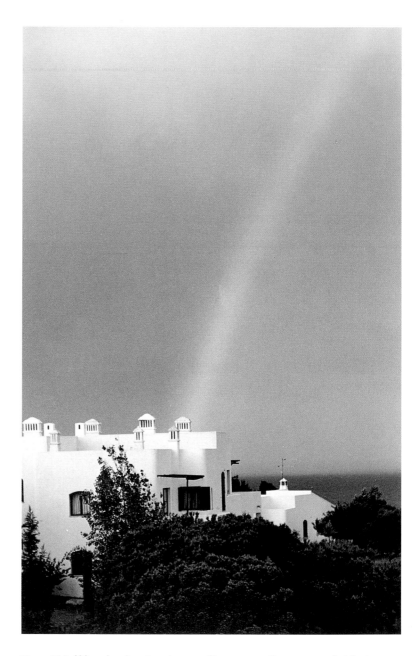

Figure 10.2 *Although colour transparency films are usually recommended for images of atmospheric phenomena, this picture emphasizes the quality of present-day negative colour films, particularly those of slower speeds. This rainbow over villas in the Algarve was recorded on Kodak Ektar 100 film loaded in a Nikon F801s camera fitted with a 35–105-mm Nikkor AF zoom lens. There was a good balance of light and dark in the scene, so reliance was placed on the exposure meter for a sequence of images. Bracketing in this case revealed the accuracy of the meter's reading as frames deliberately underexposed or overexposed were less satisfactory.*

exposures for the sky and its contents. A polarizing filter used at approximately 90° to the direction of the Sun darkens the blue sky and is a valuable accessory. Finally, you must "be prepared." While weather conditions will help in anticipating some phenomena, others occur unexpectedly and unless you have a camera ready to fire, you will miss them.

Rainbows

Primary rainbows are caused by water droplets refracting light. A rainbow is an arc of a circle centred on the antisolar point, diametrically opposite the Sun on the celestial sphere, which is always below the horizon when the Sun is in the sky. Thus, if the Sun is high the rainbow will be low, and vice versa. If the Sun is out but there are plenty of heavy shower clouds around, then be prepared to see a rainbow in the sky opposite the Sun. Fainter secondary rainbows (outside the primary) and so-called supernumerary or interference rainbows (inside the primary) are not uncommon.

A polarizing filter will not help you in photographing rainbows because the Sun will be behind you and not to one side. Take a general reading with your meter. If you are facing an extensive rainbow seen against the backdrop of a large mass of dark cloud, the meter will give a reading which will tend to overexpose the rainbow. Take a reading of the foreground for a more accurate estimate, and in any case take at least one picture with the aperture stopped down by one half-stop. Slight underexposure when using transparency film can help accentuate the saturation of colours in the rainbow. Of course, if there is a secondary rainbow it is usually much dimmer, so that it is possible the underexposure will substantially lose it. The answer is to make sure you bracket exposures (see Figure 10.2), and I would recommend two half-stops on either side of the exposure indicated by the meter.

If you have an automatic camera you can still achieve underexposure by dialling in a higher film speed than you are actually using. (But remember to change the speed back afterwards.) Your camera may appear to read only the DX coding on the film cassette, but check that this is definitely so. Some cameras enable you to overcome this problem by a manual override, or by dialling in an exposure compensation value.

Usually, a rainbow is at its most intense for only a matter of seconds. You may be able to obtain a reasonable picture in the few minutes either side of maximum intensity, but you need to be alert to get the best possible result. Foreground interest too is important: a rainbow pictured suspended in the sky is "empty." Ideally the foreground should be an attractive one, but I am tempted to say that anything is better than nothing.

Halos

Like rainbows, halos around the Sun result from the refraction of light, but by ice crystals at high altitude rather than by water droplets. They usually occur in cirrus cloud. Figure 10.3 shows the appearance of the 22° halo and the less frequent 46° halo, together with other features associated with them (these values are the halos' radii). Halos also differ from rainbows in that, once a halo (and any subsidiary features) has appeared, it usually lasts a considerable length of time – sometimes for hours – so there is no need to rush the photography.

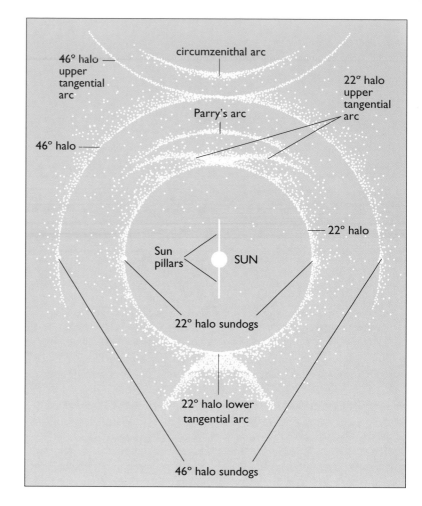

Figure 10.3 *Some of the commonest solar halo features, many of which can be seen together in the sky at the same time. The appearance and location of these effects vary with the Sun's altitude. For example, the two 22° halo sundogs are on the halo itself when the Sun is on the horizon. But as the Sun climbs in the sky they move further out, fading, and disappearing altogether when the Sun reaches an altitude of just over 60°.*

To photograph an entire halo requires a wide-angle lens, and I have tended to use a fisheye lens (see Figure 10.4). Ideally you should compose the picture so that the Sun is blocked out by a suitably positioned tree or some other feature. When there has been no convenient obstruction I have, with a *very* quick glance through the viewfinder, positioned the unadorned Sun at centre frame and made my exposures. Since a lens of very short focal length is in use the Sun will move very slowly across the frame, so that even over a lengthy programme of photography there will be no need for more than one or two quick glances through the viewfinder. During a long session of solar photography,

Figure 10.4 A 22° solar halo, photographed through a 12-mm f/8 fisheye lens. The lens distorts the foreground, but this is no disadvantage in a composition which is based on the circle. ISO 64 Kodachrome was used for a sequence of images in which the film's relatively high contrast and high resolution were valuable in recording in as much detail as possible what is a difficult subject. Extensive bracketing of exposures is advisable in situations such as this where an exposure based on the solar disk will lead to gross underexposure of the sky. In this frame the choice of shutter speed was based on an exposure meter reading of a sunlit hand.

place a lens cap on the lens between shots or, better still, cover the camera with a light-coloured cloth to keep it as cool as possible.

Subsidiary features of the halo phenomenon such as *parhelia* (see Figure 10.5) can be photographed with a moderate telephoto lens, and a zoom provides the flexibility to achieve the most striking cropping. The use of the longer lens also removes the Sun from the field of view. The exposure can be based either on a standard centre-weighted exposure meter reading, or read by one of the more sophisticated systems that sample all areas of the frame. Exposures should be bracketed, and I normally shoot at least two half-stops on either side. If the Sun is in the field of view, the meter system will tend to be overwhelmed by the intensity of its light and will heavily underexpose the sky area. That being the case, you should open up by at least one stop, and the "bracketing" should all be on the side of (apparent) overexposure in terms of the meter's reading.

There are many other attractive phenomena associated with sunlight or moonlight. A *corona* (not to be confused with the corona that is the outer atmosphere of the Sun) quite frequently occurs when the Moon passes behind light or broken cloud. Much smaller than the 22° halo, the most common form of the lunar corona is a disk of light which is bluish at its inner edge, changing to white further out, and intensifying

Coronas, light pillars, and the green flash

Figure 10.5 *A parhelion (also known as a mock sun, false sun, or sundog) in the afternoon sky over Houston, Texas. The phenomenon is associated with a 22° halo around the Sun produced by the refraction of sunlight by ice crystals. The bright white shaft of light extending to the right of the parhelion (that is, away from the Sun) is produced by light rays being refracted through ice crystals or at angles other than the minimum deviation of 22°, which causes the separate colours to overlap and thus create white light. Kodak Ektar 125 film was used in a Nikon F301 camera set to an aperture of f/8. This is the best of several bracketed exposures made on either side of the indicated meter reading.*

to a reddish-brown outer edge. This is called the aureole, which may well have a further coloured ring or rings surrounding it (normally referred to as iridescence). The corona is caused by the diffraction of moonlight by water droplets or by ice crystals in the atmosphere. (Although it is there, we do not usually notice the corona around the Sun because the area of sky close to the Sun is just too bright for our eyes.)

Since it is created by clouds which can obviously be moving, the lunar corona can vary over short periods of time, but the typical weather pattern in which it is created means that photography is not limited to a few seconds. A tripod and cable release are clearly required with a moderately long focal length lens. An ISO 200 or 400 colour film will give adequate quality for a delicate subject, and if the cloud is moving relatively fast it will be best to open the lens wide (the corona is an extended object) and keep the measured shutter speed as fast as possible. Try a centre-weighted exposure as well as a full frame sampling if you have that type of meter with bracketing of exposures of at least two half-stops on the side of (apparent) overexposure.

The diffraction effects that give rise to coronas around the Moon (and Sun) are also responsible for more localized phenomena of a less astronomical nature. The *glory* can be seen from an aircraft whose shadow, cast onto clouds below it, is surrounded by coloured rings. In the similar *spectre of the Brocken* (named after a peak in Germany's Harz Mountains), seen when a climber casts an enormous, conical shadow onto mist or cloud below, the head part of the shadow is surrounded by halos.

Other impressive phenomena are caused by reflection, rather than refraction, by ice crystals or water droplets and water. A *Sun pillar* (or *Moon pillar*) is a normally vertical column of light above a Sun or Moon close to the horizon, caused by light reflected upwards into the sky by

Figure 10.6 *A subsun photographed through an aircraft window over the Atlantic. This is a reflection phenomenon caused by the same reflection process that creates a solar light pillar, only in this case the image is formed beneath the horizon. This exposure on Ektachrome ISO 200 transparency film loaded in a Nikon F3 was based on the meter reading. A subsun can remain visible for some seconds as the aircraft flies over the area of high-altitude cloud that helps create it. Perhaps the most critical part of the photography is to avoid window reflections.*

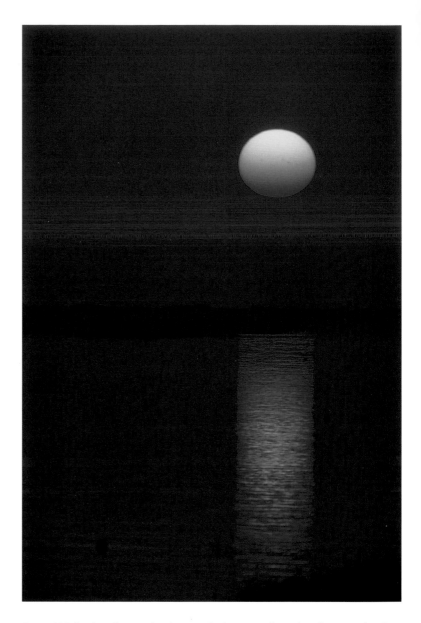

Figure 10.7 *A solar glitter path, photographed as part of a series of tests undertaken in advance of the annular solar eclipse seen from California on 1992 January 4. That eclipse took place in the late evening Pacific Time, and exposures with and without filters needed to be worked out beforehand for the time of day. Ektachrome 50HC transparency film was used, loaded in a Nikon F4S camera. A 300-mm focal length f/4 Nikkor lens boosted by a TC16A AF teleconverter was fitted, and the MF23 data back programmed for a sequence of autobracketed exposures over five frames. In this case spot metering on the Sun itself was chosen, and the exposure of 1/500 of a second created the intended colour saturation in both the Sun and glitter path.*

ice crystals. A similar downward reflection when the Sun is higher in the sky gives rise to a *subsun*, formed below the horizon. Aircraft passengers often see a subsun on cloud below them (see Figure 10.6), and it can flash with greater brilliance when its track passes over a body of water. A more common though no less dramatic sight in most people's experience is the *glitter path* extending across water toward the viewer from the Sun or Moon near rising or setting (see Figure 10.7).

If a low Sun is in the field of view when you are photographing a pillar, there is again the danger that a general meter reading will be biased by the solar disk and would result in severe underexposure. To compensate, overexpose by at least one or two stops. Such a measure should not be necessary when you are photographing a subsun and the Sun is out of the field of view. For a glitter path the exposure is a matter of choice: exposing for the Sun and the (frequently) brilliant path can isolate them and create a powerful effect. Allowing one or two stops more creates a more mellow scene of the kind that may bring back warm memories of summers past.

Another refraction effect seen at sunset is the flattening of the disk and its separation into segments. This is caused by temperature differences between non-uniform layers of the atmosphere, and can frequently take the form of a mirage. The most important photographic requirement is again to base the exposure on the Sun itself.

The *green flash* is a quite famous but very elusive phenomenon. In the final seconds of sunset on a clear horizon, out across the sea or on a distant mountain horizon, just before the Sun disappears the last visible segment of its disk may be seen to break off and momentarily flash green. The theory is that, as the Sun sinks and sunlight passes through the greatest possible thickness of atmosphere, yellow-orange light is absorbed by water vapour, and violet and some blue light are dispersed by atmospheric scattering. This leaves red light, which is refracted less (and therefore is seen lower down), and green light, which is seen last of all. While this theory is generally agreed upon, it is not understood why the green flash is so unpredictable.

Its elusiveness is what makes it a good photographic challenge, and I must confess to having hunted the flash but never to have captured it. The technique, however, is straightforward. The camera with the longest focal length lens available is placed on a tripod with a moderately fast colour film, ISO 200 or 400. The green flash appears in the last few seconds before the image of the Sun disappears entirely below the horizon, and it is such a delicate emerald colour that over-exposure must be avoided at all costs. It is best to expose on the basis of the solar disk itself. If your camera has a spot meter, which measures an extremely small area at the centre of the frame, so much the better; if not, expose with centre weighting and stop down a further half-stop as you wait with finger poised for that (hopefully successful) last picture.

The greatest care must always be taken when photographing the Sun. The usual advice is to use the correct filters, and never look at the Sun directly or through any optical instrument. However, when the Sun is *very* close to the horizon I do not use filters, and certainly never when trying to catch the green flash. I do not look through the viewfinder for more than a split second on any one occasion, and experience has taught me when I can do this and when I cannot. The rule remains: if in doubt, *don't*.

Dawn, twilight, and moonlight

There is great beauty in dawn and twilight skies. The subjects for the photographer are almost endless: *crepuscular rays* ('crepusculum' is Latin for twilight) fanning out from clouds beyond the far horizon; the shadow of the Earth cast by the setting Sun visible towards the eastern horizon; cloudscapes illuminated by the Sun in limitless profusion (see Figure 10.8). I take such pictures with just as much enthusiasm as I have for "straight" astronomical subjects, and I make no excuse for repeating that we exist on a dynamic, living planet. Little more is

Figure 10.8 *A scene on the border between astronomy and atmospheric physics but which, despite its beauty, is all too often ignored by astrophotographers. Once again, it is important to bracket a series of exposures because, as the Sun sets, large expanses of foreground cloud become very dark. With the Sun partly obscured by distant clouds a single, general meter reading would be biased in favour of greater exposure to yield more detail in the nearby clouds. This exposure of a sunset off the island of Madeira was deliberately underexposed by one stop to hold the colour saturation in the sky around the Sun and to emphasize the contrast between the rays of light and shade above it. Kodak Ektar 125 negative colour film was used in a Nikon F301 camera.*

required than basic photographic equipment loaded with good-quality transparency film. Correct exposure is the biggest test, but bracketing eases many of the problems. Given the variety and beauty of so many sky subjects, I think it is a tragedy to economize on effort, or on film.

And don't forget moonlit scenes: pictorial images both including and excluding the Moon, and particularly with broken cloud in frame, are just as attractive as sunsets, if very different in mood. Again, exposure is the prime challenge. Moonlight is nothing more than reflected sunlight, and I have seen one estimate that a moonlit scene is 2 million times (or 21 photographic stops) dimmer than sunlight. Be that as it may, if you set your camera up on a tripod, compose the picture, and let the meter take command you will end up with a daylight rendering because the meter is again aiming for an 18 percent grey. You will need to give between 25 and 50 percent less exposure to get a well-exposed moonlit scene. Making sure that the Moon is behind a convenient cloud will save you having to worry about the exposure differences between the Moon itself and the scene. Incidentally, film manufactured for use with artificial (tungsten) lighting is more sensitive to blue, so this colour will be emphasized in your moonlit scenes if you decide to try such a film.

We have all seen magnificent photographs of lightning, but they are not easily won. A few ground rules will help to increase your chances, even though you will probably face a high film consumption. Photographing a storm at night provides the best opportunities. Typically, the camera is loaded with film in the range ISO 100 to 400, set up on a tripod, and operated by cable release. The ideal conditions are a slow-moving storm some distance away with a moderate amount of foreground detail (for example, a few house or city lights) to provide a human context.

Lightning

Set the aperture at $f/5.6$ or $f/8$, fire the shutter, and hold it open for perhaps 20 seconds or so (although earlier tests might have shown that a longer exposure can be given before foreground lights become too intrusive). If a lightning stroke occurs, close the shutter immediately. Should a storm be concentrated in one location for any length of time, you could try securing multiple images on one frame of film (as in Figure 10.9). Cloud-to-cloud lightning will usually fog your exposure, so it is best to wind the film on immediately afterwards in the hope of a more dramatic stroke between surface and clouds.

Attempting to capture lightning on film in daytime is difficult. The shutter cannot be kept open, as during the night, because overexposure would quickly take place. It has been claimed that lightning strokes frequently take place in pairs and that the second one can be anticipated. There is some evidence to support this, but there must be a large element of luck – or dedication – involved. Better to concentrate on night storms where the practical difficulties are somewhat less. It is a platitude that lightning is dangerous. Considerations of safety should be paramount: a mountain would provide an excellent vantage point for photography, but (as a one-time climber who experienced storms in the mountains) I would never dream of attempting it!

Figure 10.9 *An awe-inspiring photograph obtained by Willem Hollenbach during a storm over the Cederberg Mountains north of Cape Town in South Africa. His Ricoh KR5 Super camera with its 50-mm f/4 lens was loaded with Agfa ISO 100 colour transparency film, and he made a series of 30-second exposures as the storm approached. The main stroke here was obviously very close; anyone endeavouring to secure dramatic pictures of lightning must not ignore their own safety. Although inevitably very dark, the mountain ridges in the foreground and middle ground of the photograph aid the composition.*

Protecting your equipment from rain is also important. An ideal place for protecting your person and your equipment while attempting to photograph lightning is a roofed balcony or patio facing the storm. If you decide to venture out during a storm, don't stray far from the car, and build a protective cage for the camera – or take plenty of clean dry rags with which to mop up!

CHAPTER 11

Comets and the zodiacal light

During its last appearance in 1985–6, Halley's Comet was without doubt a great disappointment to members of the general public in the northern hemisphere. Although astronomers had warned that it would not be a bright object, such is the fame of this usually once-in-a-lifetime visitor that for many people – even if they did manage to get a look at the small, diffuse ball in one of the telescopes opened up to the public – there was a sense of anticlimax. But in July 1994, there was a great resurgence of public and media interest when the fragments of Comet Shoemaker–Levy 9 collided with Jupiter.

Most of the comets that are discovered or return to the inner Solar System each year are detected by inveterate and mostly amateur comet-hunters using binoculars, or by researchers studying photographic plates. These usually very dim comets will receive considerable attention from cometary scientists, and virtually none from the public. But, while not so frequent as they were during the last century, the occasional new comet becomes a bright, naked-eye object of great beauty and impact, and well within the grasp of the amateur's fixed camera. Comets Ikeya–Seki (most comets are named after their discoverers) in 1965, Bennett in 1970, and West in 1976 (see Figure 11.1) were examples. We could be forgiven for thinking that a comet of equal prominence is long overdue.

Throughout history, comets have been popularly associated with death, destruction, plague, and other horrors. The folklore is interesting and entertaining, but comets have a much more serious place in astronomy. They are usually regarded as being the most primitive members of the Solar System, believed to have undergone relatively little change since it came into being about 5 billion years ago. Therefore, although comets vary greatly in their characteristics, the more that can be learned about them, the greater the insight that can be gained into the evolution of the Solar System. This is why comets have received so much attention since the beginning of the space era, and why Halley's Comet in particular was studied by a flotilla of space probes from various countries. The next significant development in space will be the European Space Agency's Rosetta mission in which, if all goes to plan, a spacecraft will rendezvous with Comet Wirtanen in the year 2011.

Comets

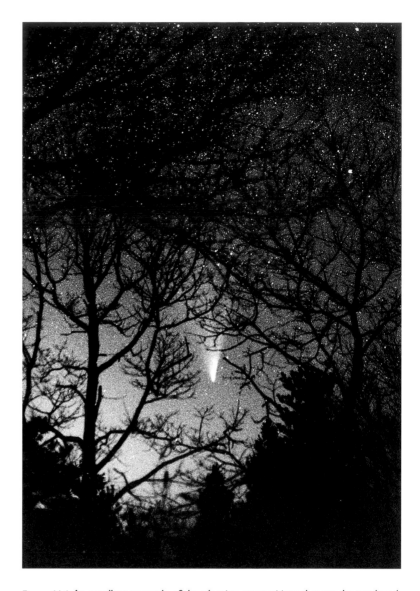

Figure 11.1 *An excellent example of the pleasing compositions that can be produced using a fixed camera. Beyond the trees is Comet West, photographed in March 1976 by Akira Fujii. He used a Nikon camera and a 35-mm wide-angle lens at f/2. The exposure was 20 seconds on Kodak Tri-X film, which was developed in Fuji Pandol at 20°C (68°F) for 10 minutes.*

When a comet is in deep space it consists essentially of just a small *nucleus* a few kilometres across. According to current theory (largely confirmed by the results from Halley), the nucleus is a "dirty snowball": a mixture of frozen gases – mostly water ice – and dust particles. As the comet comes into the inner Solar System, a *coma* (Latin for "hair") develops. This very tenuous halo, extending sometimes hundreds of thousands of kilometres into space, is composed of a mixture of dust and gases released by the warming effect of the Sun. Later, there develops a tail of two components: a *dust tail* and an *ion tail*, the latter consisting of molecules released by the nucleus that have been ionized by solar ultraviolet and X-radiation. Electrically charged particles from the Sun (the solar wind) and solar radiation pressure cause both tails to point away from the Sun. Hence the tails follow the head of the comet as it approaches the Sun but, perhaps paradoxically at first sight, precede it on its journey away from the Sun. It is, of course, the tails of comets that can be so spectacular and cover such a large area of the sky, presenting a marvellous subject for the photographer.

How bright and extensive a comet appears to observers on the Earth depends upon many factors, not all of which are understood. One which is readily apparent, however, concerns the relative positions of the comet and the Earth as the comet rounds the Sun. The reason why the 1985–6 visit of Halley's Comet was not one of the best was that for some time around perihelion (the point of its closest approach to the Sun, and when it is at its most active), it was on the opposite side of the Sun from the Earth and therefore lost in the Sun's glare. The distance between comet and Earth on the incoming and outgoing passages is also important.

So comets vary in brightness from extremely dim, and visible only in telescopes, to very bright, sometimes bright enough to be seen in broad daylight. The last occasion on which this happened was early in 1910, when the Great Daylight Comet upstaged Halley's Comet which followed some weeks later. In the face of such differences it is difficult to give valid guidance to the newcomer to comet photography, but one generalization may be proffered: if a comet is a naked-eye object, then any attempt to photograph it with a fixed camera on a tripod is well worthwhile. There is one feature of comets that works in the photographer's favour, but which frequently causes some confusion. While a comet will be moving at high speed in absolute terms (Halley's speed at perihelion was around 200,000 km/h, 125,000 mile/h), when viewed from Earth it will not be speeding across the sky "like a shooting star": it will be moving gradually against the backdrop of stars, and a few hours will need to elapse for the movement to become clearly discernible. Over the course of several nights this movement will become apparent.

Comets are extended objects so, as with everyday objects, the measure of the speed of a lens is focal ratio. Because comets typically brighten around perihelion, when they are at their best they will often be located in the western sky during evening twilight, or in the eastern sky near dawn. The sky behind them will therefore be relatively bright, so lengthy exposures are not possible. There is an advantage in these conditions, mentioned in an earlier chapter: while the eye may see little colour, film often records delightful hues which result in a most attractive pictorial image. If the comet is still up some time after the Sun has set, light pollution may become a problem near towns, but this is something the individual must resolve in the best available way. Should a naked-eye comet appear it is almost certain that it will be well covered

Figure 11.2 *Comet Levy (1990c) had a tenuous tail some 2° long when photographed from southern England in August of that year in an 8-minute exposure on hypersensitized 2415 film. The camera was a Nikon F3 fitted with a Nikkor 180-mm f/2.8 lens and mounted on a Goto Mark X camera platform programmed to track the comet. Comet Levy was in Pegasus at the time, and the bright object to its upper right is the double star 33 Pegasi.*

in the media, with newspapers giving details of when and where in the sky it will be visible – weather permitting, of course. Estimates of the length of the tails may well be given in advance, and from them the most likely suitable focal length can be worked out (as on page 78). Alternatively, direct observation can establish the most suitable focal length (see Figure 11.2). If the tail structure develops well it is probable that a 50-mm focal length lens will be required. With the prospect of a light, colourful sky, as opposed to the full darkness of a nighttime image, quality is important, and I would recommend a compromise on film speed with the use of an ISO 400 film and nothing faster.

Set the lens at its fastest focal ratio, observe the basic photographic drill (sturdy tripod, black card, and so on), and make a series of exposures from around 5 seconds up to perhaps 1 minute in 5-second increments. Some star trailing will take place in the longer exposures, but this is perfectly acceptable since it is the comet that is the prime target. If the weather is good and the comet is visible on a number of days or nights, modifications to the bracketing sequence can be introduced if the first results are not satisfactory. If the comet becomes very bright and the first results suggest the possibility, it would be worthwhile trying a slower film of ISO 200, or even ISO 100, in the interests of better quality.

Should the comet be a bright object at dusk or dawn, this again would be an occasion when an aperture priority automatic exposure system would prove its worth (careful notes being made of the shutter speeds selected by the camera), and colour negative film could be used. The image size of the comet (according to focal length selected) would affect the metering mode chosen if more than one mode is available. With a very bright comet, a keen black-and-white photographer could experiment with recording the ion and dust tails. Since the dust tail is yellowish (because of the backscattering of sunlight towards the observer) and emission from the ion tail is at the blue end of the spectrum, a yellow or orange filter in the one case and a blue filter in the other could be used to enhance detail. Kodak Wratten filters, types 21 and 47 respectively, would be suitable. Clearly, to stand any chance of success with the use of filters (which attenuate the light transmitted) on a camera which is fixed and not on an equatorial mount, the comet would have to be extremely bright. In that event, ISO 400 black-and-white film rated perhaps at ISO 800 would seem a suitable choice.

The procedures suggested here would not have worked well for photographs of Halley's Comet taken from the northern hemisphere in 1985–6. The comet did not develop an extensive enough tail structure, nor was it bright enough to capture with basic photographic equipment. However, there will be others, and we are owed a bright one. Capturing your first comet on film will be a prize indeed.

The zodiacal light

Comets can be bright, but are all too frequently dim. A genuine dim light phenomenon which nonetheless makes an intriguing picture is the zodiacal light. Quite probably it has been seen by many people, particularly those fortunate enough to take cruises to the tropics and the equator, but confused with the twilight.

The name "zodiacal light" stems quite logically from the fact that it stretches along the imaginary belt of constellations through which pass the paths of the Sun, Moon, and planets. It may be seen after astronomical twilight ends during evenings (that is, when the Sun is more than 18° below the horizon) and for some time before the Sun reaches that position at dawn. The phenomenon is caused by sunlight scattered by the *zodiacal dust cloud*, a sheet of dust particles in the inner Solar System. It appears as a luminous wedge or pyramid of light, approximately as bright as the Milky Way, and its widest and brightest part is on the horizon – that is, closest to the Sun. It has been suggested that, because of interaction between particle streams emanating from the Sun and the zodiacal dust cloud, the zodiacal light is more intense at times of sunspot minimum. The mid-1990s is such a time, so the accuracy of the claim can be tested over the next few years.

If the zodiacal light is to be seen, a dark sky is a necessity, and moonlight is certainly to be avoided. It is seen to best advantage from the tropics, where, following the line of the ecliptic, it rises up steeply from the horizon throughout the year. However, it is still clearly visible in a dark sky outside the tropics. From the northern or southern hemisphere it is best seen in the west after sunset in the spring, and in the east before sunrise in the autumn. The evening zodiacal light inclines to the left, and in the early morning to the right (that is, to the south in both cases), and under optimum conditions it can be seen stretching almost to the zenith. In the southern hemisphere, the light slants to the left after the sunset and to the right before sunrise (to the north in both cases).

As with other astronomical objects, locating or recognizing the phenomenon may well be a little more difficult for newcomers than actually photographing it. Since the zodiacal light can last for an hour or

Figure 11.3 *The zodiacal light seen in an autumn morning sky from Tenerife in the Canary Islands. The star trails at the top of the picture include Castor and Pollux in Gemini. Procyon in Canis Minor is the bright trail on the right, and plainly seen in the upper centre of the zodiacal light cone is the open star cluster Praesepe (M44) in the constellation Cancer. The wedge shape and inclination of the zodiacal light are well demonstrated here, but the light appears a good deal less bright to the eye than it does in lengthy time exposures. This exposure was 15 minutes on Agfachrome 1000RS Professional film, through a 24-mm f/2.8 Nikkor lens.*

so after astronomical twilight ends, there is no rush. Given its extent, a 50-mm or 35-mm wide-angle lens is required, and the camera needs to be loaded with ISO 400 or 1000 film. Like comets, the zodiacal light is an extended object so a fast focal ratio is essential. Using the slower of the suggested films, a sequence of time exposures (1, 2, 4, 8, and 12 minutes) is suggested. Although the zodiacal light is essentially monochromatic, colour film gives a pleasing picture since star trails will be recorded (see Figure 11.3). Greater accentuation of the phenomenon itself can be achieved by using an ISO 400 black-and-white film, overdeveloping it by about 25 percent, and printing the resulting contrasty negative on a hard grade of paper.

As with comets, but even more so, dark and unpolluted skies are essential if you are to see and photograph the zodiacal light well. The urban astronomer will have to be prepared to travel near or far to find such skies, for which there is no substitute: the use of filters, as described in Chapter 8, and other technical measures are unlikely to bring much reward to the beginner seeking to capture this faint, elusive phenomenon.

CHAPTER 12

Meteors, satellites, aircraft, and UFOs

Meteors

Everybody has at some time or other seen a "shooting star" or "falling star" – a brief trail of light in the night sky usually lasting a fraction of a second. The flash is caused by a particle of interplanetary dust impacting the upper atmosphere of the Earth. The heat generated by its passage usually vaporizes the particle completely, but a complex interaction results in the ionization of air molecules around and behind the particle, and this is the light trail that we see in the sky. The name *meteor* is given to this phenomenon; the actual particle of dust is called a *meteoroid*. Larger, more rubust objects that survive their passage through the Earth's atmosphere and reach the surface are known as *meteorites*.

Meteors occur at altitudes from 80 to 120 km (50 to 75 miles). Their entry speeds vary greatly, with an upper limit of around 70 km/s (45 mile/s). Brightness levels, too, vary widely, with an effective lower limit for the photographer of magnitude 2, rising to the brightness of the planet Venus at maximum (magnitude -4.7) and beyond. Meteors that outshine Venus are called *fireballs*, and the brightest of them can be seen in daylight.

Meteors can be seen on any night, at a rate of maybe five or so an hour. But greater numbers are seen at times of the year when the Earth encounters what are called *meteor streams*. These streams are generally believed to originate from periodic comets losing material as their orbit brings them into the inner Solar System; in time, this material becomes distributed around the comet's orbit. When the Earth's orbit about the Sun takes it through or near the orbit of a comet, a surge in the number of observed meteors takes place in what is called a *meteor shower*. Meteors from a particular shower seem to radiate from the same point in the night sky on the same dates each year. The particles are in fact moving on parallel paths, and the appearance of radiating from a point is an effect of perspective. In much the same way, if we stand on a bridge over a long straight road and look towards the horizon, the parallel lanes of the road appear to converge and meet in the distance, although we know they do no such thing. Nonetheless, the term *radiant* is still used for the apparent point of origin of meteors from a particular shower, and a shower is named after the constellation in which its radiant lies.

The major annual meteor showers are listed in Table 12.1. There are in addition many minor showers with lower hourly rates. The dates given in the table indicate when the shower is active; activity rises to a maximum, then fades away. Individual observers will see fewer meteors than indicated by the hourly rates given here, which are all-sky figures calculated as if the radiant were at the zenith. January's Quadrantid shower is named after the now defunct constellation Quadrans Muralis, and its radiant is in the constellation Boötes. The Eta Aquarids and Delta Aquarids have their radiants near two different stars in the constellation Aquarius. Perhaps the best-known shower is the Perseids, peaking on a warm mid-August evening that should not deter even the most casual observer. The Leonids are a *periodic shower*: less than 10 an hour are visible in most years, but every 33 years comes the possibility of something much more dramatic: a *meteor storm*. The last was in 1966 when, for 40 minutes, the hourly rate of Leonids in the skies of Arizona was over 150,000. Something similar could happen again in 1998 or 1999. The reason for this behaviour is that the cometary debris is not evenly spread around the orbit, but concentrated in a swarm which the Earth approaches closely every 33 years.

The dates and, in particular, the hourly rates of meteor showers show slight changes from year to year. But although a particular shower's performance in any one year cannot be predicted, the time demanded of the less than devoted specialist is kept within bounds by the existence of a recognized date for the likely maximum. Even the more elusive *sporadic* meteors (those not associated with any shower) have a diurnal peak, in the hours before dawn. This is because, as the Earth moves in its orbit about the Sun, an observer in the early hours of the morning is on the leading side. Meteoroids that are encountered enter the atmosphere head-on, generating higher energies and therefore producing brighter meteors. In the evening hours the observer is on the trailing side of the Earth, where incoming meteoroids have to "catch up"; those entering the atmosphere come in at a lower relative speed, so generate less energy and produce fainter meteors.

So, although we have an indication of the nights of the year on which there is the best chance of observing meteors, skill and luck are obviously going to be important. The task facing the astrophotographer is intriguing. When we photograph the stars with a fixed camera (and we are not deliberately trying to record star trails), their apparent

Table 12.1 *Major meteor showers.*

Shower	Dates	Maximum	Hourly rate at maximum
Quadrantids	Jan 16	Jan 3	100
Eta Aquarids	Apr 24 – May 20	May 5	20–25
Delta Aquarids	Jul 15 – Aug 20	Jul 29	35
Perseids	Jul 25 – Aug 20	Aug 12	80
Orionids	Oct 15–Nov 2	Oct 21	30
Leonids	Nov 15–20	Nov 17	Varies (see text)
Geminids	Dec 7–15	Dec 13	100

movement is very slight, and in effect for the duration of the exposure their light falls on the same area of film. Meteors, like stars, are point sources, but ones that move across the film in a period of time between about 0.1 and 1 second! It may sound quite encouraging to talk about meteor trails of, for example, magnitude +1, but photographically this is very different from a star of magnitude 1 that steadily builds up an image on film over a period of 20 seconds or more.

As we have seen, the diameter of the lens is the most crucial factor in the photography of point sources, so the natural inclination might be to opt for the long, large-diameter lenses discussed in earlier chapters. Their drawback is their relatively small field of view, which makes the chances of capturing meteors all the slimmer. At the opposite extreme, a wide-angle lens gives a far greater chance of including a meteor in its field of view, but because it has a relatively small diameter a meteor might appear very faint or not be recorded at all on the film. The best solution is compromise, in the shape of the faithful 50-mm focal length lens, particularly if it is $f/1.8$ or faster. This has a very reasonable $27° \times 40°$ field of view and a diameter of 28 mm (or more with faster lenses). For more on the subject of lenses for meteor photography, see *Sky & Telescope*, August 1993, pages 97–8, and February 1994, pages 85–7.

As in star photography, high-speed films may appear attractive, but you must bear in mind the quality of your sky. Remember that, used wide open, the lens will be doing its best with point sources, but at the same time the fast focal ratio will be causing any light pollution (or airglow) to build up rapidly on the film. If the sky is dark and of good quality there is every reason to select one of the high-speed films in the ISO 1000 range. With meteors there are no worries about reciprocity failure over lengthy exposures, and films capable of maximizing the very brief light burst are at a premium. Most meteor photography specialists use black-and-white film, and there is little to be gained in using colour, which in any case is more expensive.

Although it may seem surprising, it is not advisable to centre the radiant in the camera's field of view (see Figure 12.1). If it is in the centre, then any meteors captured will be seen head-on or nearly so, as points of light or very short trails. Based on observations over some years, meteor specialists advise pointing the camera at an elevation of 50° to the horizon and from 30 to 45° to one side of the radiant. It is claimed that an elevation of 30° is likely to produce a higher yield of fireballs.

Meteor photography is a type of what might be called patrol photography. Since it is obviously impossible to react fast enough to photograph meteors as they occur, a series of time exposures must be made of a duration and over a period that are decided upon beforehand. It is difficult to give general advice on this, but the length of each exposure depends most importantly on the darkness of the sky. If the sky is good, then exposures of 10 minutes or more should be possible with little risk of sky fog – particularly if a medium-fast ISO 400 film is being used. If you have not done so before, a sensible thing to do in advance of a

Figure 12.1 *This time exposure by Akira Fujii captured two Perseid meteors, and gives a classic demonstration of how meteors radiate from the area of the sky after which they are named, in this case the constellation Perseus. The shorter of the two trails is in fact still within the boundaries of Perseus, and the radiant itself can be traced back to just outside the top of the frame. At the bottom left are the Pleiades, and towards the top right is the Andromeda Galaxy (M31). The original picture was exposed on Fujichrome ISO 400 film in a Canon F1 camera with an f/1.4, 24-mm wide-angle lens fitted.*

meteor shower is to make some test exposures lasting for, say, 1, 5, 10, and 15 minutes on the type of film and from the site to be used. This will establish the quality of the sky and the tactics that must be pursued. Meteor photography and light pollution do not go well together, so if your tests reveal sky fog quickly developing in the images, a move to a darker site is indicated. My local sky is very bad, and when I cannot travel I restrict exposures on ISO 400 film to no more than 2 minutes. This is far from ideal, and is very heavy on film, particularly when using a battery of cameras set to fire automatically! But sometimes we have to decide on something rather than nothing. The general advice given in Chapter 5 also applies, and since meteor photography tends by defini-tion to be a somewhat protracted business if tackled at all seriously, a method of dealing with the formation of dew on lenses should be available (see page 50). Specialists use a rotating shutter spinning at nearly 1000 revolutions per minute in front of the lens to "chop"

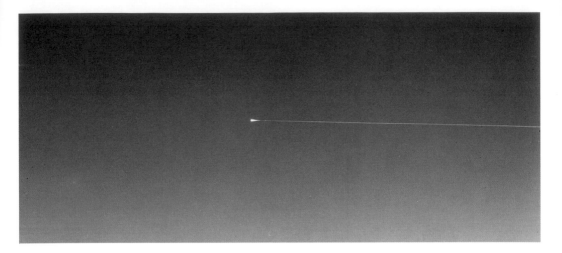

Figure 12.2 *The Teton fireball of 1972 August 10. According to Lanny Ream, who took this photograph from the Idaho/Montana border, the object was in sight for about 20 seconds and left a trail like a jet plane's, but thicker, that remained visible for half an hour. The exposure was on Kodachrome-X film loaded in a Nikkormat camera fitted with a 50-mm lens.*

meteor trails into segments, from which the velocity of the incoming meteoroid may be calculated. These devices also enable meteor trails to be distinguished from the otherwise similar trails left by artificial satellites and aircraft.

In the past the Earth, like most other bodies in the Solar System, has been subjected to meteoritic bombardment of great intensity. Relatively few large bodies have impacted the surface during recorded history, but this has not prevented the evolution of theories about the role of such impacts in the Earth's more distant past, for example in the extinction of the dinosaurs. Often no bigger than specks of dust, the particles that burn up to produce meteors are at the opposite end of the size scale, but occasionally we are reminded of what might be. On 1972 August 10, for example, a fireball was seen over a large area of the US and Canada in broad daylight. Because of the oblique angle and high velocity of its approach, it cut through the Earth's atmosphere and went back into space without striking the surface. Its weight was estimated to be a possible 1000 tonnes, and, had it impacted, the energy released would have been the equivalent of a thermonuclear explosion. More prosaically, a lesson of its appearance was the wisdom of carrying a camera at all times (see Figure 12.2). On 1994 February 1 a body estimated to have weighed 400 tonnes exploded 20 km (12 miles) above the Pacific Ocean, producing a fireball with a magnitude of -23, almost as bright as the Sun. Although the only eyewitnesses seem to have been the crews of fishing boats, the fireball was picked up by at least six surveillance satellites.

Satellites Artificial satellites in orbit about the Earth are much more predictable than meteors, although natural forces acting on them may cause them to be a little later or earlier than predicted. Military radars are currently tracking over 7000 objects in space (many of which are defunct spacecraft and the remnants of numerous launch vehicles, well deserving the description *space junk*) and at any one time 500 or more may be above the horizon. They are so numerous that an experienced binocular observer can spend the entire night tracking satellites as they cross the sky, a new one appearing every few minutes.

Earth-orbiting satellites shine by reflected sunlight, so it follows that the best times to see them are after sunset and before sunrise against the darkness of the sky above. Depending on how far the Sun is beneath the horizon and on the altitude of a satellite, it will either remain lit by sunlight for its entire passage overhead, or enter the Earth's shadow (in the evening) or come out of it (in the early morning) part way through its traverse of the sky. Not infrequently the surface of a satellite catches sunlight at a critical angle and a brief flash is seen – doubtless the cause of some UFO reports.

Satellites seen by the naked eye or through binoculars fall into two broad categories. Weather and earth-resources satellites (as well as many military spacecraft) are usually in what are called *polar orbits*, in which they travel in a north–south/south–north direction and cross the equator more or less at right angles. This orbit is selected because over a given period of time all of the Earth's surface passes beneath the satellite's cameras or other sensors. Many other satellites are in orbits that do not take them so far to the north and south of the equator: thus one which is said to be in a 50° inclination orbit will never pass beyond 50° north or south latitude. Most communications satellites and some meteorological satellites are placed in what is called a *geosynchronous orbit*, at an average altitude of just under 36,000 km (over 22,000 miles), where their period of revolution matches the rotation of the Earth below them. A satellite in such an orbit which is circular and in the plane of the Earth's equator appears from the Earth's surface not to move, and is said to be *geostationary*. These satellites are extremely difficult to photograph, but it can be done (see *Sky & Telescope*, June 1986, pages 557, 563–7, and 606–7).

Depending upon their purpose, satellites differ too in their altitude, and thus in the time they take to complete an orbit and in how rapidly they move across the sky. The lower they are, the faster they travel. Thus a satellite at an altitude of about 200 km (125 miles) will take around 90 minutes to complete an orbit of the Earth, and will move across the sky in one observer's field of view in perhaps 2 minutes. Another at an altitude of around 5000 km (3000 miles) or more could easily take 3 hours to circle the Earth, and 10–15 minutes at least to pass across the sky as seen from one vantage point.

Brightness also varies enormously, depending on such features as the size and shape of the vehicle as well as its altitude and the angle at which it is illuminated by the Sun. Many satellites require binoculars to be seen, while others – such as the Russian space station Mir and the US space shuttles (see Figure 12.3) – can be at least as bright as Sirius, the brightest star in the sky. Similarly, whereas satellites usually move in their orbits with apparent ease and grace, there can be occasions of

Figure 12.3 *The space shuttle* Columbia *flies over southern England during the early evening of 1983 November 28. The vehicle was carrying the European Space Agency's Spacelab module on its first flight, and this was also the first of only a few occasions when the inclination of a shuttle's orbit has brought it sufficiently far north to be seen from the UK. The exposure was for 45 seconds on Tri-X film, and an f/2.8, 24-mm Nikkor wide-angle lens was used.* Columbia *was already in the field of view to the west when the exposure was begun, and it moved into eclipse almost at the zenith. Vega in Lyra is the bright star towards top left, and the "handle" of Ursa Major can be seen over the poplar tree at bottom right. The light on the horizon is a mixture of twilight and light pollution.*

great drama, as when a spacecraft re-enters the Earth's lower atmosphere in a brilliant firework display, or (as has happened for some years) a Russian Soyuz manned spacecraft approaches and docks with the Mir station. Not infrequently, parts of rockets used to launch spacecraft can be seen periodically flashing as they tumble end over end in orbit overhead.

During any period of observing it is very likely that a satellite of some kind will be seen. This is of little use, however, for those wishing to make a study of them, whether with a camera or by eye. Fortunately, details of satellite orbits appear on NASA electronic noticeboards, and may be accessed by bona fide observers; members of the Artificial Satellites section of the British Astronomical Association in the UK can arrange to receive data by post at approximately weekly intervals; and some daily newspapers publish details of a small number of satellites. According to taste, you can either draw the track of a satellite across a terrestrial map and estimate its path relative to the viewing site, or, armed with information on its position in right ascension and declination at given times, you can plot its passage on a starchart. With information about the track and time available, basic photography is quite straightforward.

Satellites are point sources which are sometimes brighter, and invariably moving much more slowly, than meteors. Moreover, the advance information about their orbits means that, while there may be some small discrepancies, the photographer can await the appearance of satellites without the need to adopt the patrol approach necessary with meteors. Once again, the standard 50-mm lens at maximum aperture provides both reasonable speed and large sky coverage, which will be welcome news for the novice. (Later, when experience has been gained and the passage of a satellite can be predicted with greater accuracy, longer focal length and faster lenses can be used.) Because the shutter is rarely held open for more than half a minute or a minute at most, there is little fear of light pollution having too much effect on the image, particularly as there is no need to use a very high-speed film: one of ISO 400 (whether colour or black and white) is entirely satisfactory.

The normal basic procedures described in Chapter 5 should be adopted. Once the camera has been aimed, it helps to memorize quite accurately the area of the sky covered by the lens's field of view, or even to draw a rough sketch-map. When the satellite has been spotted, you can open the shutter on the B setting using the black card technique, wait until the satellite is just a short way from the edge of the field of view, withdraw the card, and then cover the lens again once the satellite has moved out of the target area. Of course, there is no reason at all why an exposure should not be begun or ended with a satellite in the middle of the field of view, but this is more likely to be by accident than design, when the satellite has been spotted at the last moment or has moved unseen and unexpectedly into an exposure being made for other reasons.

Your notes should include not only details of the lens and exposure, but also timings for the entry and (if possible) exit of a satellite from the camera's field of view, together with information about the location's longitude and latitude, and the starfield in the image. If there is then any subsequent query about the identity of the satellite, the image and notes should together be enough to provide the answer.

When a satellite's passage is across the entire sky and is picked up very early, there is a temptation to try a series of pictures. With a single camera in use this should be attempted only after having practised smooth and efficient readjustment of the tripod/camera pointing angle between exposures. It is better to get one excellent image of a satellite (as near the zenith as possible) than risk knocking the tripod over or some similar mishap. If maximum coverage is required, it is sensible to arrange two cameras on two tripods pointing at different parts of the sky.

Since satellites were first put into orbit around forty years ago, professional and amateur observers have conducted an intensive study of the effects of gravity, variations in the upper atmosphere, and other factors on orbiting spacecraft, and much new knowledge has been gained. By devoting a great amount of time and developing observational skills of a high order, amateurs have played an important role in this work, and for the newcomer to satellite photography there is the prospect of eventually becoming part of this effort. Then the simple enjoyments of locating and photographing satellites will give way to the need for highly precise timings of the passage. Specialists use a rotating shutter that "chops" the trail of the satellite recorded on the film into several segments, corresponding to equal time periods, from which detailed

(a)   (b)

Figure 12.4 *These two images were recorded during an automated camera patrol. The aircraft in (b) passed directly above the camera, and its full complement of strobe and fixed lights was recorded. The aircraft in (a) was probably banking, so few lights were recorded, but at least one of them was a flashing strobe. At critical angles and without visible strobes aircraft can resemble satellites in the trail they leave on film. On those relatively rare occasions careful analysis is required to identify them accurately.*

information about the satellite's orbit may be derived. The use of computer programs, together with updated information about satellite orbits supplied in the first instance by NASA, greatly facilitates such studies by providing a wealth of data.

Aircraft – and UFOs

Many images of meteors and satellites are quite unmistakable. Meteors range from faint and delicate needle-like traces to the far more robust and denser trail of a fireball. Satellite trails are often of uniform density, although where they enter or leave eclipse there may well be a "feathering" effect before the reflections from the spacecraft are extinguished (as in Figure 12.3). Sometimes, however, the trail may be broken into segments as a satellite rotates or tumbles, while somewhat less dramatic perturbations of this kind may introduce a pulsing of the trail that is discernible only under a magnifier. Under less than perfect sky conditions (and if visual observations were not taking place at the same time) it can be difficult to decide on the likely cause of some trails, and this situation is compounded by aircraft lights.

Civilian airliners display a whole battery of lights. A constant red light is located at the end of the port wing, and a constant green light on the starboard. A constant white light is usually fixed to the tail, and flashing anti-collision beacons, usually orange in colour, are located both above and below the fuselage. Finally, very bright landing lights on the inner leading edges of the wings are often switched on at night as a further collision-avoidance measure once an aircraft has descended below 3000 m (10,000 feet).

When seen (or photographed) from directly below at night, an aircraft cannot be mistaken for anything else. However, as angles get more oblique an image can become less easy to interpret, and the presence of light cirrus cloud can complicate the problem. The two photographs in Figure 12.4 were taken during an automated camera patrol. One shows a trail from beneath an aircraft, and the other shows the trail of an aircraft at an angle to the camera. Both interpretations are indisputable, but it only needs the flashing strobe lights to be hidden from the camera for a teaser to be set for the newcomer to astrophotography, and sometimes for the more experienced too. Often other evidence, such as knowledge of satellite passes or aircraft movements, will provide the answer, but not always. Figure 9.7, on page 100, shows another aircraft trail.

This leads to the occasional need for detective work to solve a mystery. I live about 60 km (35 miles) southwest of London's Gatwick Airport, under one of the main approach paths. Years ago, shortly after taking up astrophotography, I became puzzled by bright, seemingly stationary lights to the southwest of the camera site. Thorough observation over a short period revealed these to be landing lights on aircraft making a head-on approach a considerable distance away. No engine noise was audible, lateral movement was minimal, and over a period of a few minutes there was no apparent movement of the light source. If the lights were watched for long enough the eventual movement of the aircraft was clearly revealed. This type of sighting may well be the origin of some UFO reports.

Sometimes, even for the knowledgeable, celestial objects can provide a brief puzzle. During an evening's photography one spring I saw a bright point of light in which green and red elements were discernible. It was to the northeast, in the general direction of Gatwick Airport. My first thought was that this was an aircraft that had just taken off, and that I should not let it intrude into a picture. A few minutes later the light was still in the same position, and I thought a helicopter might be operating in that area. After a few minutes more, with the light still in approximately the same position, the truth dawned: the beautiful star Vega was rising and displaying some of the classic features of twinkling (or scintillation), when atmospheric turbulence refracts the light from a star and causes flashes of different colours.

If you ever see an object in the sky that puzzles you, endeavour to make full notes of place, time, direction, elevation, and any other relevant details. If at all possible, photograph the object in a series of time exposures (say 5, 10, 20, and 30 seconds on ISO 400 film or faster) that hopefully will record background stars if the sky is clear. If time allows, use lenses of different focal length and change the position

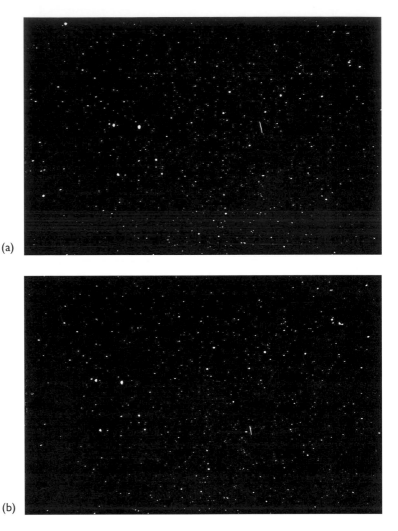

(a)

(b)

Figure 12.5 *An IFO (identified flying object). These two images are of the Corvus/Crater/Hydra region of the sky, centred at declination 20°S, and were obtained in 1987 during a programme of fixed-camera constellation photography. Two 20-second exposures were made, (a) first, then (b), using an f/1.4 35-mm Nikkor lens and Agfachrome 1000RS Professional film. During the photography no movement in the sky was observed, but when the film was processed two short trails were revealed quite clearly. These indicated a bright object at considerable altitude and moving quite slowly in a southerly direction. The object was subsequently identified by Russell Eberst as the largest remnant of the Pageos balloon satellite, which was launched in 1966 and which disintegrated in 1975. It took about 180 minutes to orbit the Earth in a near-polar orbit, but has now re-entered.*

of the object in the field of view (see below). In at least some of the pictures include a foreground object, even if it is a totally dark hedge, tree, or house. Note as accurately as you can the time at which each exposure was commenced. It will be surprising if any mystery remains after subsequent analysis of notes and pictures (see Figure 12.5).

Figure 12.6 *A mystery object (see the text). One of the original colour transparencies, exposed on 1988 November 2, has been printed so that stars appear black on a white background. Jupiter is the major object, with the Pleiades above and the Hyades with Aldebaran below. The small unidentified object is arrowed. Under microscopic examination the image of the object did not have the typical characteristics of a "ghost," and subsequent tests with Jupiter in the field of view failed to recreate anything like it. The object appeared on four consecutive exposures, from 30 seconds to 2 minutes, on Agfachrome 1000RS film loaded in a Nikon F3 camera mounted on a driven platform. The lens was a 58-mm f/1.2 Noct-Nikkor stopped down to f/2.8 and fitted with a Lumicon Deep-Sky Filter™.*

However, I have to report one astrophotography experience where later research and analysis failed to identify an object convincingly. A sequence of four different time exposures I took in November 1988 included the Hyades and Pleiades in Taurus and a very bright Jupiter. On later examination, an uncharted, starlike object appeared in all four frames (see Figure 12.6). Because it was in all the frames, the object could not be the result of a processing fault. Neither did it possess the typical characteristics of a ghost image, even under microscopic examination. Subsequent tests of the same camera/lens/filter/film combination were inconclusive, and in the absence of any positive, corroborating evidence from other sources I concluded (perhaps too easily) that the object was probably an unknown artifact of the photographic system. In retrospect, of course, a simple test would have provided the answer. If, using the same equipment, the camera had been moved between frames so that Jupiter occupied different positions in the field of view, then on the film a ghost image would have moved too. But this was being wise after the event, because I was not aware of the mystery object when taking the pictures.

If you do find an uncharted object in a photograph you have taken, do research it thoroughly. You may have (unknowingly) recorded an asteroid, a nova, or a comet – who knows, you may even have *discovered* one!

CHAPTER 13

Processing

For many photographers "home processing," whether for black and white or for colour, is half the fun. This chapter is directed not at them but at newly enlisted astrophotographers who have not hitherto processed their own films. Why should they now contemplate doing so? Putting aside the increased enjoyment to be had from the hobby and the question of the safeguarding one's efforts (discussed in Chapter 4), the main attraction is the convenience. We have to take advantage of periods of good weather when we may be able to devote consecutive nights to astrophotography, and it is advantageous to be able to see the results of one night's work before the following night. If there is a good, fast processing laboratory in the neighbourhood then all is well, but many of us will not have access to such a service. Even if we do, a laboratory might well be shut for a lengthy period over a holiday – exactly when the astrophotographer might have the time and therefore a greater inclination to take advantage of clear nights. It is also easy for the home processor to take a compact kit away on foreign travels so that results can be checked between photo sessions, and also to ensure that no damage results from X-ray screening of unprocessed film at airports (see Chapter 14).

It is quite natural to wonder how the costs of commercial and home processing compare (both vary somewhat according to locality and, of course, country). Although it is possible that over a period of time somebody who exposes and processes a considerable number of films might save money, I would not recommend home processing for that reason. Clearly, a colour slide kit with an effective life of four weeks (once processing has begun) and a capacity of six or eight 36-exposure 35-mm films provides greater value if it is used to the full, but this is not always possible. Another important consideration is quality. If you are prepared to follow a small number of detailed instructions carefully (and can read a thermometer accurately), the quality you can achieve by using a home processing kit will leave nothing to be desired. Moreover, it will not entail a great expenditure of time.

The guidance that follows cannot be as lengthy or as detailed as that found in a specialized book on processing or in manufacturers' instruction leaflets (which are first class). It is, however, intended to be sufficient for you to decide whether to go ahead and purchase the few items of equipment that are needed and try home processing for yourself.

This may be described as the dry stage. The exposed film has to be removed from its cassette in total darkness and placed in a light-tight container before processing. You can do this in a photographic darkroom – but if you have access to one, you will not be reading this chapter. One step up from such primitive methods as unloading film under the bedclothes is to use a dark cupboard. The problem is that cupboards are very rarely dark, as will become clear if you shut yourself inside one and allow time for your eyes to get dark adapted. Making a cupboard dark enough for handling films (particularly fast films) is a laborious business. The simple and very modestly priced answer to the problem is the *changing-bag*. This is made of a black fabric and looks rather like a cushion cover. It has a large zipped flap in an inner lining, and a flap in an outer cover which is closed by several press-studs. In two corners of the bag are shaped cuffs through which you insert your hands, and which are kept light-tight by elasticized bands. (The bag is an excellent purchase for it serves also, for example, as a means of tackling such problems as opening the back of a camera in which a film has apparently jammed, and unjamming it without losing any frames through exposure to light.)

The large flap of the bag admits a daylight *developing tank*. This consists of four main parts: a two-sided, grooved plastic reel onto which the film is wound; a hollow spindle that passes through the middle of the reel; a cylindrical tank that accepts the spindle and reel; and a tank lid moulded in such a way that a central spout (into which processing liquids are poured) fits down inside the spindle, thereby rendering the inside of the tank light-tight (see Figure 13.1). A rod for agitating the reel is supplied with some tanks, and all have a tightly fitting cap for the lid.

These tanks have improved steadily over the years, and some current models have rather strangely shaped lids through which processing liquids can be poured in no more than a second or two – an important factor in securing an optimum result. Into the changing-bag with the film cassette and tank go an opener for extracting the film from the 35-mm cassette (this need be no more than an ordinary hook-type bottle opener) and a small pair of sharp but preferably blunt-nosed scissors.

The two ends of the reel can be set at different distances from each other to take various sizes of film. The tanks themselves come in a number of sizes, and some will take more than one reel at a time, which is an obvious advantage when several films of the same type are to be processed. As a reminder to the user, the tanks normally have moulded somewhere on the outside details of the volume of processing liquids required by different sizes of film.

Before inserting the film into the reel, the leader has to be cut off in between the perforations across the full width of the film. (If the cut runs through one or both of the perforations it is likely that the film will not enter the reel without difficulty.) This is why the habit of winding the film completely back into the cassette after the final exposure is not recommended. With a film not fully wound back it is an easy matter to extract all of the leader and cut carefully and at right angles across the full width of the film. If the film has been wound in fully then the

Preparatory stage

Figure 13.1 *A modern, highly efficient daylight developing tank. The main shell of the tank is at centre left. To the right is the light-tight inner lid shaped for fast pouring of developing solutions; at the far right is the reel onto which the film is wound, with a hollow spindle inserted through the reel core. In the foreground is an agitating rod, and at far left is the outer lid which seals the tank completely so that it can be inverted without solutions leaking.*

operation has to be done within the changing-bag when the cassette has been opened (and then there is a very good chance of cutting across the perforations because we obviously cannot see precisely what we are doing); either that, or an attempt must be made to extract the leader.

One way of extracting the leader is to cut a piece of acetate or very thin but stiff plastic into a strip measuring about 10×2.5 cm (4×1 inches). The corners of one end are rounded off so that the film is not scratched when inserting the strip through the lips of the cassette, and a piece of double-sided adhesive tape roughly 2 cm (0.8 inch) square is fixed on one side of that end. About half the length of the strip is pushed through the lips of the cassette with the adhesive tape towards the film core. The core is turned clockwise, which presses the film against the tape, to which it will hopefully stick so that it can be withdrawn, though several attempts may have to be made. The moral for home processors is not to wind the film fully back – although a camera with auto-rewind will usually put the matter beyond their control.

Extracting the film from its cassette and loading it onto the reel requires practice. The changing-bag is somewhat restricting to the inexperienced, so it is a good idea to practise the technique first of all in ordinary light on a table, and then in the dark on the table, before attempting to use the changing-bag. This requires the expenditure of two or three films (perhaps outdated ones which have been around for a long time, or a particular brand you have come to dislike), but this should not be regarded as a waste.

Gather together the film cassette, the tank (with lid lightly on, but reel and spindle separate – this saves a needless extraction of the reel from the tank once it is inside the bag), the opener, and the scissors. Pull the leader out from the cassette and cut it off at the point where the film becomes full width. Clipping and chamfering the corners of the film makes it less likely to jam when it is being fed into the spindle. Place the hook of the opener under the edge of the cassette cap opposite the long end of the spool, and remove it. Take out the film (still on its spool) and discard the empty can. Put the film down for a moment – it will not unravel if you take care – and take up the reel. Align the two entry points (which have ball-bearing ratchets to facilitate the entry of the film) and take the reel in one hand with the entry points facing you. Take up the free end of the film between the thumb and first finger of your other hand, and draw it gently between the entry points until several inches of it are through and it is secure (see Figure 13.2(a)).

Place the fingers of each hand along the edges of the reel with the thumbs acting as guides to the film at the entry points, and rotate the two sides back and forth in opposite directions until almost all of the film has been loaded (see Figure 13.2(b)). If the two little fingers of each hand are kept extended underneath the reel while the film is being wound, they can be used as sensors to check that the film end is close with the spool still attached. (If you cannot feel this, you risk damaging the film if the spool jams into the reel ends.) Hold the reel in one hand, pick up the scissors, and cut off the spool. Rotate the sides of the reel again until the film is completely loaded. Taking care not to touch the surface of the film, insert the spindle through the centre of the reel. Put the reel and spindle down for a moment and remove the lid from the tank. Place the reel and spindle (reel first) into the tank, and snap the lid in place. If the lid is kept on the tank until the last moment, it should prevent the empty cassette and loose end-cap from finding their way into the tank, and causing confusion when the operation is taking place in the changing-bag.

If several films are being processed in quick succession in a single film tank, it is essential to ensure that the reel and tank are completely dried between films. If there is any water in the spiral grooves of the reel, the film will swell and become sticky, making loading virtually impossible. Occasionally, for no apparent reason, the film may not load smoothly. On no account should it be forced once resistance has been felt, since this can result in damage to the film and possibly in light flashes on the developed photographs caused by physical deformation. Try tapping the reel with your knuckles. If this has no effect, flex the end of the film that is still free by pushing the edges together slightly, and pull the film free with the reel rotating in the other hand. (If much of the film is on the reel, it should be pulled very slowly so that, as it comes away, the film coils up on itself loosely, and does not hang free, vulnerable to damage.)

In daylight and with a reasonable working space, this first practice session should go quite smoothly. Before the second practice, place all the items close to hand before cutting off the leader and then switching off the light. The main difference between the practice in the dark and

(a)

Figure 13.2 *(a) In the darkroom or in a changing-bag, this is the way the film is drawn past the entry points or ball-bearing ratchets of the reel. Notice how the leader of the film has been neatly cut at right angles to facilitate entry. (b) Once the film has been taken up by the reels, it is wound in by counter-rotation of the reels.*

the third practice in the changing-bag is the greater restriction on space. I find it best to work on a table-top so that the various items in the bag are supported, and I can take the weight on my elbows.

The tank, with the lid lightly in position, and the spindle are placed to one side of the bag; the reel is positioned in the centre; and the cassette, scissors, and opener are put in the opposite corner. The bag is then closed. Once the cassette has been opened, the film is placed carefully by the reel for a moment, and the end-cap, together with the empty cassette and opener, are replaced in their corner of the bag. This is important because there is then no risk of the objects touching and scratching the film as it hangs beneath the reel during the loading operation. Once this is completed and the film spool is cut off (and placed in the right-hand "refuse corner" of the changing-bag), the spindle is inserted into the reel with its base at the bottom. Both are placed in the tank and the lid is fixed firmly in place. The bag can then be opened, all objects can be removed, and processing can commence.

With a little practice you will be able to carry out this procedure with few if any problems. The main difficulty will be the occasion when, with hands within the bag, you sneeze or get an itchy nose!

Processing black-and-white film

A brief description of what happens when an image on black-and-white film is developed will help make clear the practical requirements. When film is exposed in the camera, light affects silver halide crystals in the emulsion and forms what are called *development centres* in the crystals. These make up the latent image. If we could see the film at

(b)

this stage, no image would be visible: a developer is needed to act on the development centres where the silver halides are reduced to black metallic silver, the extent of this action being broadly proportional to the amount of light striking the film in the original exposure. The silver halides not affected by the light have no development centres, so none should develop, but when this does happen for a variety of reasons it causes a chemical fog that degrades the image.

When enough silver has been produced to give the desired result, the action of the *developer* (which is alkaline) must be stopped. This is done by removing the film from the developer solution and placing it in a mild acid solution known appropriately as a *stop bath*. The remaining silver halides, which are still sensitive to light, must be removed, and this is accomplished by the *fixer*. This is a selective solvent which reacts with the halides to form soluble silver salts that dissolve into the fixer solution. Finally, once removed from the fixer, the film has to be washed to remove residual fixer chemicals, dissolved silver salts, and other by-products of the various stages.

This is a very simple outline of what is a complex process. The ultimate result depends on an enormous number of variables including the properties of the film, the nature of the original exposure, the characteristics of the developer, and the manner of the development. Fortunately for the newcomer, the manufacturers of film and processing chemicals usually issue excellent instruction leaflets with their products.

Although the exact details of the processing steps vary somewhat according to the particular film and chemicals, the basics are very similar. The film is developed for a period of time (roughly 4 to 10 minutes) that is determined to a considerable degree by the temperature of the developer solution. The film is then placed in the stop bath for up to 30 seconds, and then in the fixer for several minutes. The traditional working temperature for black-and-white film development is 20°C (68°F), although processing at higher temperatures has become more popular in recent years. Holding to the chosen temperature of the developer is critical to the result, but the acid bath, fixer, and washing water may be a degree or two either side without any ill-effects to the image. If water from the tap cannot be held to approximately the desired temperature while the film is being washed, it is safer to fill a bowl with water at this temperature and to wash the film by repeated changes of water from the bowl. After washing, the film is given a final rinse in a wetting agent (which helps prevent the formation of drying marks on the film) and hung up to dry. The drying place must be dust-free, and preferably warm and well-ventilated. Detailed guidance on, for example, the type and amount of agitation of processing liquids required in the different sorts of development tank will be found in the manufacturers' instructions, but it is pertinent here to indicate the items of equipment (as distinct from chemicals) required by the newcomer.

The developing tank has been discussed in detail already. The next most important item is the *thermometer*. Various types are available, the differences largely concerning accuracy and ease of reading, and there-fore cost. Spirit and mercury versions are popular, usually accurate to about 1°C (0.5°F) and 0.4°C (0.2°F) respectively, but I confess to having had difficulty over the years in reading thermometers of this type. Dial thermometers are very easy to read but are somewhat unreliable in accuracy. Digital, LCD display thermometers are accurate to about a tenth of a degree and are easy to read, but are about three times as expensive as a good mercury thermometer. Contamination is a problem during the preparation of processing solutions, and care must be taken to wash the thermometer thoroughly in cool (not hot) water.

Working solutions of acid bath and fixer can be used repeatedly until they near exhaustion. With many developers you need to make up a working solution from a powder or liquid concentrate. Therefore at least three appropriately sized and dedicated containers or bottles will need to be purchased; most people seem to prefer glass containers. A small graduated vessel or measuring cylinder with a capacity of at least 300 ml and marked graduations of at least 25 ml is needed for measuring out the solutions, although again thorough and frequent washing is essential in order to avoid contamination. (In general, a little developer will have no detrimental effect on acid bath or fixer, but a little acid bath or fixer will have a potentially severe effect on developer.) A mixing jug and a mixer or mixing paddle facilitate the preparation of the processing solutions, the mixer particularly if the developer concentrate is in powder form, which dissolves with greater reluctance than a liquid concentrate. Again, take care to avoid contamination.

If tap water can be mixed to the desired washing temperature, use a *film washer*. This is a simply a tube that fits onto the developing tank at one end, to ensure maximum washing efficiency, and over the tap at the other. It costs very little. Holding processing liquids and washing water at steady temperatures can be accomplished by using a *water jacket*, which can be as elaborate as a thermostatically controlled tank designed specially for the job, or as simple as an adequately sized kitchen bowl containing water a few degrees warmer than the solutions. Pairs of *film clips* (one of which is weighted) are used to hang the film up for drying; they are inexpensive and are more efficient than drawing pins/thumbtacks at the top and clothes pegs/clothespins at the bottom. Some people recommend using a film squeegee with soft rubber blades to drastically reduce the amount of water left on the film after putting it through the wetting agent. I do not use one because, however much care is taken, it is a potential source of scratches on the film. While some of us have skins which are far less sensitive to chemicals than others have, it is sensible to wear a pair of ordinary household rubber gloves during all processing operations. Finally, a countdown timer with a very clear display is essential, particularly at those stages in the process where the processing liquids need to be agitated at specified intervals so as to optimize development.

Processing colour film

Despite the additional complexity of colour transparency film, processing it is only a little more involved than for black and white. Leaving aside Kodachrome film (which requires complex processing that can be carried out only in major laboratories), the industry standard is based on Kodak's E-6 process, which is well suited to home processing and which can be used for virtually all other transparency films.

Whereas black-and-white film is composed basically of one sensitive layer, colour film has essentially three layers, one sensitive to each of the primary colours of blue, green, and red. After exposure, a first developer produces a black metallic silver image that, as with black-and-white film, represents the highlight areas of the original. Unlike black-and-white film, however, this silver is developed in the three basic layers according to the colours in the original scene. Since the film is intended to yield transparencies (or positives) and not negatives, the negative images have to be turned into positive images by reversal processing. This is accomplished by the use of a colour developer that fogs the hitherto unexposed and undeveloped silver halides in the positive areas of the image, and then creates in them dye images of the correct hue in each colour-sensitive layer. Since the positive and negative silver images now serve no purpose, they are bleached out of the film, and the film is fixed by a combined bleach fix solution to leave only the colour dye images.

If you decide to use colour negative film you will find film processing just as easy as for transparency film, although there are some differences of detail. Kodak's own E-6 home processing kit contains four processing solutions, but those of some other kit manufacturers contain, as indicated above, only three: a first developer, a colour developer, and a bleach fix. One major difference from black-and-white processing is the high temperature that is regarded as optimum for colour processing – typically around 38°C (100°F). Obviously this makes it more demanding to keep the solutions at their required temperatures. An equally important difference is the need to maintain the critical balance between the images formed in the three colour-sensitive layers, and this is accomplished by strict adherence to the required solution temperatures and processing times.

The following is a summary of the processing steps using the Chrome Six 600 ml kit produced by Photo Technology Limited. This widely available kit is typical of several such commercially available kits (Unicolor Rapid E-6 is another), and I have used it for some years with complete satisfaction. All kits are available in convenient sizes for the amateur, typically to make up solutions in about 500 or 600 ml quantities.

1. Bring the processing solutions up to 38°C by standing the containers in a large bowl of water at about 40°C (104°F).
2. Preheat the tank and film by filling the tank with water at 43°C (110°F) and standing it in the water-bath for 1 minute. Empty the tank.
3. Pour in the first developer. Agitate (see below), and stand the tank in the water-bath (it is kept there throughout the process). Develop for 6½ minutes at 38°C, including the time taken (10–20 seconds) to pour out the developer. The developer is kept for re-use.
4. Wash the film for a total of 2 minutes in at least four complete changes of water at 34–42°C (93–108°F), and drain the tank.
5. Pour in the colour developer. Agitate. Replace the tank in the water bath. Develop for 6 minutes at 38°C, including the pouring-out time. The developer is retained for further use.
6. Rinse with three changes of water for a total of 1 minute, and drain the tank.
7. Pour in the bleach fix. Agitate continuously for at least 1 minute, and thereafter at about 30-second intervals for 10 minutes. Extra time will do no harm. Retain for re-use.
8. Wash the film for a total of 4 minutes in water at 34–42°C using at least six complete changes.
9. Add a few drops of wetting agent to the final wash.
10. Hang the film up to dry in a warm, dust-free place. It may be heat-dried, but the temperature must not exceed 60°C (140°F), and care must be taken to avoid local overheating if a hair-dryer is used. The transparent parts of the film will have a milky appearance when wet, but will become clear on drying.

Note on agitation: At the commencement of each processing step, tap the tank on a hard surface to dislodge any air bubbles adhering to the film. Then immediately agitate, either by inverting the tank seven or eight times in succession or, with tanks having an agitating rod, by rotating the spiral reel four or five times. Thereafter invert the tank (or rotate the reel) twice at 30-second intervals throughout the process. Replace the tank in the water bath between inversions.

Copying slides

If you want a good-quality, accurate copy of one of your slides, it is probably cheapest to go to one of the film manufacturers or one of the independent photo labs that cater for the amateur photographer.

Getting sufficient accuracy is very difficult, but accuracy may not be what you are after. You may want to increase the contrast of the original to bring out more detail, or adjust the colour balance to give a more faithful rendition of the original scene as you remember it, or as you wish it had appeared. These objectives are not so difficult to achieve, and are well worth trying for yourself as you get more deeply involved in astrophotography.

The main requirement is for a duplicator assembly that will reproduce the original slide at least at the same size. The simplest such system consists of a tube in which is mounted a dedicated, fixed-aperture lens. At one end of the tube is a slide-holder, and at the other an adapter for mounting a camera. Daylight may be used as the light source for illuminating the original slide during copying, and for reliable calculation of exposures you cannot beat an SLR camera with its through-the-lens metering. At the other end of the scale are bellows copying units made by the major camera manufacturers for their own models, employing lenses specially designed for close-up work, although a standard 50-mm lens can be used if it is reversed when fitted to the bellows. These dedicated units are usually versatile and come with a host of features, but they are expensive. While it is possible to make use of daylight as the light source, greater control can be exercised by using an electronic flash or a tungsten light positioned behind the original slide.

The film used will depend on the light source. If it is daylight or electronic flash, then a slow (say ISO 25 or 50), high-resolution, high-contrast slide film balanced for daylight is the best choice. A tungsten light source will require a film balanced for that type of light. In your choice of film, however, you will in another aspect depart from the usual photographic practice. Dedicated copying films are intended to limit the contrast that builds up when an original is copied. However, you will almost certainly be wanting to increase the contrast, and so will choose a conventional (non-copying) film balanced for daylight or tungsten light. Experience will teach you whether you need to modify the exposures indicated by the SLR's through-the-lens system. For example, you may have a dense transparency which, when illuminated by a strong light source, shows considerable detail. One or two stops of overexposure in terms of the meter reading might well be required to bring this detail out.

If you are attempting to correct a colour cast in the original, then you will need to understand a little about filters and the nature of colour. A particular filter passes its own colour, but blocks others. Thus a red filter will pass red light, but absorb the other primary colours, green and blue. Much use is made in photography of the so-called subtractive primary colours (sometimes called secondary colours) of cyan, magenta, and yellow. In terms of their filtering properties, cyan is composed of blue and green, and so passes them, but absorbs red; yellow is composed of red and green (yes!), and so passes them, but absorbs blue; and magenta is composed of red and blue, so passes them, but absorbs green. If you need to get rid of an unattractive greenish cast in a slide, then give a light red or magenta filter a try. If there is a red bias in the slide, a cyan filter could well improve things.

Kodak and other manufacturers make a range of colour-compensating filters that are available in gelatine and are reasonably priced. Duplicating is a technique with a special significance for the astrophotographer because it can help correct some of the deficiencies in an original, and it offers a few of the opportunities open to the user of CCDs and computers (see Chapter 16). It is something to be tackled further along the learning curve. More detailed accounts are given in books and articles listed in the Bibliography.

I have not attempted to give any guidance on black-and-white or colour printing. I have recommended home processing principally as a means of checking easily and quickly that all photographic systems are working well. Printing and darkroom work represent a further stage, one best left to specialized books and guides or tutorial courses. The information given in this chapter should be sufficient to help the newcomer decide whether to start home processing. Home processing has many advantages and, with attention to detail, good quality can be achieved. Moreover, even for those who have lost count of the number of films (black-and-white or colour) they have processed, the thrill of "seeing the image come out" rarely dies.

CHAPTER 14

Foreign skies

These days, holidaying abroad is popular and relatively cheap. While the motive of many people who journey to foreign countries is to combine rest and relaxation with assured sunshine, the principal attraction for those interested in astronomy is the chance to see constellations and other objects not visible at all, or only partly and with difficulty, from home. By going no further than the Mediterranean, for example, those of us living in the UK can see such impressive constellations as Scorpius and Sagittarius in their entirety, and within their boundaries the impressive Milky Way star clouds towards the centre of our Galaxy. Further south, from Tenerife in the Canary Islands, for example, the splendid southern constellation Centaurus containing the finest globular cluster in the sky (Omega Centauri) comes into view during spring evenings. If a holiday is taken in the opposite direction, in Scandinavia and perhaps as far as the Arctic Circle, there could well be plentiful aurorae to enjoy and photograph, as well as the midnight Sun.

The challenge of the South

Should a trip take us to Australia, New Zealand, South Africa, or South America, we can enjoy the glories of the southern sky (including our companion galaxies, the Small and Large Magellanic Clouds), which are almost overpowering at first. In addition, northerners need to accommodate to major differences of orientation. Sun, Moon, and planets track through the northern part of the sky; and not only does the Moon's face appear upside down, but it waxes and wanes from left to right. The constellations need relearning too, and a star map of the southern skies is essential. At first, it is difficult to recognize or accept clearly delineated constellations (such as Orion or Leo) which appear upside down or side-on, or Gemini being lower than Orion in the sky, while Sirius is higher. Slowly, however, it all begins to make sense.

When we return home we need to readjust again, even if we have been to just another part of the northern hemisphere. For example, as seen from the Canary Islands (28°N, 16°W) in the spring, the beautiful steel-blue star Vega in the constellation Lyra clears the northeastern horizon around 23.00 local time. When I return to the south coast of England (51°N), it is easy to be puzzled briefly by the bright star very high in the northeastern sky at 23.00. Yes, it is Vega – acting as a reminder of the differences of geographical location which speedy air travel tends to make us forget.

A major attraction of foreign travel for astrophotographers is the possibility of very dark skies. Of course this is far from certain, and it is likely that if a holiday is taken in the most popular areas then the amount of light pollution will be as bad as in urban areas back home. But a location or tour chosen with some care can be rewarding. A fly–drive holiday to the southwestern United States for Europeans (or for Americans living in less astronomically favourable areas) will reveal dark skies in large areas of Arizona and New Mexico, while the blackness of the sky from Monument Valley in Utah is almost beyond belief when first seen by a city-dweller. The holiday resorts in the south of Tenerife yield poor skies, but just a few miles inland by car, around the volcanic peak Teide, the stars are gloriously clear. Holidays in desert (and therefore thinly populated) areas generally yield dark skies, and it is easy to imagine the delights there would be, weather permitting, for keen and hardy astronomers whose work took them to the Arctic or Antarctic during the winter months.

A third attraction of foreign travel for the astrophotographer is the possibility of exotic foregrounds for unashamedly pictorial images (see Figure 14.1). Of course, this is not to underrate such opportunities at home, but a planetary conjunction and crescent Moon photographed with minarets or a magnificent saguaro cactus in the foreground (as in Figure 8.2 on page 80) would be worth travelling many miles to secure.

What sort of tour?

The opportunities for the astrophotographer will depend greatly upon the type of holiday. With a package tour your chances of finding out much in advance about an area's suitability for astrophotography are severely limited. Most tour operators and travel agencies are selling holidays in a fiercely competitive market, and will not have the time, inclination, or local knowledge to answer questions from those with special interests. (Just try asking whether you'll be able to see the setting Sun from your hotel room during your two weeks in July!) However, all is not entirely lost. At least the individual can choose a holiday date that coincides with the most suitable phases of the Moon, for example, and hopefully with other events such as planetary conjunctions.

There are other possibilities. Tour operators offer many choices of holiday location, and the astronomer or astrophotographer prepared to do a little advance research may find that the weather conditions in some of the locations offered were analysed in detail in publications such as *Sky & Telescope* when a solar eclipse or other major astronomical event was due to be visible from there. From time to time the *Journal* of the British Astronomical Association, and similar publications in other countries, publish accounts of the experiences of members on trips abroad, and these too can make helpful reading. Nonetheless, while initiatives taken by the individual can yield some results, the fact must be faced that astrophotographers get nothing special out of the typical package-tour holiday. In the end, it may be a question of just taking the binoculars and enjoying new constellations.

Figure 14.1 *Local architecture in the Algarve provides an exotic foreground for this picture of a crescent Moon in the evening sky recorded with a Nikon F301 camera on ISO 800/1600 Ektachrome film. A 35–105-mm Nikkor zoom lens was found to be most useful for pictorial compositions of this kind. Earlier in the evening, the camera's automatic exposure system was relied upon for images of a colourful and still light sky, but as the sky darkened manual exposures based on previous experience were used. This exposure was for 1 second at f/3.5, and the camera was of course fixed on a tripod. The colour cast of the white villa walls results from illumination by streetlights.*

Infinitely preferable is the specialist astronomical tour, usually organized for a specific event like a solar eclipse. While they are not usually as cheap as an ordinary package tour, their party rates normally make them cheaper than an individual would pay for a privately arranged trip, and there is the added attraction of being with fellow enthusiasts in a group probably led by knowledgeable specialists. The learning potential is therefore high. Even here, however, it is wise to take care. In my experience some astronomical tours can fall between the two stools of providing ordinary holiday-type attractions and catering for the more specialist interests. Indeed, it is not unknown for so-called star trips to have been offered at a time when the Moon hampered observations and photography. It is essential that the tour operators or leaders should have familiarized themselves with the viewing and other conditions at the destinations and to be aware of any problems. A newcomer contemplating such a trip will be well advised to seek out others who have been on trips organized by the same operator, and to take their opinions into account.

There is a third possibility which, on grounds of cost, is not open to too many: the privately arranged astrophotography trip abroad. Obviously it has many advantages. The location can be chosen without any need for compromise, and even such details as a balcony facing east (or west) for convenient dawn or dusk photography can be arranged. A hire

149

car gives maximum mobility in finding dark sites. Once found, it is likely that a suitable area will receive further visits from the serious enthusiast.

Astronomical centres

An excellent development in recent years has been the appearance of small centres providing facilities for astronomers to indulge their hobby at the same time as they and their families enjoy a holiday. Telescopes, mounts, and other essential equipment are usually provided or can be hired, and informed and helpful guidance is at hand. I have visited two such centres on a number of occasions, and can highly recommend them. The Star Hill Inn is situated in magnificent wooded mountain country at Sapello, not far from Albuquerque, New Mexico, and the Centre for Observational Astronomy in the Algarve (COAA) has been set up by an English couple not far from Portimão in the popular tourist area of the Algarve in Portugal. Places at both can be booked for just a few nights or for longer periods, and since both areas also have many attractions for the non-astronomers in a family or group they are well worth serious consideration.

Whatever the type of holiday or trip, it is best to take with you all the films and most of the equipment you will need. The films you plan to use, whether colour transparency or black and white, may not be available abroad, and this will certainly be the case in popular resort areas where the films on sale locally will be largely amateur colour negative–positive films (which may not have been kept in temperature-controlled conditions). Any consideration of possible price advantages should be disregarded. It is also vital to take reserve supplies of any other expendable items such as batteries. While few of us are likely to have the ability to repair a camera, a jeweller's screwdriver set can be useful for tightening small screws that work loose, as well as opening the battery compartment cover of some cameras (though for this job a coin is frequently more suitable). In case a film becomes jammed in the camera, a light-tight changing-bag (as described in Chapter 13) is a valuable addition to the photographic kit, and in case of possible malfunctions it is as well to take the instruction booklet for the camera since it may contain a troubleshooting checklist. Of course, if you take the booklet you may even learn something new about the camera!

Sun lotions will be used extensively during a holiday in warm countries. A determined attempt should be made to keep one's hands away from the exposed surfaces of lenses, but the occasional failure of good intentions is to be expected, and lens cleaning tissues should be packed for the trip. Better still, take a small bottle of lens-cleaning fluid. Finally, although on holiday and relaxing, we need to remember good, everyday photographic practice. If it is hot, keep the camera and other equipment out of direct sunlight, and always away from such things as sand, water, and drinks.

X-ray problems

The advice to take with you all the film likely to be required raises the question of current security measures at airports. Hand baggage is generally subject to X-ray screening. While the screening equipment is now more sophisticated than when first introduced, and X-ray inspection levels are claimed to be below the level at which photographic film starts to fog, the situation is complicated by the different sensitivities of different films and the variety of X-ray equipment in use in various parts of the world. International airports in the UK now use X-ray equipment giving such low levels of X-rays that even very high speed films remain unaffected. Tests carried out at London's Heathrow Airport in 1993 showed that X-ray screening produced no visible changes in films of speeds up to ISO 3200, even after 32 inspections. Similar equipment is used in other developed countries such as the US, Canada, Japan, and Australia. Where this is the case you can safely allow your films to be passed through the X-ray inspection. But older, high-intensity devices are still in use in some Third World countries and elsewhere. These can damage unprocessed films by just one inspection, the fogging showing up as density streaks on the subsequently processed film. Such streaks are more pronounced if the film slot of the cassette happened to have been facing the X-ray source during the screening.

Such undesirable effects on photographs are to be avoided whatever the subject matter. This applies even more to the astrophotographer's images since they represent much application and patience, and frequently contain faint and minute objects that are especially vulnerable to degradation by fogging. The best policy is to place all your films (exposed and unexposed) in a clear plastic bag, and to ask for a visual examination if this is allowed (it is not at London airports). Clearly the traveller is in the hands of the security staff, but on the whole I have encountered few difficulties with such a request in the US and elsewhere, especially if the plastic bag is packed so that it can be retrieved easily from hand luggage, and an attempt is made to pass through the security check when it is less crowded and the security staff are under less pressure. Bags that are claimed to protect films from X-ray screening can be purchased, but the results are unpredictable and depend on a number of factors (such as film and X-ray machine variations) beyond the traveller's control. Experience indicates the clear plastic bag to be a cheaper and more reliable solution – and one, moreover, that does not attempt to defeat the whole purpose of a security check directed to the common good.

Processing films

Of course, the surest way of preventing any harmful effects from X-ray screening of exposed films on the way home is for the films to be processed before departure. While colour processing is available in many resort areas, it is almost entirely limited to handling amateur negative–positive films. Even where colour transparency film or black-and-white processing is available, the special nature of astronomical images and possible language problems in explaining your requirements point to the advisability of either bringing the films back for processing or processing on the spot. Home processing has been covered in Chapter 13; for on-the-spot processing all the essential equipment can be packed into a small kitchen bowl (which is used as a water jacket to maintain required temperatures) that occupies a relatively small volume

Figure 14.2 *Basic processing equipment for a foreign astrophotography trip. At right rear is a daylight developing tank with a pair of rubber gloves in front. The items in the centre foreground are placed on a changing bag. They are (right to left) a pair of scissors, a hook-type bottle opener for opening the film cassette, a digital thermometer resting on a film washer tube, two film clips and a reserve dial thermometer. In front is a plastic measuring cylinder. At far left are three 600-ml colour processing solution bottles with a small bottle of anti-static film wetting agent in front. On location, the bowl at the rear can be filled with hot water and used as a water jacket for maintaining the correct temperatures of the processing solutions in the developing tank. All the other processing equipment can be packed into the bowl, which is in turn packed in a suitcase.*

in a suitcase, as shown in Figure 14.2. A portable, thermostatically controlled processing jacket would be a welcome innovation from the manufacturers, but there probably would not be a high enough demand for it to be commercially viable. Anyway, the high daytime temperatures at many foreign holiday destinations make it much easier to maintain high processing temperatures than at more temperate latitudes.

It is of course for the individual to decide whether holidays abroad are to be used for total relaxation, mostly for rest with a small amount of observing, or chiefly for serious astrophotography. If you go for the last of these options, you will find that there are enthusiasts the world over, and that warm friendships are there to be made.

CHAPTER 15

Project photography

W hen we first start astrophotography, we are pleased if we manage to secure sharp and well-exposed images of targets such as the Moon or the constellations. Once we have gained experience and the number of failures has decreased, we may find as time goes by that getting individual pictures of reasonable quality is not enough to hold our interest. Motivation is important in any chosen field of activity, and what we might call project photography can provide it in astrophotography. By project photography I mean the study of an astronomical event or phenomenon using photography that is somewhat more involved or demanding than is required to obtain a single image, no matter how competently that image may have been obtained. The purpose of an advanced project might be to contribute to original research, but it is more likely to be of an educational or informational nature: to obtain, for example, a photographic record of a phenomenon which extends over a period of time and which our eyes cannot therefore encompass. Project photography does not necessarily require complex or expensive equipment, although that will, of course, expand the scope. Most of the examples in this chapter use little more than basic photographic equipment. Some projects can be attempted at any time, while others have to do with astronomical events that must be recorded as and when they happen.

T he first sighting of the new Moon has considerable religious importance for Moslems. Spotting a very young new Moon (or a very old one just before new) has long been a challenge for amateur astronomers, and photography of the event is a good test of technique. Properly documented sightings of a Moon less than 20 hours from new are rare, and what may be the record was established on the evening of 1989 May 5 when a Moon just under 13½ hours old was seen with binoculars (and also possibly by the naked eye) from the US. Witnessing the event is more than just having the luck to be in a location where the Moon has become old enough to reveal the thinnest of crescents in a twilight sky. Very important too are the steepness of the ecliptic to the horizon and the Moon's position relative to the ecliptic, which must be such that its angular separation from the Sun is as great as possible. Moreover, the Moon must be close to perigee (the closest position to Earth in its orbit) because then it is travelling at its fastest, and that increases its angular separation from the Sun more quickly than at

The slender crescent moon

any other time. These conditions were favourable in May 1989, and the new Moon was spotted from a location which was close to ideal because from there the Moon was standing directly above the Sun as the sky darkened sufficiently for it to be seen. For more on the subject, see *Sky & Telescope*, July 1994, page 14.

There is sufficient interest in such sightings for astronomy magazines to publish information about forthcoming opportunities and the best vantage points in advance, so the need for detailed knowledge of the event itself is not a problem. Photographically it is demanding because by definition the thin crescent Moon will be relatively low on the horizon where it can easily be obscured by cloud, haze, and atmospheric pollution. In addition, the slender crescent will be seen against a comparatively bright twilight sky in middle and higher latitudes, although this is less of a problem the closer the photographer is to the equator.

The exposure may confidently be based on a meter reading since the crescent Moon and sky do not present a severe lighting contrast, and a general reading should suffice; although I always bracket at least two half-stops each side of the indicated exposure. With such a large expanse of sky the film chosen should be no faster than ISO 400, otherwise grain will become too intrusive. The lens should be a telephoto of at least moderate focal length. One of around 200 mm

Figure 15.1 *The Moon was just over one day old, and could easily have been missed in the bright twilight. The difficulty with photographing a very young Moon is not one of exposure — a general reading of the sky will suffice. Rather, the problem is to obtain sufficient contrast between sky and crescent, achieved here by using a long lens and a high-resolution, high-contrast film. This picture (which also includes Venus) was taken on 1989 June 4 using a 300-mm f/4 Nikkor lens at maximum aperture and an exposure of 1/8 of a second on Fujichrome ISO 400 transparency film. A slower film would have afforded higher quality, particularly as there is such a large expanse of clear sky in the scene.*

would provide a pictorial type of image, particularly with an attractive foreground, whereas longer focal lengths of up to 2000 mm will direct attention to the Moon only. For optimum results, observe closely the advice on procedures given in Chapter 5, such as use of tripod and cable release, and especially of mirror lock-up and shutter-release delay if available in the camera. A picture of a 14½-hour Moon was obtained from the southwestern US on 1989 May 5. Figure 15.1 shows a photograph of the Moon a little over 25 hours old taken in England during the following lunation, on 1989 June 4.

Earthshine

This phenomenon, referred to in Chapter 6, could be developed as a project for both observation and photography. Earthshine could be photographed at regular intervals from the earliest possible occasion after new Moon until the time when the growing daylit crescent of around three days begins to swamp it. Alternatively, a similar study could be made of the waning crescent Moon. Since the phase of the Moon as seen from the Earth is the reverse of that of the Earth as seen from the Moon, earthshine would be expected to be at its brightest immediately after new Moon. Atmospheric conditions would almost certainly vary over the two or three evenings for which earthshine remained visible, as it would from one lunation to the next. Nonetheless, it is quite possible that careful observation and recording of the atmospheric conditions over the period of the study could lead to meaingful conclusions about variations in the nature of earthshine. For example, might the different levels of earthshine resulting from a cloudy or less cloudy Earth, or from more of the Antarctic as distinct from the Arctic being seen from the Moon, be recorded convincingly? The extent of the difference would be revealed by gains or losses in the detail discernible among the recognizable surface features on the lunar nightside (see Figure 15.2).

Although I have photographed earthshine quite frequently, I have not attempted a study of this kind, but it is an attractive proposition. The photography is not difficult; the salient points were made in Chapter 6. For optimum results a long focal length lens of 1000 mm (or more) should be used, and the camera mounted on a platform (or telescope) tracking at the lunar rate. Extensive note-making will be essential.

The size of the Sun

The Earth travels round the Sun in an elliptical orbit, and is at its closest to the Sun (at perihelion) early in January each year and its furthest (at aphelion) early in July. At these times its distances from the Sun are 147 million km (91.5 million miles) and 152 million km (94.5 million miles), respectively. The difference has a significant effect on the size of the solar disk as seen from the Earth, and this can be demonstrated in a simple photographic experiment.

The Sun is photographed on black-and-white film through suitable white-light filters (see Chapters 7 and 16) early in January, and again early in July using exactly the same equipment. The lens should be of at least 500 mm focal length, the longer the better. The resulting negatives are then enlarged by exactly the same amount, and printed. The most

Figure 15.2 *Earthshine is recorded clearly in this picture of a two-day-old Moon. A 1000-mm f/11 Nikkor mirror-reflex lens was boosted to 2000 mm by the use of a ×2 teleconverter, and the camera was mounted on a platform tracking at the lunar rate. The original exposure was 8 seconds on Fujichrome ISO 1600 transparency film. While the daylit crescent is overexposed, the exposure is generally satisfactory in that there is no flare. However, flare does become apparent in the long exposures required for earthshine once the Moon is about three days*

dramatic way of demonstrating the difference in the size of the two disks is to carefully cut each print in half, and then mount the left half of one with the right half of the other on a black background, leaving just a thin gap between them. An example is reproduced in Figure 15.3.

The fact that Earth is closer to the Sun during the northern winter can puzzle those with scant astronomical knowledge. The fact is, of course, that both the northern and southern winters occur at those times of the year when the 23½° tilt of the Earth's axis causes those parts of the world to receive less solar energy – the Sun totally disappearing for some time within the Arctic or Antarctic Circle.

Solar activity

With the same equipment described above for photographing the Sun, we can demonstrate the rotation of the Sun, using sunspots as markers. The Sun completes one rotation as measured at its equator in just under 27 days; the rate slows progressively towards its poles. Movements of sunspots across the visible disk can therefore be seen for a little less than two weeks, weather permitting.

Figure 15.3 *It is relatively simple photographic exercise to demonstrate how the apparent size of the Sun varies during the course of a year. The main constraint is that the same focal length of lens be used to obtain the winter and the summer image, and that the means of presenting them be strictly comparable – for example, giving the negatives exactly the same degree of enlargement, as here. These images were obtained using an Inconel white-light solar filter and Technical Pan 2415 film. Both exposures were for 1/1000 of a second, using an f/10 telescope. The left-hand image was photographed on 1989 January 11 (perihelion was on January 1), and the right-hand one on 1988 July 2 (aphelion was on July 6), both from a period when sunspot activity was close to maximum.*

Using a neutral density filter (or a special solar filter – see below) and as long a lens as possible to achieve maximum detail, the Sun is photographed on as many days as possible. The film can be high-resolution Technical Pan 2415 black-and-white film, or one of the medium-speed colour transparency films such as Kodak Ektachrome ISO 100. Given favourable weather, an impressive multi-image display consisting of five or six prints can be produced. If of good enough quality, as in Figure 15.4, the sequence can also demonstrate how individual sunspots or clusters of spots change with the passage of time. It is important in displaying the images to ensure that the orientation of the Sun's axis is consistent so that the sunspots' tracks across the disk can be followed.

A hydrogen-alpha filter will reveal active regions and other details of the solar chromosphere – but it is expensive. Its use is dealt with in

(a)

(b)

(c)

(d)

(e)

Figure 15.4 *Pictures of sunspot activity can be used to demonstrate the rotation of the solar disk. This sequence of photographs charts the movement from east to west (left to right) of a large group of spots across the face of the Sun's northern hemisphere in August 1990: (a) day 3, (b) day 5, (c) day 8, (d) day 9, (e) day 11. All five images were originally recorded on ISO 100 Ektachrome transparency film through an Inconel type solar filter placed over the full aperture of a Celestron C8 telescope. The camera was a Nikon F3, and the exposures varied from 1/125 to 1/500 of a second. A full sequence of images covering a complete rotation of the Sun could be turned into an even more striking demonstration by using a video camera to copy the individual images and presenting them as a time-lapse movie.*

Chapter 16, but it is appropriate to mention here that with such a filter it is possible to obtain a sequence of images of the Sun recording changes over minutes rather than days. The two images in Figure 15.5 show the development of a solar prominence – plasma shooting up for sometimes tens of thousands of kilometres into space – over the course of 15 minutes.

O ften we photograph stages of eclipses and other events such as occultations as they progress on separate frames of the film. But they also make suitable subjects for multiple images on a single frame of film, and three excellent examples by Japanese astrophotographer Akira Fujii are reproduced in this chapter. The first two, Figures 15.6 and 15.7, show how a fixed camera, a lens of the correct focal length, and accurate pointing of the camera combine to record an entire astronomical event on one frame. The third, Figure 15.8, was obtained with a driven camera, and required the greatest care in timing the individual exposures. Planning is the essence of success with pictures of this kind. Exposures have to be worked out in advance, as does the positioning of the camera on tripod or platform so as to achieve an accurate and hopefully pleasingly balanced track of images across the film frame. Of course, it is essential to use a camera on which the double-exposure prevention mechanism can be overridden.

Eclipses and occultations

Solar eclipse: India, 1980 February 16

The two most important aspects of planning this record of a solar eclipse (Figure 15.6) were choosing the focal length of lens that would accommodate a large number of images on the film, and the correct positioning of the camera on the tripod so that the Sun tracked fully through the frame. You will need the correct neutral density filter to photograph the partial phases of the eclipse, and this will be removed for the one image exposed during totality. High-speed film is not required, so you can opt for the quality of, say an ISO 100 or 200 film. The camera is, of course, fixed, the Sun itself doing the tracking. Since a typical solar eclipse lasts for 2 hours or so, you will probably need at least the 40° horizontal field of view of the 50-mm standard lens to fit the Sun's movement across the sky onto the one frame. Although the solar diameter is then only about 0.5 mm, this is sufficient (particularly if you subsequently have the frame enlarged by a laboratory).

Having decided on the lens, you will have to run some tests. Set up the camera complete with filter, film, and so on, just as you plan to do on the actual day. Check the track of the Sun across the sky, and lock the camera on the tripod so that the Sun appears in one corner. If you are going to use a right-angle viewer incorporating a magnifier for ease of operation, remember that it reverses an image right to left, so that the track of the Sun will appear to run in the opposite direction to the way you see it directly. Start your exposures (for which guidance is given in Chapter 7) and, not forgetting that you must deactivate the film wind-on each time, make an exposure every 5 minutes. This will be valuable experience, and will quickly show up any significant

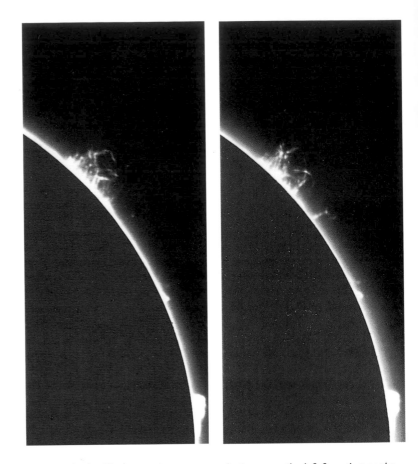

Figure 15.5 *In the 15 minutes that separates the image on the left from that on the right, the large prominence towards the top of the solar limb has evolved rapidly. The two pictures were taken through a DayStar 0.7-Å bandpass hydrogen-alpha filter attached to a Celestron C8 telescope. Each exposure was for ¹/₂ a second on Technical Pan film. An exposure of this length is necessary to record prominences but totally overexposes the solar disk, which can be blanked out, as here with pre-cut black paper disks.*

problems. You may decide to record only part of the eclipse sequence, around totality, for example, in which case you can choose a longer focal length lens, say 180 or 200 mm; the testing procedure, though, is just the same.

Once you get to the eclipse site, it is important to check on the track the Sun will follow at the time of the eclipse. This can be done the day before, and having already decided on the shutter speed/focal ratio combination to be used all you need do is set up the camera and make a note of the angle that gives the correct track. Think this through, and think about what you would do in more detail; now look at what Akira Fujii did, and notice how beautifully the totality exposure is balanced in the frame. This was not luck.

Lunar occultation of Venus, 1989 December 2

Less time is required for a multi-image picture like Figure 15.7. An occultation occurs when the Moon, travelling eastwards in its orbit, moves in front of a star, or in this case the planet Venus. Because the Moon moves through its own diameter in about one hour, that is the maximum approximate length of an occultation. This particular event was shorter because as seen from Earth Venus was not moving behind the lunar disk along its central diameter, but well to the

Figure 15.6 *The progress of a total solar eclipse as seen from India on 1980 February 16, recorded on a plate camera by Akira Fujii. A solar eclipse lasts in all for around 2 hours, so quite a wide-angle lens is needed to encompass the large amount of sky traversed by the Sun and Moon in tandem during that period. The use of a solar filter during all but one exposure, that for totality, renders the sky dark.*

Figure 15.7 *A lunar occultation of Venus on 1989 December 2, recorded on a plate camera by Akira Fujii. The occultation took place in twilight, thus yielding pleasing colours as well as the attraction of a foreground carefully chosen by the photographer. The lens was of longer focal length than the one used for the solar eclipse sequence because the Moon moves through its own diameter in around an hour, the maximum possible duration of any occultation.*

south, "tracing" a shorter line across the disk. The first image taken was the one at the top of the frame in Figure 15.7, and by the third exposure Venus had been occulted by the leading, dark limb of a waxing crescent Moon. The planet appears again on the lower lunar cusp in the eleventh exposure, but is not seen easily for two more exposures.

No filter is needed for a picture like this, and only a moderately fast film, certainly no faster than ISO 400. The camera would be mounted on a tripod. The exposure for both Venus and the Moon has to be a compromise, and guidance on this was given in Chapter 9. Akira Fujii's picture has an exquisitely coloured twilight sky and a pleasing foreground. The sky in a picture of this kind can be a problem because, if the occultation takes place in a relatively bright sky, multiple exposures of Venus and the Moon can easily result in the sky being grossly overexposed. Of course, a picture such as this could be a composite, with the occultation photographed in a dark sky and the image later combined with an attractive twilight scene!

Figure 15.8 *The total lunar eclipse of 1982 December 30: another multi-image composition on one frame, but with a difference. The camera was not fixed but mounted on a platform tracking at the sidereal rate. As seen against the background stars, the Moon moves eastwards in its orbit and through the large shadow cast by the Earth. A lens of relatively long focal length can be used. The greatest skill shown by Akira Fujii in this picture lies in his timing of the exposures such that the images balance pleasingly on either side of the single image of totality. The lunar disk was in the penumbra for six of the images, and the exposures were based on the photographer's previous experience. Experience could play a part too in estimating the exposure for totality, but here the state of the atmosphere (which can vary enormously) would have been a major factor, and one difficult to predict.*

Lunar eclipse, 1982 December 30

A lunar eclipse can be photographed like a solar eclipse, as described above. But there is another, much more graphic way of recording it which shows the Moon moving through the Earth's shadow. This requires the use of a camera platform tracking at the speed of the stars (the sidereal rate). Relative to the stars, the Moon moves eastwards, and by a careful choice of lens focal length, frame positioning, and exposures a result like Figure 15.8 can be obtained. Details of the timing of eclipses are published well in advance. The aim in this picture was to record images of the Moon wholly within the penumbra; about halfway into the umbra, when a just a sliver remained outside the umbra; and at mid-totality; and corresponding images in the second half of the eclipse. If moving on a central path through the umbra the Moon can be totally eclipsed for about 105 minutes, but it was clearly well to the north in this picture, so totality would have been considerably shorter.

Exposures during the various stages would be based, for the film and focal ratio chosen, on previous experience. The one marked variable is the Moon's disk during totality, which can be quite light or dark according to the state of the Earth's atmosphere. No elaborate tests are necessary to establish what focal length of lens to use. Only seven exposures need be made if Akira Fujii's model is followed, and the simple formula

Figure 15.9 *The analemma. Recording it is is another project involving multiple images on one frame of film, but it differs from the others described in this chapter in the time encompassed – an entire year. The azimuth and altitude of the Sun at the summer and winter solstices dictated the focal length of lens chosen for the camera, which needed to be bolted into position for an entire year so that the track of the solar analemma on the single film frame would be accurate. A white-light solar filter was in place for every image. A successful outcome to the project stemmed largely from precise accuracy in the time of day that each of the weekly exposures was made, and good fortune in the sky being clear at that time. At the conclusion of the project the series of solar images was combined with an image of a sunlit scene to make the final result more pleasing.*

of focal length divided by 100 will yield the approximate size of the lunar disk on the film. Since some of the images overlap, a total span based on seven separate disks is more than enough, although there will need to be some black sky at left and right for balance. The calculations would point to the use of a 400- or 500-mm lens with a 35-mm camera.

The analemma Figure 15.9 records the passage of a year from 1988 January 14 to 1989 January 11. On a single frame of film in a 35-mm camera, I recorded the passage of the Sun from winter into summer and back again by making one exposure at precisely 08:30 UT regularly on one day each week (weather permitting). The resulting shape (called an

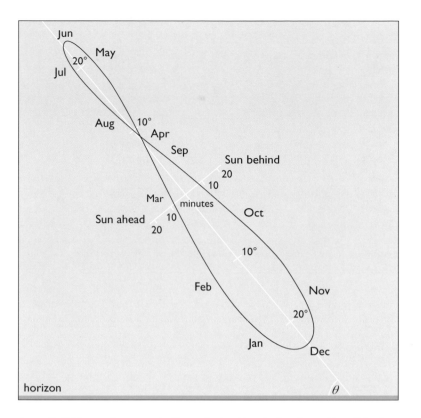

Figure 15.10 *The analemma – the figure obtained by plotting the position of the Sun in the sky, at the same time of day, at regular intervals for a whole year. The long axis, graduated in degrees of arc, represents the effect on the Sun's position of the Earth's axial tilt. The short axis represents the effect of the Earth's elliptical orbit, and for reasons explained in the text is graduated in minutes of time. The angle (θ) that the long axis makes with the horizon is equal to the observer's latitude.*

analemma, from the Greek for "lofty structure") has a characteristic figure-of-eight outline, which was frequently included on globes of the Earth many years ago. This exquisite celestial phenomenon – which only the time-lapse camera can record – results from the combined effects of the tilt of the Earth's axis and the elliptical nature of its orbit about the Sun.

The 23½° tilt of the Earth on its axis is well known, and is represented in Figure 15.10 by the long axis of the analemma. Understanding this presents no great problem, but the spread of the solar track along the short axis, which is graduated in minutes (of time), is a little more complex. If the Earth's orbit about the Sun were circular and its axis not tilted, the Sun would appear to move eastwards throughout the year at a constant rate and it would constitute a perfect clock. This *mean Sun* is what our clocks are designed to emulate, and they keep what is called *mean solar time*. But actual or true solar time is less perfect. At the solstices, the real Sun's effective eastward motion is faster than the mean Sun's. Therefore, at those times (twice a year), the Sun arrives at a location's meridian later and later – that is, it runs slow. Around the time of the equinoxes, its motion is slower than the mean Sun's, so at those times it arrives earlier and earlier – that is, it runs fast. Actual solar time can be ahead of, or behind, mean solar time by as much as 16 minutes, and the difference between the two is called the equation of time. It is this difference that produces the east–west spread of the analemma as shown in Figure 15.10.

The lower loop of the analemma is larger than the upper one because the Earth's elliptical orbit brings it closest to the Sun (to perihelion) in January. During the northern winter months, therefore, celestial mechanics causes the Earth to move faster, and this in turn causes the Sun's apparent motion along the ecliptic to be faster than at other times of the year; hence the greater size of the lower loop.

Equipment and procedure

The camera used for the photograph in Figure 15.9 was positioned so that it framed the view from an "up and over" sloping loft window facing due east, with a clear horizon. Any jarring would disturb the smooth outline of the analemma, so it was essential to eliminate even the slightest movement of the camera body. This would be most likely to happen when the window was opened and closed for an exposure. So a strong platform fixed to the window frame was specially constructed. The camera was placed on wooden supports shaped so as to orient it at the correct angle to the horizon, and bolted to the platform. Window stops were also screwed to each side of the window frame to prevent the back of the camera from being struck when the window was opened for photography.

A motor-driven Nikon F3 was selected. Its readily accessible multiple-exposure lever was a valuable feature in this project, and the use of a motor drive reduced the possibility of slight camera movement on the platform resulting from the operation of a lever wind by hand. Critical to the choice of lens was the angular movement of the Sun's position between the winter and summer solstices. Information supplied by the Royal Greenwich Observatory for my latitude indicated that between December 21 and June 21 there was a movement of 40° in altitude and 30° in azimuth. Some additional margin in altitude was necessary to allow for a foreground in the (hoped for) final picture, as well as for peace of mind. My eventual choice was a 24-mm Nikkor wide-angle lens with a 55° vertical and 80° horizontal field of view. The latter was much more than necessary, but the vertical angle of view was the critical factor. The solar disk would be very small, but I had always envisaged enlarging a successful image at the darkroom stage of the project.

With the first exposure due to take place in mid-January, the camera was fixed to the platform so that the solar disk was located in the lower right corner of the field of view with the reasonable expectation that the Sun's image would not run out of frame in June. Come June, I was (thankfully) able to confirm this visually, thanks to the choice of an SLR camera. Before the first exposure was made the camera was fully checked, new batteries were installed, and the lens was taped to a focus setting of infinity and an aperture setting of $f/11$. Even so, these and other settings and arrangements were checked for accuracy regularly throughout the year.

The camera unit would be subjected to considerable extremes of temperature in the loft over the course of the year (despite the provision of a thermal blanket). For this reason I selected an amateur colour negative film, as such films are less prone to temperature variations than the professional transparency films I normally use. Exposures were to be made through an ND5 gelatine filter pack, which does not require a fast film when photographing the Sun, and I eventually chose Kodacolor Gold 100. Previous tests with the proposed equipment/filter/film combination indicated an exposure of 1/250 of a second at $f/11$.

The day chosen for each weekly exposure throughout the year was Saturday, but such is the English weather that one day either side was regarded as acceptable. Far more critical was the precise time of day, 08:30 UT, which had to be accurate to the split second. Also important was remembering to keep to UT throughout the year, making allowance for when daylight saving time was in operation.

The procedure on a morning when an exposure was scheduled was first of all to set a countdown electronic timer accurately according to a radio time check. Then a regular drill – removing the lens cap, moving the motor drive control from L (lock) to S (single firing), and so on – was observed. This drill was written down for those occasions when I could not be present personally to make an exposure. It was rather difficult to look through the camera's viewfinder while holding the window fully open, so whenever broken or cirrus-type cloud made me wonder whether an exposure should be made, I looked through a second, hand-held filter. Doing that, holding the window open and firing the shutter all at the same time required some dexterity, but it could be done.

Since the view from the loft was pictorially boring, a more interesting scene was selected for a single daylight exposure with which the analemma could be combined carefully. Over the course of the year 40 solar images were obtained out of a possible 51, and light cloud cover caused a few other images to be fainter than optimum. I considered this quite acceptable for a location in the UK. If I were to undertake the project again, I would modify at least two photographic elements. First, the density of the solar images exposed during winter was less than expected, obviously because of the attenuation of light resulting from the Sun shining through a greater thickness of atmosphere when close to the horizon. A half-stop increase in exposure would have solved the problem. A second problem arose when the film was processed. Having been wound round the take-up spool in a fixed position for a year, the colour negative film had "taken set" – it had become kinked. The direction of the set was the opposite of what was needed for smooth entry into the small developing tank reel, and I failed to get it to take up on the reel despite several attempts. Loading the film from the other end was successful, but not before the failed attempts had caused stress "flashes" to appear on the film perilously close to the single image. Clearly, any film left in a camera in a fixed position for a long time should be unrolled and loaded trailing end first into the developing tank.

Nonetheless, the relief and pleasure when I processed the film and saw the result can be imagined!

Figure 15.11 The progress of Mars as it performed a retrograde loop as seen from Earth in 1992–3 was the subject of another multi-image photograph, but this one was largely a darkroom project. An in-camera solution (as for the analemma) was ruled out by the risk of fog building up as a result of many exposures on the same frame of film and of gross (and unsightly) overexposure of Castor and Pollux, two of the stars which would be in the field of view during the course of the loop. Instead, a series of individual frames taken at different times were accurately combined and set against a starscape of Gemini in the darkroom. The different angular diameters of Mars were a result of the different exposures in the individual frames dictated by sky conditions (especially light pollution) from various different locations. The ideal would have been an identical exposure on each occasion with Mars at a predetermined altitude, but this was not possible. The track of the loop, however, is demonstrated well.

At certain times in their orbits, the normal eastward movement of planets against the background stars as seen from Earth appears to halt. They then appear to move in a westward direction for some time before again halting and resuming their movement eastwards. This apparent westward movement is called retrograde motion. It is a line-of-sight effect which (for planets from Mars outwards) occurs when the Earth is at its closest to a planet and in effect performs an overtaking manoeuvre as it speeds by between the planet and the Sun. The inner planets, Mercury and Venus, can also display retrograde motion but this is not usually seen as clearly as in the case of Mars, for example, because they are so frequently in a twilight sky without stars to reveal the apparent retrograde movement.

A retrograde loop

Because the planets' orbital planes are all slightly different from the Earth's (see Table 1.1 on page 14), the path of a planet's retrograde motion shows intriguing variations of shape that depend on the planet's distance from the Earth and its location above or below the ecliptic. Thus Mars can perform "S" or "Z" shaped zigzags or loops. Mars performed such a loop between September/October 1992 and early May 1993, and I decided to record it (see Figure 15.11). Publicity about the event indicated that the retrograde movement of the planet would be about 19° in the constellation Gemini, so the field of view of a normal 50-mm lens would be more than ample to record the entire loop. There were, however, two possible ways of accomplishing the task. Given a satisfactory location, a camera could be dedicated to the project for the entire period, as for the analemma, multiple images being exposed on a single frame of film. I was aware of one previous attempt of this kind, but while an exact timing of the exposures could doubtless be arranged (for example, fixing a telescope of some kind which would be sighted on a target star) there were two objections. Multiple exposures of a night sky – even if fairly dark, which I could not guarantee – would eventually build up a fog level, and since Castor and Pollux would be in the field of view a series of images of them would quickly lead to gross overexposure.

As a result I decided to make separate exposures of the Gemini area over the period of retrograde motion and to combine them in the darkroom. This decided, I chose Ektachrome ISO 400 HC film as the standard with the $f/1.4$ 50-mm lens stopped down to $f/2.8$ on every occasion, to limit off-axis coma as much as possible. The individual pictures were taken from a variety of locations, some of which (abroad) had excellent dark skies, while others (such as at my home) suffered badly from light pollution. Exposures of up to 10 minutes were given in the former case, and as little as 1 minute or 30 seconds in the latter. These shutter speeds required the use of a camera mount tracking at the sidereal rate. The cameras used were a Nikon F3 and a Nikon F4S. The area photographed did not need to be exactly the same during each exposure, provided Mars and some target stars which ensured correct vertical and horizontal coverage were in view. Several images of different exposure lengths were taken on every occasion to ensure that there was at least one usable frame.

By May 1993 images had been obtained on 57 different dates. Sequences where images would be almost on top of one another were thinned out, leaving 31 for the composite. One 5 × 7 inch colour print was made from each to exactly the same degree of enlargement, and each print was duplicated under copying lights onto one frame of Ektachrome 160 film balanced for tungsten lighting. This was loaded into my Nikon F2AS copying camera with the $f/3.5$ Micro-Nikkor lens fitted.

There were two major requirements in this operation. First, the starfields appearing in the individual frames clearly had to be exactly in register. This was accomplished by marking up an acetate overlay with target stars. Before copying, each print was carefully placed underneath the overlay in register, and taped down before the overlay was removed from the field of view. The second requirement concerned Mars itself. One of the best frames would be used for copying the entire background constellation, but in all the others only Mars was to be copied. At first I thought that a sheet of matt black paper with a very small hole perhaps 2 or 3 mm in diameter would suffice. But more than thirty exposures of a black sheet under bright copying lights produced a very washed-out sky. A little thought produced the solution. I made a rough-and-ready cone, the broad end of which fitted up and around the lens barrel of the Nikon, and the tip of which just cleared the surface of each print. A small hole cut in the tip enabled Mars to be located in each print and permitted the copying lights to illuminate just that small area, with the rest of the print excluded.

In a few of the frames it was not possible to match all the stars to the overlay because of differential refraction through the atmosphere, and for these a "best fit" policy was adopted. Also, because of the different exposures given, as well as distended images resulting from the proximity of Mars to the horizon in some frames, the apparent diameter of the planet varied. Because of this one can draw no quantitative information about Mars's magnitude or diameter from the composite, which is simply a record of the planet's changing location tracing out a retrograde loop. A more aesthetic balancing of the individual images would have been pleasing, but that, and a more desirable consistency in length of exposures, would be possible only if the project were carried out in a very favourable climate.

The attraction of project photography is that if successful it can provide a great sense of satisfaction and achievement. As time goes on, you may develop special interests which can form the basis of a project or projects. For example, you might like to make a record of Jupiter's four Galilean moons at various points in their orbits, or photograph the constellations so that differences in star colours are brought out as clearly as possible. I want to make a comprehensive photographic record of halo phenomena, and also demonstrate photographically the manner in which we are enabled to see more than 50 percent of the lunar surface as a result of various forms of libration (see Chapter 6). It is just a question of the weather – and finding the time!

The way ahead

S ome readers may have reached this point after sampling previous chapters, and decided that observing rather than photography holds the main attraction for them. Others may have worked through the book in a determined manner, steadily gaining knowledge about the sky and the photographic skills used in recording its greatly varied treasures. Hopefully the hard work will have been rewarded and photographs produced that at least show promise when compared with those published in the astronomy magazines. The primary purpose of this book has been to bring readers to this stage. Now the obvious question is, where do we go from here? This final chapter outlines the route ahead.

A s we turn to photographing more difficult celestial objects requiring exposures of many minutes, the performance of even the fastest films used in a fixed camera is outpaced, and we must look to equipment that will enable us to track the stars. A first step in this direction, the simple Haig mount, was discussed in Chapter 8. Cameras with standard photographic lenses fitted still have an important role to play in photographing astronomical objects that cover large areas of the sky, for example (see Figure 16.1). The means of enabling them to track the stars lies in two directions: dedicated camera drives, and telescopes upon which cameras will ride "piggyback."

Camera drives

Various dedicated drives, normally powered by conventional batteries, are commercially available. It is important for the newcomer to realize that, no matter what any advertising may say, even when a camera mount or telescope is correctly aligned on the north or south celestial pole and the equipment is performing to specification, the gears and other mechanical components of the system cannot of themselves track a chosen celestial object with absolute accuracy. This is of no great significance when wide-angle and normal focal length lenses are in use, but once a focal length of around 100 mm is reached a control unit is required which allows the photographer to make small adjustments to the speed of the motor while monitoring the target's position. This is known as *guiding*.

The mounts often have a boom that is driven by the motor. A camera can be placed at each end, but more usually one end is used for a guidescope. This is focused on the target object, and used by the photographer to track it throughout the exposure, making adjustments as necessary with a hand-controller. The units are portable, and are particularly

Figure 16.1 *The North America Nebula in Cygnus (NGC 7000) recorded in a 5-minute exposure on hypersensitized Technical Pan 2415 film. A Nikon F3 camera was mounted on an equatorial, driven camera platform and fitted with a 180-mm f/2.8 Nikkor lens. This lens is made from extra-low-dispersion (ED) glass, which limits the chromatic aberration inherent in telephoto lenses, and yields "tight" stellar images and improved contrast. The exposure in this case was carefully calculated so that the image of the nebula did not swamp the discrete stellar images in the same area.*

suitable for low-power photography. The more expensive models have better provision for accurate alignment on the celestial pole, and a mount with guidescope is comparable in essentials to a small telescope. Figure 16.2 shows an advanced mount sophisticated enough to incorporate not only lunar and solar drive rates, but one that could be programmed to track comets too. Basic, lower-priced mounts are suitable for taking good-quality constellation images in a matter of minutes with cameras fitted with wide-angle and normal focal length lenses. More expensive mounts can deliver good performance with lenses of up to 200 or 300 mm focal length, but in my view that should be regarded as the limit: we have now reached the province of the telescope.

Using the telescope for photography

For the general public, the telescope is the instrument that epitomizes astronomy and which (for the good reasons stated at the beginning of the book) we have been largely ignoring. Even now I am not going to go into great detail about the different types that are available. I shall concentrate on astrophotography with one of the most popular types of commercially produced telescope: a 200-mm (8-inch) aperture f/10 model with a focal length of 2000 mm (see Figure 16.3). The optical system embraces both lenses and mirrors (not unlike the mirror-reflex photo lenses discussed in Chapter 3) and is called a *Schmidt–Cassegrain* in honour of the two pioneers whose optical researches (greatly separated in time) led to the development of this instrument. These telescopes have become steadily more advanced over the years, and it is now quite common, for example, for them to incorporate a computerized

Figure 16.2 *An advanced camera platform (with its heavy tripod out of frame) which can be used in a number of configurations. It can accommodate up to eight cameras at any one time, which could be useful for, say, meteor patrol photography. A sophisticated drive system allows the choice of sidereal, lunar, or solar tracking rate, and also (almost certainly a unique feature in such a mount) the ability to programme the drive to track comets.*

system which can locate a large number of celestial objects whose positions are stored in its memory. Be that as it may, let us assume we have one of these telescopes with a dual-axis drive corrector with which to make corrections in both declination and right ascension, and a number of eyepieces of various powers.

Piggybacking

This highly versatile instrument makes an admirable mount on which to piggyback our camera fitted with its own lenses. Many popular astronomical objects, such as the famous spiral galaxy M31 in Andromeda, are too large to fit within the film frame of a 35-mm camera when photographed through a 2000-mm focal length instrument. The solution is to purchase or make a special fitting that permanently attaches to the upper rear of the telescope to which the camera can be threaded or clamped. The camera is then fitted with a more convenient 300- or 400-mm focal length lens to record the glories of M31, which is sighted along the top of the telescope barrel, and the normal viewfinder is then used to frame the galaxy.

The telescope, of course, plays a vital role. Aligned correctly on the celestial pole, it will be tracking in right ascension quite well. It may be that the focal length of the lens being used will be such as to reveal few signs of the minor fluctuations in the rate at which the telescope is being driven by its motor, but most photographers will usually guide nonetheless (see Figure 16.4). A *star diagonal* is fitted at the rear cell of the telescope to direct the light rays upwards at right angles, and in it is placed an *illuminated reticle*. This is a high-power eyepiece with single or

Figure 16.3 *A basic 200-mm (8-inch) aperture, 2000-mm focal length Celestron Schmidt–Cassegrain telescope prepared for deep-sky photography, with off-axis guiding via a unit fitted between the camera and the rear cell of the telescope. Notable features are the large dew cap with counterweights beneath it, the permanent piggyback camera mount (not in use) at the top rear beside the guidescope, and the polar axis finder projecting to the left of the telescope base. This is the sort of instrument that has greatly expanded the number of keen observers and photographers working with telescopes over the past two or three decades.*

double cross-hairs that are illuminated by a red light whose brightness can be controlled. The telescope is aimed at the area to be photographed, and when the correct field of view for the camera lens has been confirmed, a target star is focused in the telescope's eyepiece. Then, throughout the exposure, a hand-control is used to make slight adjustments in right ascension (and less likely in declination) so that the target star remains on the illuminated cross-hair. This is an admirable means of guiding for moderate focal length photography because, obviously, if a 2000-mm telescope is being used for the guiding and is holding steady on a target star, the results produced by a lens of only 300 or 400 mm focal length should be excellent.

Photography through the telescope
The telescope can be used for photography in a much more direct fashion. If the camera lens is removed, the camera itself may be attached by means of an adapter and a T-ring (designed for the particular camera) to the rear end of the telescope. Now the skies are viewed

Figure 16.4 *Some of the glories of the southern-hemisphere sky as recorded from the Cederberg Observatory, north of Cape Town. A Nikon F4S was loaded with Ektachrome ISO 400 film which was exposed for 10 minutes through a 35-mm f/1.4 lens stopped down to f/2.8. The camera was piggybacked on a Celestron C8 telescope which, despite the use of the wide-angle lens on the camera, was guided to achieve maximum accuracy. Clouds of stars fill much of the frame. The constellation Sagittarius is located left of lower centre, and much of Scorpius is to the right, with Antares very prominent. Numerous Messier objects can be seen, including the Lagoon and Trifid nebulae (M8 and M20), above and to the west (right) of the "lid" of the Sagittarius Teapot shape, and the open clusters M6 and M7, west of the Teapot's "spout."*

through the *f*/10 optics of 2000 mm focal length. This is normally (if not too accurately) referred to as *prime focus photography*. The focal length is such that the Moon and Sun fit conveniently into the 35-mm film frame: when other objects are too large a tele-compressor lens can be fitted which reduces the telescope to an effective *f*/5 1000-mm system – which is faster, of course.

Since the photography is taking place through the main optics of the telescope, the problem arises of how to guide during lengthy time exposures of deep-sky objects. This is usually accomplished by a technique known as *off-axis guiding*. A hollow T-shaped accessory screws directly into the rear cell of the telescope, and the camera is fitted to the other end to receive the light down the tube. Part way down the guider tube is a small prism which reflects light from the edge of the field of view and directs it up at right angles to an illuminated reticle which is fitted at the top of the long stem of the T accessory. A suitable star is selected as the target, and, once the exposure is under way, any drift is revealed by the star beginning to move off the cross-hairs. Such movement is corrected (as in piggyback photography) by using the drive corrector control unit. The technique sounds very straightforward, but is in fact demanding and can become very tiring.

Figure 16.5 *Eyepiece projection through a 26-mm objective fitted to an Astro-Physics, Inc. f/9 178-mm (7-inch) StarFire refractor tracking at the lunar rate was used to obtain this image of the eight-day-old Moon. The exposure was on Ektachrome ISO 100 Plus film for $^1/_2$ a second. Mare Imbrium is the major feature of the picture, together with a number of prominent craters. Towards the top is Plato, with the cleft of the Alpine Valley just to its right. At the bottom is the famous crater Copernicus, with one wall in shadow and the other brightly lit by the Sun. North of Copernicus is the smaller but clearly illuminated crater Eratosthenes, above which run the Apennine and Caucasus Mountains that separate Mare Imbrium from Mare Serenitatis and Mare Vaporum. The large, partially filled crater within Mare Imbrium is Archimedes.*

Eyepiece projection photography

One more stage remains with the telescope as far as mainstream photography is concerned. A focal length of 2000 mm is insufficient for some purposes, such as meaningful photography of the planets or close-ups of the Moon (see Figure 16.5). At this stage the eyepieces used for visual observing are pressed into use. An eyepiece is screwed into the back of the telescope. A *tele-extender*, which is a projection tube, screws over the eyepiece and the camera fits at the other end of the tube. This arrangement is known as eyepiece projection photography, or EPP.

Expressed in this way it may sound straightforward, but it most certainly is not, and EPP may be regarded as the toughest test for an astrophotographer. There is a wide range of eyepieces to master, typically from 40 mm focal length (low power/magnification) to 4 mm (very high power). Eyepieces come in a number of different designs, but I think most experienced workers would agree that orthoscopics are the most suitable for astrophotography as distinct from observing. Having made a choice, which might begin with, say, 25 and 12 mm eyepieces to give a spread of magnification from relatively low to reasonably high, and fitted the chosen eyepiece to the telescope, some of the problems will become quickly apparent. To start with, if the astrophotographer is using one of the popular Schmidt–Cassegrains, the tele-extender with the camera fitted to the end will unbalance the telescope. Counter-weights, which may have to be specially purchased, will have to be added at the front of the telescope.

So we fit an eyepiece and magnify the image of part of the Moon or of the disk of Jupiter. But while magnification is the whole object of the exercise, we have to pay for it: higher magnification spreads a fixed amount of light over a larger area, so the image becomes dimmer. A normal SLR focusing screen is quite inadequate when the camera is being used for EPP, and in my view one of the special screens (see Chapter 3) is essential if good results are to be achieved. The dimness of the image (which in addition may of course be intrinsic to the celestial object) calls for long exposures. For dim deep-sky objects such as galaxies or nebulae, exposures can be an hour or more, and the main challenge then is guiding accuracy and endurance. With lunar or planetary photography, in which exposures often fall into the difficult "no-man's land" region of around a second or so (see Chapter 5), operating procedures need to be at their best.

There is something else about EPP that needs to be stressed. As astrophotographers we may have improved and gained considerable experience, and we may be fortunate enough to own good-quality equipment. But if the seeing (the state of the atmosphere) is not good, then no amount of skill or hard work is going to lead to a happy outcome. Experience is also knowing when to stay indoors. Finally, although I have pointed out the difficulties, my intention has certainly not been to discourage anyone, because it is with the move to EPP that the astrophotographer comes of age, beginning to use focal lengths and ratios that would astonish the ordinary photographer – for example 28,000 mm at $f/140$!

Film

Reference to such a low focal ratio inevitably raises the issue of film, particularly as the spectre of reciprocity failure affecting exposures of more than a few minutes has risen on a number of occasions in previous chapters. Deep-sky photography is the realm of the professional observatories and of many devoted amateurs. Over the years, Eastman Kodak has evolved a number of astronomical products for the observatories which were designed with specific sensitivities and to reduce reciprocity failure to a minimum. These films and plates are still used, but the technique of *hypersensitization*, or *hypering* for short, has grown greatly in popularity and is now used widely by advanced amateurs and in the observatories with wide-field telescopes employed for surveys of the sky.

Film is hypersensitized by baking it in a special vessel containing a "forming gas" mixture of nitrogen and hydrogen for several days at around 30°C. A small amount of fog occurs, but reciprocity failure is greatly reduced and certain films exhibit what can only be described as astonishing speed gains. Kodak Technical Pan 2415 is one of the most successful of the hypersensitized films, and a tenfold speed gain has been claimed for it. The equipment for hypering films, as well as pre-treated films, are available from a small number of suppliers in the US and elsewhere. For many years, dedicated astrophotographers reduced reciprocity failure by using specially constructed *cold cameras* containing dry ice which chilled the emulsion. The technique was very demanding, but introduced little fog into the emulsion and colour balance was scarcely affected. Now, however, among deep-sky photographers it has been largely superseded by film hypersensitization.

CCDs

Discussion of the means of improving a film's performance leads us directly to a revolution in amateur astronomy that began in the late 1980s and shows no sign of stopping. With the exception of wide-field mapping, since about 1970 all imaging in the great observatories of the world has been done almost exclusively with *charge-coupled devices*, usually referred to as *CCDs*. The CCD is essentially an imaging chip in the form of a grid containing thousands of picture elements (*pixels*). The pixels convert the photons of incoming light into electrical charges which cumulatively build up a picture that may be stored in digital form and displayed on a monitor. The system has some significant advantages over photographic film.

The CCD is far more efficient than film in converting available light into the form of an image. It does not suffer from reciprocity failure: its response is linear, with the result that doubling the length of an exposure doubles the amount of information recorded. In addition, its dynamic range (latitude) is also superior to that of film. Added to these major considerations is the fact that the information is digital in form and may be processed by computer. The images thereby lend themselves to various forms of manipulation to extract the maximum amount of data.

With the coming of the computer and electronic age, professional astronomers quickly saw how the new systems could be applied to their studies. However, the cost of CCDs and suitable computers initially placed them beyond the range of almost all amateur astronomers. But subsequently the great growth in ownership and falling cost of personal computers, and now the reduction in the prices of CCDs, has brought these formerly professional tools within the grasp of the amateur.

The CCD cameras available today include the Santa Barbara Instrument Group's ST-4 and ST-6 units, SpectraSource Instruments' Lynxx systems, Electrim Corp's EDC-1000, and the British Starlight Xpress systems. Their prices are according to specification, and cover much the same price range as amateur telescopes, and they can now be used to produce colour images. Knowledgeable amateur astronomers have quickly recognized that, because of the CCD's efficiency, much shorter exposures are possible: what took hours with photographic film can be achieved in minutes with a CCD, and what took minutes can be done in seconds. And short exposures mean that clear images can be recorded in heavily light-polluted urban skies (and moonlight). It is no exaggeration to say that amateurs using CCDs are now securing images of deep-sky objects that ten years ago could only have been obtained at professional observatories. Some CCDs can also be used as autoguiders for the more lengthy deep-sky photographic images so that tedious guiding by eye is no longer necessary. And amateurs too are indulging in the computer processing that can greatly improve CCD images.

But it is necessary to keep a sense of proportion. Although the situation may well change, CCDs in the sizes that amateurs can afford continue to be very small in area (a centimetre or so square, compared with much larger film sizes) and therefore of very limited field of view. Film is markedly superior in its resolution, and the starting costs for the CCD user – remember that a computer is necessary – are higher. The astronomy magazines are very helpful in evaluating the relative merits of film and CCDs for their readers, and in any case I feel that the two forms of imaging are complementary: for advanced workers, photography with its high resolution is ideally suited for such subjects as sky surveys over a wide area and for the Sun, while the CCD comes into its own with, for example, dim, deep-sky objects and the planets where its small field of view is no disadvantage and its efficiency is at a premium (see Figure 16.6).

It is certain that both electronic imaging and film technology will advance further in the years ahead. The former's appeal will doubtless develop as a generation that has grown up with the personal computer takes up astronomy as a hobby, and we may expect continued technical improvement. Film too will also improve: we should not forget the comment by Dr Edwin Land (of Polaroid fame) a few years ago that film was still in the stone-age, and Eastman Kodak has reported the successful preparation of "hollow" silver halide crystals which may well lead to another jump in film speed and quality. We astronomers will be the beneficiaries of the competition and – since the picture is the thing, not how it is obtained – perhaps we should now be talking of *astroimaging*, rather than of photography or CCDs.

The Schmidt–Cassegrain telescope has perhaps done more than anything else to bring astronomy, and in particular astrophotography, to a wider, participating audience. Of course, other types have their protagonists. The Newtonian reflector (which uses mirrors to form the image, with the eyepiece the only lens) is relatively cheap, has a fast focal ratio, and is a popular choice for studying planets and deep-sky objects. The refractor (and particularly the apochromatic type) yields superbly sharp and contrasty images but is relatively slow and, aperture for aperture, is the most expensive type of telescope. If you decide to proceed further with your astrophotography you will find the

Specializing: Sun, Moon, planets, deep sky

(a)

Figure 16.6 *The charge-coupled device (CCD) comes to astronomy and makes a significant contribution to both planetary and deep sky imaging. These two pictures were taken by Terry Platt using one of the Starlight Xpress cameras that he designed and developed. These cameras differ from most other models currently available in a number of significant ways: they incorporate an interline transfer CCD as distinct from the more normal frame transfer device, and they also have a dedicated electronic memory (known as a frame store) to capture and hold the digital image. The frame store allows an image to be read off in less than $1^{1}/_{2}$ seconds and instantly displayed on a TV monitor, thus avoiding the delay involved in using a computer to read and display images.*

The Jupiter image (a) was obtained at the f/40 focus of an off-axis 318-mm ($12^{1}/_{2}$-inch) reflector (a Buchroeder tri-Schiefspiegler) in a $^{1}/_{4}$-second exposure. The telescope's normal f/20 focal ratio was amplified using a Barlow lens. The image was processed with an unsharp mask to enhance the fine detail, and a median filter was used to smooth out "noise." The wide-field image of the Andromeda Galaxy (M31) (b) was taken with a 135-mm telephoto lens attached to the CCD camera. The exposure was 320 seconds at f/3.5, and the fainter regions of the galaxy were subsequently enhanced by rescaling the image brightness with a logarithmic contrast boost followed by renormalizing with a linear contrast stretch.

pros and cons of different telescopes well analysed in the various magazines, and knowledgeable staff at retail outlets as well as astronomy club members should be able to help.

Inevitably we tend to specialize as we progress. The following brief comments on four popular subjects are based on my own experience.

The Sun is a fascinating subject, but the specialist filters needed for serious work are expensive – as is the refractor, which, in my view, is unmatched for solar photography. The best known of the broadband filters are of the Inconel type, made of glass coated with an alloy of cobalt, nickel, and iron, and they reject 99.999 percent of the Sun's radiation (see Figure 16.7). An aluminized mylar product is popular

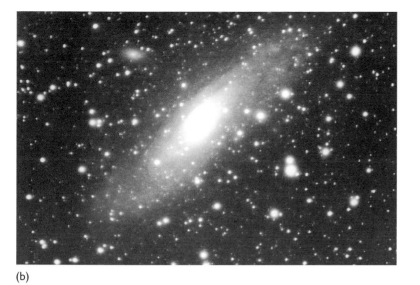

(b)

in the US as a cheaper alternative, although unless corrected by an extra filter it gives a rather incongruous looking light blue Sun. Specific solar features can be studied in more detail by using special narrowband filters that pass only a very small part of the spectrum. A *hydrogen-alpha* filter concentrates on the strong hydrogen line at 656.28 nm (6562.8 Å), and reveals prominences, flares, and other activity not visible through the broadband filters (see Figure 16.8). Eyepiece projection is normally used very little, and the serious solar astrophotographer uses the high-resolution, high-contrast, black-and-white film Technical Pan 2415 almost exclusively.

The Moon may seem at first sight an easy photographic subject, but to get high-quality images of lunar surface features requires excellent technique and much skill. Eyepiece projection is normally used (as for Figure 16.5) and is essential, for example, if the photographer is a participant in a group studying TLPs (transient lunar phenomena), occasional localized changes on the surface believed to be caused by outgassing from the lunar interior. The telescope should be tracking at the lunar rate. Depending on the Moon's phase, either high-contrast (2415) or lower-contrast (T-Max type) black-and-white film is used, and a variety of development techniques may be chosen from for optimum results. Colour film can be used, but little is to be gained since the Moon is essentially a monochromatic subject.

It is easy to obtain moderately satisfactory photographs of the Moon, but excellent results require close attention to the procedures outlined in Chapter 5. You also need the ability to recognize when conditions will not permit good results. If you do not have an observatory then it is pointless trying to take pictures of the Moon (or anything else) if the tripod of your Schmidt–Cassegrain is being buffeted continually by a strong wind. The "seeing" is very important, and I feel that it is of far greater significance than any consideration of the different merits of various types of eyepiece.

The altitude of the Moon, too, is critical in obtaining optimum results. A few serious lunar photographers in the UK argue that to photograph the Moon when its altitude is any less than 30° is a waste of time. This may be considered too severe an attitude, but it is certainly true that there are good times and bad times to try for high-quality images of the Moon. If you want to get the best results, then – all other things being equal – the first quarter Moon is best photographed in March, near the equinox; the full Moon near the winter solstice in December; and the last quarter Moon at the September equinox.

Planets are arguably the most demanding subjects to photograph well. Eyepiece projection is essential, and all three of the major types of telescope have their protagonists. Filters are frequently used to emphasize colour differences in the surface and atmosphere of planets such as Mars and Jupiter (respectively). Once again, good results come from attention to detail, application, and experience. CCDs have much to offer the planetary specialist, since short exposures take advantage of momentary improvements in seeing, and subsequent computer processing will bring out detail that would remain hidden in a conventional photograph (see Figure 16.6(a)).

Deep-sky objects are probably what appeal most of all to beginners, inspired by images of exotically coloured nebulae, of star clusters, and of distant galaxies. But this too is a very demanding area. The relatively fast focal ratios of Newtonian reflectors, the use of hypersensitized films, and a competence in off-axis guiding will all improve your chances of success. Often, though, you are dealing with dim objects

Figure 16.7 *The innermost planet Mercury in transit across the south-southwest limb of the Sun, giving an excellent demonstration of the difference in size of the two bodies. The transit took place on 1993 November 6, and was seen at midday in Australia. The original image was obtained using a 26-mm Plössl eyepiece fitted to a Celestron C8 telescope. Technical Pan 2415 film was loaded in a Nikon F4S camera and was exposed for 1/60 of a second through an Inconel solar filter. The image was subsequently copied onto colour transparency film through an orange filter.*

Figure 16.8 *The Sun photographed with a 0.6-Å DayStar hydrogen-alpha filter reveals active regions, sunspots, and filaments on the disk and a major prominence on the limb. Using a system which includes a negative Barlow lens to boost the size of the solar image, two pictures were taken of the Sun within a few seconds of each other on standard Technical Pan 2415 film loaded in a Nikon F4S camera fitted to an Astro-Physics, Inc. f/9, 178-mm (7-inch) StarFire refractor. The exposure for the disk was 1/60 of a second, and that for the prominence $^1/_2$ a second. Prints enlarged by exactly the same amount were prepared from the negatives, and the two images copied as a single image through an orange filter onto Ektachrome film. This last procedure is purely cosmetic, but it does increase the impact for a general audience.*

which to the eye can be lost in light-polluted urban skies and which (even when skies are good) require very long and demanding exposures. These factors are virtually certain to assure the place of CCDs since, as mentioned earlier, they do so much to overcome just these problems.

Advanced darkroom work may seem a somewhat paradoxical theme in the light of the comments about CCDs, but it is very relevant. David Malin, the head of the photo laboratories at the Anglo-Australian

(a)

Telescope in New South Wales, has a worldwide reputation for his magnificent colour images that result largely from skilled darkroom techniques such as unsharp masking and photographic amplification which he uses to bring out detail not readily discernible in the original images. Malin's work has inspired some highly skilled amateur astrophotographers and darkroom workers. In the US it is by no means uncommon to see superlative deep-sky images resulting from darkroom skills in which colour negatives are stacked in the enlarger as a means of producing colour prints and transparencies with superior colour, contrast, and grain characteristics. For many years both professional and dedicated amateur astrophotographers have overcome the deficiencies of ordinary colour film by taking separate pictures through red, green, and blue filters on black-and-white film, and subsequently reconstituting a composite image on colour film in the darkroom. A more recent development has been to take advantage of film's high

(b)

Figure 16.9 *Stonehenge makes a marvellous foreground for astronomical images, and two different treatments are reproduced here. The composite image (a) was created by combining a moderate telephoto record of the Sun with a colour negative of a trilithon stone grouping. A high-contrast, black-and-white positive of the stones was made from the original colour negative, and this was combined with a transparency of the Sun and sky. It would be impossible to secure a Sun of this powerful size in a single image which also contained an entire trilithon. Two trilithons are in the foreground of the second image (b). In this dawn picture, Venus climbs above the trilithons with the standing stones and lintels of the sarsen circle beyond. The planet was in Gemini at the time (August 1988), and Gamma Geminorum can be seen clearly below and to the right of Venus. Betelgeuse is at the extreme right. This was a 6-second exposure taken on Ektachrome ISO 400 film loaded in a tripod-mounted Hasselblad 500/CM camera fitted with an 80-mm f/2.8 Zeiss Planar lens.*

resolution and spatial coverage in the initial capture of the image, but then to convert the three black-and-white negatives into digital form with scanner and computer, and use the computer to generate – and enhance – the colour composite. The best of both worlds, indeed! Of course, any photograph can be digitized, and it is likely that some everyday photographers now turning to astrophotography will have experience of converting pictures to digital form with the Kodak Photo CD system. This is available from the usual retailers. If Kodak's PhotoEdge software is purchased as well, the user will have an admirable introduction to the world of digital image manipulation which is somewhat less daunting than the more advanced packages.

**The chance of
some reward**

Perhaps by now you have come to a decision on astronomy. Maybe it is simply a matter of the delight of roving free through the heavens without specializing, or using relatively inexpensive binoculars to search for comets or novae, or to time satellite passages. Perhaps the study of variable stars appeals. But hopefully astrophotography may have taken a firm hold on you.

If you make the grade, your pictures may well see the light of day in the astronomy magazines. In addition, the opportunity to earn some money from your new skills should be borne in mind if the quality is good enough. After all, a hobby often demands a considerable outlay, and the chance to recoup some of it should not be neglected. High-quality images can attract the attention of picture editors. If there has been discussion about a new Russian space flight or US shuttle mission, and you secure a good photo of the spacecraft flying over your home area (there is need for very quick processing in cases such as this), ring up the picture desk of the local newspaper and ask if they would like to see it. Even if the photograph does not get printed on this occasion you will have made a useful contact for the future. But your photography does need to be very good. If a regional magazine is published in your home area and frequently uses colour landscapes on the cover or inside, think about planning a dramatic skyscape at night or twilight with a recognizable feature such as a famous church in the foreground. Make a point of studying the layout of the magazine, however: if you are attempting a cover picture, keep the area where the title and any other information is located free of any distracting detail.

Provided poetic licence is not pushed too far in the direction of the impossible, talented darkroom workers – and those familiar with digital techniques – should think of constructing composite images containing two or more elements. I have long considered that most "natural" images of Stonehenge at sunrise or sunset lack impact. Therefore some time ago I prepared a high-contrast copy from a conventional image of the standing stones and combined it with a specially taken image of the Sun (see Figure 16.9(a)). The Sun was deliberately enlarged to achieve maximum impact.

Other commercial opportunities can arise unexpectedly. I was once approached by a manufacturer of aircraft fire-control equipment about the cover of a new brochure. Fire in aircraft is an emotive subject, and the company wished to suggest the message without a literal (and inevitably staged) treatment. I remembered having taken a sequence of pictures at dawn when aircraft vapour trails had framed the rising Sun which could be seen through light cirrus cloud. The connection was made – aircraft and fire – and the cover problem was solved.

If you are making progress with your astrophotography, then think seriously about moving onward into the new areas outlined in this chapter. Enjoyable work can be done with a fixed camera and everyday photographic equipment, but once you progress to a driven camera and the telescope, the metaphorical chains are broken and you are free to roam wherever your skill can take you.

Postscript

One of the fascinating things about astronomy is the contribution that the amateur can make to new knowledge. It would be understandable to assume that all areas of the sky are studied continuously by professional astronomers working in observatories around the world. In fact such astronomers number but a few thousand. Perhaps half of them are theoreticians who rarely look at the sky, or are working with radio or other wavelengths. Most of the rest will be fighting for very limited observing time in the pursuit of important but very restricted research projects. Hardly any will ever conduct broad, sweeping surveys of the night sky.

This is where amateur observers and astrophotographers have a role to play. For example, in the study of the Moon, planets, asteroids, meteors, and variable stars, and in the search for comets and novae, it is amateurs who as a group can contribute the time and enthusiasm, and also the ever-developing skills that have come to be so highly regarded by professional astronomers. In the eyes of the general public, astronomy is regarded as a high-tech science that requires sophisticated, costly telescopes and spacecraft. It is in fact a revelation to realize how much can be achieved with a pair of binoculars – or even the naked eye.

In the late 1960s and early 1970s, I was much involved with the photographic programmes on NASA's Apollo lunar missions. When looking in particular at the superb, high-resolution images of the Moon's surface obtained by mapping cameras flown from Apollo 15 onwards, it was easy to question why anybody, anywhere back on Earth should ever again bother to photograph the Moon. Shortly afterwards I took up astrophotography seriously, and the answer was provided. Nothing could rival the Apollo images, but equally there was nothing to compare with the thrill and elation of roaming over the lunar maria and mountains at the eyepiece of a telescope, and – whatever the problems with the Earth's atmosphere – of personally recording these features with growing skill on photographic film.

This is the delight of astronomy: our interest may be more casual than those who devote much time, effort, and skill to "patrol" activities or other programmes, but all can share the emotions roused by the never-ending mystery, drama, and beauty of the sky. Astrophotographers have an advantage over their colleagues in virtually all other branches of photography, for in a very real sense we can begin to appreciate the true meaning of infinity. If this book helps readers part of the way towards that appreciation, I shall be well content. May we all successfully defy Spode's law – and enjoy clear, dark skies!

Bibliography

General

Burnham, R. Jr, *Burnham's Celestial Handbook*, Dover, 1978.

Crossen, C., and Tirion, W., *Binocular Astronomy*, Willmann-Bell, 1992.

Harrington, P.S., *Touring the Universe through Binoculars*, Wiley, 1990.

Muirden, J. (editor), *The Sky Watcher's Handbook*, W.H. Freeman, 1993.

Ridpath, I. (editor), *Norton's 2000.0*, Longman, 1989.

Ridpath, I., and Tirion, W., *Collins Pocket Guide to Stars and Planets*, second edition, HarperCollins, 1993.

Tirion, W., *Cambridge Star Atlas 2000.0*, Cambridge University Press, 1991.

Tirion, W., *Sky Atlas 2000.0*, Sky Publishing Corp., 1981.

Specific themes

Long, K., *The Moon Book*, Johnson Books (Boulder, Colorado), 1988.

Price, F.W., *The Moon Observer's Handbook*, Cambridge University Press, 1988.

Rükl, A., *Atlas of the Moon*, Hamlyn, 1990.

Phillips, K.J.H., *Guide to the Sun*, Cambridge University Press, 1992.

Wentzel, D.G., *The Restless Sun*, Smithsonian, 1989.

Allen, D., and Allen, C., *Eclipse*, Allen & Unwin, 1987.

Harris, J., and Talcott, R., *Chasing the Shadow*, Kalmbach, 1994.

Littmann M and Willcox, K., *Totality: Eclipses of the Sun*, University of Hawaii Press, 1991.

Schaaf, F., *Seeing the Sky*, John Wiley, 1990.

Schaaf, F., *Seeing the Solar System*, John Wiley, 1991.

Schaaf, F., *Seeing the Deep Sky*, John Wiley, 1992.

Greenler, R., *Rainbows, Halos and Glories*, Cambridge University Press, 1980.

Meinel, A. and M., *Sunsets, Twilights and Evening Skies*, Cambridge University Press, 1983.

Minnaert, M.G.J., *Light and Color in the Outdoors*, Springer-Verlag, 1993.

Schaefer, V.J., and Day, J.A., *A Field Guide to the Atmosphere*, Houghton Mifflin, 1981.

Bone, N., *Meteors*, Philip's, 1993.

Yeomans, D.K., *Comets*, Wiley, 1991.

Scagell, R., *Astronomy from Towns and Suburbs*, Philip's, 1994.

Astrophotography

Astrophotography Basics, Publication P-150, Kodak.

Covington, M., *Astrophotography for the Amateur*, Cambridge University Press, 1985.

Dobbins, T.A., Parker, D.C., and Capen, C.F., *Observing and Photographing the Solar System*, Willmann-Bell, 1988.

Gordon, B., *Astrophotography*, Willmann-Bell, 1983.

Malin, D., *Extracting the Image in Astronomical Photography*, Kodak Techbits P-3-90R, 1990.

Malin, D., and Murdin, P., *The Colours of the Stars*, Cambridge University Press, 1984.

Martinez, P., *Astrophotography II*, Willmann-Bell, 1987.

Wallis, B.D., and Provin, R.W., *A Manual of Advanced Celestial Photography*, Cambridge University Press, 1988.

Photography

Attridge, G., *Photographic Developing in Practice*, David & Charles, 1984.

Book of the Darkroom, Paterson Products, 1987.

Kodak Black and White Darkroom Dataguide, revised edition, Publication R-20, Eastman Kodak, 1992.

Kodak Color Darkroom Dataguide, revised edition, Publication R-19, Eastman Kodak, 1993.

Kodak Editors, *More Joy of Photography*, revised edition, Addison-Wesley, 1988.

Kodak Professional Photoguide, Kodak, 1993.

Lansford, H., *Photographing the Sky*, The 11th Here's How, Kodak, 1979.

Neblette, C.B., *Photographic Lenses*, Fountain Press, 1973.

Copying and duplication

Copying and Duplicating in Black & White & Color, Publication M-1, Eastman Kodak, 1984.

Kodak Ektachrome Duplicating Films (Process E-6) Publication E-38, Kodak, 1990.

"Duplicating your success," *Astronomy*, February 1993, pp. 66–71.

"How to revive dull astrophotos," *Astronomy*, January 1986, pp. 62–68.

"Improving astrophotos by copying," *Sky & Telescope*, September 1987, Vol. 74, pp. 326–328.

CCDs

Berry, R., *Choosing and Using a CCD Camera*, Willmann-Bell, 1992 (includes software).

Berry R., *Introduction to Astronomical Image Processing*, Willmann-Bell, 1991 (includes software).

Buil, C., *CCD Astronomy*, Willmann-Bell, 1991.

CCD Astronomy, Sky Publishing Corp., PO Box 9111, Belmont, MA 02178-9111, USA (quarterly magazine).

Addresses

Telescope manufacturers and distributors
Astro-Physics, Inc., 11250 Forest Hills Road, Rockford, IL 61115, USA.
Broadhurst Clarkson & Fuller Ltd, Telescope House, 63 Farringdon Road, London EC1M 3JB, UK.
Celestron International, 2835 Columbia Street, Torrance, CA 90503, USA.
David Hinds Ltd, Unit 34, The Silk Mill, Brook Street, Tring, Hertfordshire HP23 5EF, UK.
Meade Instruments, 16542 Millikan Avenue, Irvine, CA 92714, USA.
Orion Optics, Unit 12, Quakers Coppice, Crewe Gates Industrial Estate, Crewe CW1 1FA, UK.
Tele Vue Optics, Inc., 100 Route 59, Suffern, NY 10901, USA.

Filters, hypersensitization kits, and other aids
Astrotech, 39 Periwinkle Lane, Dunstable, Bedfordshire LU6 3NP, UK.
Baader Planetarium KG, Zur Sternwarte, D-82291 Mammendorf, Germany.
Broadhurst Clarkson & Fuller Ltd (address as above).
Daystar Filter Corporation, PO Box 5110, Diamond Bar, CA 91765, USA.
Lumicon, 2111 Research Drive #5S, Livermore, CA 94550, USA.
Orion Telescope Center, 2450 17th Avenue, PO Box 1158-S, Santa Cruz, CA 95061-1158, USA.
Thousand Oaks Optical, PO Box 4813, Thousand Oaks, CA 91359, USA.

Organizations
International Dark-Sky Association, 3545 N. Stewart, Tucson, AZ 85716, USA.

CCDs
Electrim Corporation, 353 Wall Street, Princeton, NJ 08540, USA.
Santa Barbara Instrument Group, 1482 East Valley Road, Suite #J601, Santa Barbara, CA 93108, USA.
SpectraSource Instruments, 31324 Via Colinas, Suite 114, Westlake Village, CA 91362, USA.
Starlight Xpress, Briar House, Foxley Green Farm, Ascot Road, Holyport, Berkshire SL6 3LA, UK.

Holiday centres
COAA (Centre for Observational Astronomy in the Algarve), Casa Adelina, Poio, Mexilhoeira Grande, 8500 Portimão, Portugal.
Star Hill Inn, PO Box 1A, Sapello, NM 87745, USA.

Index